The Charles Bowden Reader

Edited by Erin Almeranti and Mary Martha Miles

FOREWORD BY JIM HARRISON

Printed in the United States of America
First edition, 2010

♾ The paper used in this book meets the minimum requirements of ANSI/NISO Z39.48-1992 (R1997) (Permanence of Paper).

Library of Congress Cataloging-in-Publication Data
Bowden, Charles, 1945–
The Charles Bowden reader / edited by Erin Almeranti and Mary Martha Miles ; foreword by Jim Harrison. — 1st ed.
p. cm.
ISBN 978-0-292-72322-1 (cloth : alk. paper) —
ISBN 978-0-292-72198-2 (pbk. : alk. paper)
I. Almeranti, Erin. II. Miles, Mary Martha. III. Title.
PN4874.B6295A25 2010
814'.54—dc22

2010001235

CONTENTS

PART V

FOREWORD BY JIM HARRISON

FAR TOO LONG AGO, I think it was in the ninth grade, a teacher gave me the work of Joseph Wood Krutch to read. I was immersed in literature and drama, especially my own self-drama, but then one Krutch volume I discovered was devoted to the Arizona desert. I come from an agricultural family, hence was not ignorant of botany, but then every single growing thing in the desert looked alien. Later, in my nineteenth year, I hitchhiked out Route 66 to California and saw the northern edge of some of the flora but was mostly struck by the emptiness and fabulous vistas. I had picked up a ride in Terre Haute, Indiana, from a squirrelly, confessed bigamist (and God knows what else), and he never drove less than eighty until he dropped me off in Barstow, where I headed north to San Francisco to become an official beatnik, of which there were many in 1957.

My first true flirtation with the desert came in 1971 when I traveled to Arizona for the National Endowment of the Arts to read my poems on Indian reservations and at the University of Arizona. It was then on a drive to Douglas with Neil Claremon that I discovered my eventual winter home in Patagonia. On this trip and others in the seventies and early eighties I met the desert rats Doug Peacock and Ed Abbey and also read part of Chuck Bowden's *Killing the Hidden Waters* that someone had loaned me overnight. As the years passed all of the people I call "edge people," meaning those on the cutting edge, talked about Chuck Bowden, so I started reading him in earnest. You don't simply read Bowden, you become a Bowden addict, and the addiction is not always pleasant.

I will make bold to say that Bowden is America's most alarming writer. Just when you think you've heard it all, you learn you haven't in the most pungent manner possible. Bowden is an elegant stylist, but then the paragraphs unroll like a bail of razor wire to keep you inside them.

Why is a man out in the Cabreza Prieta at 1:00 A.M. when it's still a hundred degrees? Looking for bats, of course. Who else would call a companion rattlesnake Beulah? Who else would spend so much time in the charnel house, the abattoir, of Juárez where the heads roll like bowling balls and virgins say farewell encircled with burning tires?

Way back in the twelfth century the Zen philosopher Dogen said, "When you find yourself where you already are, practice occurs." I've long made it a habit to study a place before I make a substantial visit, whether it's Modena, Italy, or Veracruz, Mexico, or the Sandhills of Nebraska. You can't know a place until you look into its history, its botany, its sociological factors, its geology (my weakest point), its creature population, and Native tribes. With minimal research you discover the astounding fact that most people don't know where they actually are. One day in a Patagonia saloon I said that in the late 1800s you could take a small ferry on the Santa Cruz from Nogales to Tucson, and no one believed me.

With *The Bowden Reader* in hand you get a taste of it all, and any literate resident or visitor should want this book. It will lead them back to a close, alarming reading of the entire oeuvre. It is to ride in a Ferrari without brakes. There's lots of oxygen but no safe way to stop.

About ten years ago I finally met the author at a party given for the renowned scholar Bernard Fontana. There is a bit of the recluse in both of us, but when I'd drive to Tucson for groceries not available on the border we began to have occasional, then habitual, lunches where we would chat for a few hours about the state of the area, the country, the world in these woeful times wherein you have to be a proctologist to deal with news. At present it is a moral act to get drunk and throw yourself on the earth before a statue of the Virgin of Guadalupe. It is definitely not a moral act to call your broker or erect a worthless fence along the border.

Bowden is unflappable at these lunches and I am enriched. He never says "I told you so" to the world. He retains the air of the *amateur* in the old sense, a true lover and student of life. Read him at your risk. You have nothing to lose but your worthless convictions about how things are.

INTRODUCTION BY THE EDITORS

CHARLES BOWDEN'S OFFICE looks out on a garden of desert plants, brazenly green in the flat, white light. At his desk he hunches forward, eyes piercing through a haze of cigarette smoke as the words on the screen build. At certain intervals—the end of a paragraph, a chapter, a thought—the drumming from the keyboard is interrupted by the snubbing out of a cigarette, a slug of high-octane coffee. And then the words begin to build again.

You don't have to be in his office to sense this. The words on the page have intensity and immediacy, employing mood as much as meaning. They demand attention and hunger equal to the writing. Reading Bowden, you feel the urgency of insight followed by a rush of responsibility, for it is our collective future in this troubled world that he is wholly focused on.

Bowden's first book, *Killing the Hidden Waters* (1977), explores the "mining" of water, a non-renewable resource in the deserts of the southwest. The book asserts that the water we pump to make the desert bloom—the water that supplies our golf courses, subdivisions, and swimming pools—will not last, no matter how many wells are drilled. It was a controversial stance, but it won the support of Edward Abbey, who proclaimed Bowden "the best social critic and environmental journalist now working in the American southwest." The thesis of *Killing the Hidden Waters*—that resource problems are nearly always cultural problems and not the result of scarcity—began a path of exploration that Bowden would follow in nearly everything he has written since.

In the early eighties Bowden became a reporter at the *Tucson Citizen*, quickly distinguishing himself by covering complex stories that other reporters either ignored or saw as insignificant. He spent months covering a miners' strike and years writing about sex crimes—a beat many reporters flat-out refused. The resulting stories were not the usual beefed-up police reports, but hard-hitting portraits of people whose lives were changed forever. Bowden, like others, was horrified by the sex crimes but he believed, as he did in writing *Killing the Hidden Waters*, that we have no hope in managing our destructive appetites if we are afraid to acknowledge their existence.

Bowden also began covering the U.S./Mexico border while at the *Tucson Citizen*, and subsequent magazine pieces and books on border issues have become some of his best-known work. More than two decades before it became commonplace for reporters and humanitarian rights activists to expose the dangers of illegal immigration, he made his own illegal trek into the United States from Mexico in 1983 following the same trails immigrants suffer on today. His life has been threatened for exposing drug trafficking and murder in Juárez, Mexico. Yet Bowden continues to cover "the line" because it is a trip wire for issues—migration spawned by global inequality, the rise of stateless criminal cartels—that will shape the twenty-first century. In *Juárez: The Laboratory of Our Future,* he writes, "The future has a way of coming from the edges, of being created not in the central plaza but on the blurry fringes of our peripheral vision."

While Bowden has a gift for humanizing complex issues such as the border, his profiles often work differently, separating the unique from the universal rather than joining them. Distilling personalities—be they hit men, artists, or neighbors—is another kind of gift, but even those accustomed to the process are impressed by Bowden's perceptiveness. Max Cleland, the former Georgia senator, Vietnam veteran, and triple amputee, said of Bowden: "I've been interviewed by . . . literally hundreds of people in the last thirty-one years. He is the single finest interviewer, storyteller, writer that I've ever come across. He has an ability to capture people, who they are, who they really are, below the surface. He knows the surface story but he captures, and certainly did for me, a psychological dimension that I'm not even aware of myself."

Bowden's gift for insightful profiles grows out of his own introspective nature. At times, his writing can be deeply personal, exposing his own unsavory appetites, his own violations of the law and the land.

Yet Bowden's explorations inevitably lead outside of himself and into the hard, real world. Ultimately, this anthology attempts to document Bowden's journey of exploration—a journey, in large part, guided by the question posed in *Some of the Dead Are Still Breathing:* "How do we live a moral life in a culture of death?" No metaphor; Bowden is referring to the people, history, animals, and ecosystems that are being extinguished in the onslaught of twenty-first-century culture.

Given the demands of editors, advertisers, and prescribed audiences, it's nearly impossible for Bowden to be so personal and far-ranging in his journalism. So it is in his books that Bowden is able to fully synthesize his explorations. He travels disparate roads, not subject to linear notions of time and space, and so, in *Exodus,* for example, we may pass Pancho Villa and corrupt coyotes and Bowden himself crossing the same dusty trails on the same page. Some readers find Bowden's books hard to follow at first, but connecting every dot is less important than accepting the alternate reality Bowden reveals, the new people he challenges us to become. "I want to get the reader in the room and then nail the doors and windows shut," Bowden says. Readers willing to give him such time and commitment are seduced by Bowden's distinctive rhythm and lyrical prose, and inevitably persuaded by his ideas.

The hard examinations Bowden delivers throughout his body of work have prompted some to describe him as angry. But it is a mistake to confuse his condemnations for cynicism. In *Mezcal,* for instance, Bowden looks at the destruction of the desert by human beings and notes the contrast between the filth of modern human settlements and the open desert. He believes that in this contrasting landscape, we may be able to see ourselves in a way that we haven't before. He writes:

> The deserts force us to think rather than argue. I sense a new way of thinking emerging from the contact made in this century between the modern Americans and the ancient ground surrounding them. On the face of it, such a change in thinking would appear unlikely. The recent boom in the desert is not the kind one expects to produce a bumper crop of insights. It is crass, bustling, vulgar, cheap, ugly and has the soul of a real-estate swindler. But ideas tend to come from grubby places.
>
> I will bet my life on this place. The emptiness will tell us what we need to know. Whether we listen or not.

So, yes, there is hope and the hope is not found on some distant mountaintop or in some grand building with steeples and stained glass. The hope can only be found within us and in our own grubby places.

And if it is up to each of us to find and feel that hope for ourselves, we still owe Bowden something for articulating the behaviors that will lead us there: Appetite is a part of being human, desires drive us, and reality wins out every time.

THE CHARLES BOWDEN READER

Part I

We are fascinated by this thing we call nature because of our fear of death and we believe that within nature is a harmony and a balance that can be applied like a salve to this fear. But of course, this thing we label nature is about death and all its jaws and fangs and maws create death everywhere and every time and by that act, make death meaningless and absolute.

FROM *INFERNO*

Coming to Arizona

From *Arizona Highways*, December 2007

THE PINES OF THE PLATEAU gave way at the Mogollon Rim, and then came the cottonwoods of the Verde River, the climb up to the grasses and junipers of the bench at Cordes Junction, and, finally, the slide down Black Canyon to the burning desert floor of saguaros, creosotes, and mesquites. Somewhere in that strand of earth, I decided to toss aside my life as I'd been living it, come back to the hot ground and be a writer. I remember staring out the windshield of an International Harvester pickup into the glare hour after hour, my mind slowly tumbling half-formed thoughts like rocks in the barrel of a mineral-polishing machine.

I can remember the low roar of the engine—a six-cylinder with four in the floor—the pitted glass, the brown of the ground as I slipped down the Rim to the river. The days before are hazy, something about the ponderosa forest around Flagstaff, a walk down into the wilderness of Sycamore Canyon, that large elk antler I spied on the ground with its whiff of lust and freedom. Here was the deal: I'd had my ticket punched and could not live with my sentence.

I was teaching American history at the University of Illinois, Chicago Circle Campus. I'd gone to a national meeting of historians in Boston, and the ratio of applicants to jobs was around fifty-to-one. Somehow, I'd lost and gained steady work. There'd been a spring some years earlier when I was wrapping up my undergraduate degree at the University of Arizona, an obligation to my parents, who had never had the pleasure of college life. All those last months, I dreamed of taking my finals and hitting the road. My plan at that time was to hitchhike with a friend to Veracruz, ship out on a freighter to Europe, and then either find life or have life find me.

But just before my escape, a letter came offering me a full ride plus living expenses at any university in the United States. I lacked the moral fiber to say no. So for six years I'd been either a serf of graduate school in Madison, Wisconsin, or writing my dissertation in Massachusetts, or for the past year, living in a basement in Chicago with a Newfoundland dog and teaching.

The dog had been part of my survival scheme: I figured I could not live in a bad place with a huge black dog. I was wrong. My other tactic was a 17-foot fiberglass canoe I'd bought in Wisconsin on the assumption that it would force me to stay near wild rivers. This tactic also had failed, though I'd fled from time to time to free-running streams and cold nights and dawns as fresh as Eden as I paddled down rivers and out of dreams.

So now it is summer, I am scheduled to return to Chicago and my career, and all I want is flowing past the window of my truck as I speed from the plateau to the desert. I dream of starting a magazine to capture it all, or maybe writing a book to capture it all, to do something that matters to me rather than something that matters to a world I want to leave. Arizona and the Southwest tell you one sure thing: Everything that matters is here and it is in peril. I felt I'd somehow faltered and gotten shanghaied into a dead zone called the American university. And the work was easy—I taught only 10 hours a week on three successive days and then promptly fled to a cabin in Michigan by the lake—dunes and endless waves.

In novels and the movies, there is always this moment when everything becomes crystal clear, a decision is reached and suddenly the music comes up with heroic resolve. Life, in my experience, is not like that. It's more like the ice going out on a river come spring. Day after day the huge jams seem immobile, the ground remains frozen, and finally anyone standing on the bank gives up all hope, decides there will never be a thaw or one more flower, and resigns himself to permanent winter. And then one night there is a grinding sound, some loud cracks, and with dawn the river is opening up and with days and weeks the snow goes out—though there are always those late storms—and leaves emerge, scent fills the air, and birds missing for long, gray months suddenly appear at the feeder in the yard.

So I decided to leave a safe and sane job and become a writer in a kind of staggering way. There is the ride from Flagstaff down to the lower desert, those hours with things shape-shifting in my mind, the beckoning of the land and the sense that I was wasting my life with a job I did not want. I am crossing Dry Beaver Creek, and off to the south and west rises Mingus Mountain, the Verde flows, and I realize no one in my family is a writer, that I have no background in this business, no English beyond the freshman requirement, no journalism school, nothing but a history of sitting under a tree with a book, spellbound. I've never met a writer or a reporter. Well, at least I'm pure, I decide.

But I hear things in my head and I don't find these things in newspapers and magazines. And so I decide I must find a way to put them down on paper.

That was the first phase of this staggering move toward a new life. I got to Tucson, picked up a phone, called the chairman of my department, and told him I was walking out on a three-year contract. Then for some years, I did odd jobs like mowing lawns and trimming trees and picking up little editing stints here and there. Somewhere in there I had a book published. Finally, I talked my way into a job with a daily newspaper (I was down to less than 50 bucks at the moment) and stayed three years, although to be accurate I quit three times.

To stay somewhat balanced, I'd disappear at times and walk the western deserts of the state, a hundred to two hundred miles at a crack. That was my cure for covering murders and other mayhems, and that was essentially the undoing of me, also. About 75 miles out of Rocky Point, Sonora, I was in the Growler Valley of the Cabeza Prieta National Wildlife Refuge when I realized something had to give. The newspaper was my way of life, but my life was not enough. This part was hard for me since—then and now—I've never had a single complaint about the newspaper business. A part of me was born for such noise. I remember sprawling under a creosote bush in the heat of a late April afternoon and reading a memoir of the Mexican Revolution. Pancho Villa roared through my head and behind me lay at least 20 miles of a greasewood flat, ground I'd walked without seeing a single human footprint.

I decided I had to roll the dice, give up my day job as it were, simply write and live with the consequences. Of course, there'd been nudges. By this time, I'd met Edward Abbey and we'd become friends, had those long lunches where little seemed to get said and everything I needed seemed to be communicated. Ed was a kind of living reprimand to me. He'd simply gone and done it, lived hand-to-mouth for years, and moved through all the places I loved. I remember the hot, dry wind blowing through, the slender lines of shade from the greasewood and then the long walk out, going up to Charlie Bell Well, and then heading east until finally, at Ajo, I wandered into the world of cars and electric lights. All in all, the trip took days and something ended out there, and began.

One fall day I went into the Huachuca Mountains and spent a long afternoon with Bil Gilbert. He'd first stumbled into that border range when he was writing a book on coatimundis, *Chulo*. But I'd met him when he was touring *Westering Man*, his biography of Joe Walker, possibly the least-known and most significant mountain man of the early West. The book had become living tissue to me and told me what I'd failed to do with my life and what I must make amends for in the future. Walker was the ultimate lover of the West, and like all of us who become bewitched, he'd helped destroy it.

We whiled away the afternoon with Bil hearing me out and giving advice, and me ignoring everything but the whisper through the oaks of the mountains and the blue sky screaming over my head. Once Bil had tracked a coyote in the snow of the mountain and this trail led to a roadrunner with broken wings and a coyote blinded in both eyes by the bird. He had to destroy them both, but still that memory of his tracking lingered in my mind as we talked.

I remember this: a few weeks later putting on an old, green Pendleton shirt favored by my late father and walking into the newsroom, throwing down my press credentials, and walking out.

I went up into the Santa Catalina Mountains and six months and hundreds of miles of walking later came out with a book about the range. Since then, it has been financial insecurity, words, and ground. But at least I finally got started. It was a kind of three-part dance—plateau, desert, and mountain.

Like everyone who comes to this place, I've hardly scratched the surface. This last part is, of course, the blessing.

Bats

From *Blue Desert*

THE AIR SCREAMS, rustling movements feather against the skin, squeaks and screeches bounce off the stone walls, and a sweet acrid stench rolls across the room. My mouth chews the darkness like a thick paste.

We stand in feces, hills of feces, and the grey powder slops over our running shoes and buries our ankles. Behind us the light glows through the cave entrance, a slit sixty-five feet high and twenty-four feet wide. Above us the screams continue, the rustling frolic of life. The rock walls feel like cloth to the touch; a wilderness of fungus thrives in the warm room.

We climb. The hills of feces roll like trackless dunes. Our feet sink deeply into the grey powder as we move up toward the ceiling. Here and there a feather: a primary off a turkey vulture; a secondary off a black hawk. There is no explanation for their presence. The odor seems to ebb as our senses adjust to the stench. The dunes toss like waves and in between the dark mounds writhe masses of beetle larvae. Here we find the bones—skulls, femurs, rib cages, and the like.

This is the forbidden place, the dark zone claimed by nightmares. The air can be rich with rabies and people and animals have died from visiting such places. Up high, up near the ceiling, the rustling grows louder and louder. They are disturbed as we march into their world. The eye sees blackness but the skin feels the rustling, the swoosh of something near our brows, our throats, our mouths. We are enveloped in a swirling mass of energy and we keep walking toward the center of this biological bomb.

Something is crawling up our bare legs, across our bellies, down our arms, past our necks, and onward into the curious contours of our faces. Mites move up from the dunes of feces and explore us like a new country. When we pause and look up, our eyes peer into a mist, a steady drizzle of urine and feces cascading from the ceiling.

I have no desire to leave. The feces and urine continue to shower down, the mites tickle the surface of my body, the atmosphere tastes like a bad meal, and always the air drifting like a thick fog promises the whisper of rabies.

We have come to the charnel house, a bastion of a world in the twilight of its life. The crackling energy swirling in the air around us is dying. And we and our kind are the killers.

This is the bat cave and 25,000 *Tadarida brasiliensis mexicana* wrap us with their anxiety. Night is falling outside the cave. Soon our world will become theirs.

Then they will exit and plunder the canyons, the mesas, the hillsides, the towns, the fields. They will bring back deadly reports of our world, details buried deep in their bones and body chemistry.

The sound tightens now, a shrill spike of screeches and squeaks. The mites scramble across the skin. The larvae writhe like shiny stones at our feet.

We stand inside a brief island of life, a hiding place of our blood kin.

WE HAVE KNOWN EACH OTHER a good long while. We would pluck the eye of a live bat, stick it in a wax figure of a dog, put the effigy at a crossroads, and hope a lover would come to our bed. We would make an ointment of frankincense, the blood of a lizard, the blood of a bat, and treat trachoma. We would carve the image of a bat on the tip of a rhinoceros horn to ward off demons. We would cut the head off a live bat and place it on someone's left arm to cause insomnia. We would crucify live bats, heads downward, always downward, and place the result over our doors to fight evil, to protect our sheep, to insure our wakefulness.

We have hated bats. We still hate bats. They own the night and mock our helplessness. Their faces to our eyes look cruel, fierce, ugly.

For thousands of years, they rode through our dreams, they drank our blood, they stood as symbols of a world we were reluctant to enter but a place we lusted for—the black nights, the witches' sabbaths, the magic chants, the scream under a full moon.

THIS TIME WE HAVE COME for them wearing the mask of science. Ronnie Sidner is in her thirties now and she was raised in a tract house along a wooded draw outside Philadelphia. She wanted to become a veterinarian and found her path blocked by a male-dominated profession. She is a small, light-boned woman with red hair but she looks large and angry when she recalls this part of her life.

She decided to go West and wound up a schoolteacher in Parker, Arizona, a small town in the hard ground along the Colorado River where the Mojave and Sonoran deserts rub against each other. She stayed six years and then the emptiness of the American classroom burned her out and left her barren of ambitions. She took a summer course at Northern Arizona University in Flagstaff and the class focused on bats.

Something quickened in her, perhaps the memory of walks along the wooded draw behind her childhood home, the drive to be a veterinarian, or some simple, animal need. She enrolled in the University of Arizona at Tucson and rode to a Master's degree in biology. And she rode bats.

I first met her in the Chiricahua Mountains. She was wearing a T-shirt that proclaimed: I LOVE BATS. By then she was deep into her doctorate, a sprawling, undefined investigation held together solely by bats, thousands and thousands of bats. We talked and then there seemed nothing to do but go to the dark stone room.

I keep thinking it is something about the newspaper business, something about the killings and the people with defeat on their faces that has kindled a bad appetite within me for gore, for ruin and bankruptcy, for bulldozers knocking down giant cactuses so that shopping centers may flourish. But I constantly reject this sense of myself and am angered when others force this black cloak on my shoulders. I like to remember being a boy on that Illinois farm and I am holding a cane pole down by the creek and the fish are jumping. The sun skips off the quiet pools of water and the air comes fresh from Eden. Up by the house the old man and his cronies are drinking beer from quart bottles and marching toward a Saturday afternoon drunk. Below the barn, the Holsteins graze and cool spring water skims across the limestone floor of the milk house. And I am in the sun, and this is what I want and who I am.

I sit at my desk at the paper and stare at the blank wall and when the call comes, and it always comes, I volunteer for the bad deaths, the slaughters called meaningless in our silicon chip society. The ones that do not compute. Because for me, on some level I cannot say, they do compute. I am the one basking in the hot blaze of the Sunbelt who always senses these periodic eclipses when the land goes suddenly dark.

The assistant city editor is standing before my desk with a crooked smile. I can see him just past my boots propped up on my idle typewriter. He wears an Izod shirt. He tosses a police report down and says, "You'll like this one, Captain Death." And I go, I always go, and my entire being picks up and rises. I can sense this eclipse and I want to write it down. The Sunbelt has so much energy, so many slabs being poured, so much land being slain, so much action and I know amidst this frenzy there are these eclipses when the sun goes black and the temperature drops, these little deaths of the blazing white light. And I do not want these moments to go unnoticed. I am certain of this lunatic mission when I flip on the evening news and see the smiling faces or when I read the front page and the headlines chatter about growth, new jobs, booms, and dreams of freeways.

So when I hear of this hole in the earth where bats linger, I must go. Right now, not a moment's delay. There is a huge eclipse of the sun taking place and attention must be paid. I know my job.

The cave is near Clifton and Morenci, two eastern Arizona mining towns at the foot of a wilderness country stretching northward toward Blue River. In the early 1960s, millions of bats lived in the colony. E. Lendell Cockrum, a University of Arizona professor in the Department of Ecology and Evolutionary Biology, tried to tally them once. He made sample counts, multiplied, and came out with 50,000,000 bats. Trying to be conservative, he published a figure of 25,000,000.

The big colony once devoured 80,000 pounds of Arizona insects a night. By the late 1960s, there were 25,000 bats and they ate about ninety-eight pounds of insects a night. The devastation of the bat colony came quickly and that fact is what has brought us to the cave. A holocaust has taken place here and I want to visit the place of the great death. Few have noticed this event; fewer cared.

The walk in means miles of wading a stream guarded by light brown canyon walls. As we hike, a zone-tailed hawk explodes from a tree and slashes across the canopy of cottonwoods and sycamores. A red hepatic tanager and his mate watch from a mesquite, the blaze of a vermilion flycatcher spins and twirls off a bare limb. Half-wild steers charge through the brush before us. The water feels warm, the stone bottom slippery under our shoes. Fish dart from our footsteps. Stretches of the stream form still ponds reflecting the high canyon walls and the blue sky.

This is a throwaway canyon in Arizona, a place that in much of the United States would qualify as a national monument, but here in the careless riches of the West's wild land is regarded as simply another slit through the high country, a name on a map that few visit.

The smell hits us like a slap in the face. We look up and there is the huge vaulting door to the cave. We have found the core of the dying.

We pitch our packs under cottonwoods on the canyon's far side and wade back across the stream. Ronnie leads the way and her excitement quickens our steps.

LIKE US, THEY ARE MAMMALS. Their blood is warm and they nurse their young. One out of every five species of mammals is a bat. Forty-five million years before the first beast that looked like a human being walked this earth, bats took to the sky. The early bat jumped from tree to tree after insects and over time the arm became the wing and the air became a new floor for life.

Eight hundred fifty species now swirl across the planet's skin, and twenty-four can be found in Arizona. *Tadarida brasiliensis mexicana*, the Mexican free-tail, roams from Texas westward and winters deep in Mexico. This small bat rides on a wingspan of about a foot. The hair runs from dark brown to dark gray. They favor caves—thirteen in Texas, five in Oklahoma, and one each in New Mexico, Arizona, and Nevada.

These hunters search the desert and sometimes feed as high as 9,200 feet. They can live in colonies of millions, huge masses of bats squeaking, chattering, and crawling across each other. When big colonies once exited from their caves, the sound, according to early observers, thundered like the roar of white water and the dark cloud could be seen for miles. They fly into the night at about thirty-five miles per hour, then accelerate to around sixty. At dawn, they make power dives back into the cave, sometimes brushing eighty miles per hour.

They feed on small moths, ripping the abdomens from them in flight, and may travel forty miles in any direction seeking prey. The young, one per female per year, immediately crawl up the mother hunting the breast. At first, the mother returns several times during the night to nurse and then less frequently. No one is certain if the females find their own young in the huge colonies or nurse the first young bat they encounter. They can live perhaps fifteen years—no one is sure.

Bats remain a mystery in many ways. Science has come to them late in the day. They have been banded and migrations of 1,000 miles recorded. They have been kidnapped and released to test their homing instincts and a return of 328 miles has been observed.

And they have been dying. Oklahoma had 7 million Mexican freetails and is now down to fewer than 1 million. Carlsbad Caverns had around 9 million and is down to 250,000. And the cave on the creek in the canyon near Clifton and Morenci had its 25 million or perhaps even 50 million and is down to 25,000 or fewer.

There have always been ways for bats to die. In the 1960s, man offered them a new way.

WHITE BONES LACE ACROSS the dark guano like thin wires. The remnants outline a wing that fell from the ceiling. Small skulls peek through the feces, the tiny craniums empty of brains. Ronnie and I keep moving further into the cave. The room stretches 288 feet across, 65 feet high. Up at the peak runs a deep crevice where the bats now live. We have forgotten about the outside world and joined the darkness.

Ronnie picks up a skull and runs her fingers over the white smoothness.

"Oh, skulls," she says, "look at the baby skulls. It's a graveyard."

Bats circle over our heads. They are warming up for the evening flight. At 6:32, they suddenly swoosh out of the cave and stream from the top of the vault. A funnel forms in the center of the canyon and vanishes as the cloud of bats goes north. The flight is over in moments. It is merely the preliminary to the main evening takeoff.

We look back down at the bones, the lacework of bones on the dark guano in the hot cave squeaking with the life of the dwindling colony.

AROUND THE TURN OF THE century, they packed guano out on burros and then loaded it onto trains for the fertilizer needs of the West Coast. The haul reportedly earned a profit of $30,000. Later owners of the cave would mine it every five years or so, with the last excavation occurring in 1958.

Scientists heard of the cave in the fifties and Cockrum came in 1958. He had been banding bats since the early forties and published books on the mammals of Kansas, Arizona, and the Southwest.

He tried various schemes to catch the bats for banding and finally found a trap that worked. Bats present special problems. Rabies shots are often necessary because the caves form a perfect medium for the virus. Caged animals placed beneath the colonies have died from the disease although no bat could possibly have reached through the mesh containers to bite them.

Banding offered its own woes. The bats chew off bands within six weeks, and less than one tenth of one percent of the banded bats were ever recovered.

Cockrum reveled in the bat colony at its height—one estimate made in June 1964 pegged the population at 50 to 100 million bats. By June 1969 the census estimate was 30,000.

Cockrum remembers the cave in the good times, when the first evening flight required thirty minutes and the main event began at dusk and roared on until midnight.

"At dawn," he laughs, "we'd be sitting there banding these goddamn bats and you could hear the flutter of the bats as they came in on a power dive."

Inside the cave, the ceiling and walls were covered, the crevice could not even be seen under the mass of bats, and the animals hung far down the sides. Cockrum could just reach up and pluck them.

Cockrum is a hearty man now in his sixties. He sits in his university office and drifts easily back to the bat cave of the sixties.

"It was a constant, loud, intensive noise," he says, "a constant stream of bats flying. A constant rain of mites as well as urine and guano. After you'd been in there ten minutes, you could feel things crawling on your skin and you'd go out and see these dots crawling up your arms."

But what he remembers best is the seething mass of beetle larvae on the cave floor.

"This was fresh guano," he says. "This surface was almost a sea of larvae and any bat that died or baby that fell to the floor was immediately devoured. Within thirty minutes you'd have a clean skeleton."

OUTSIDE GREEN BLAZES OFF the trees and the stream slides like a brown skin over the rocks. Light ebbs from the canyon. We climb down from the dunes of guano, slip off the rock shelves to the cave opening. The night begins to come down.

Ronnie holds a feather and the delicate finger bone of a bat. And then it begins.

"Oh, my God," she says. "Oh, look at them all. This is great!"

Urine and feces rain down on us. We look up and we cannot look away. Bats storm across the top of the vault, a torrent of wings and squeaks. They streak to the canyon center and swirl and then funnel off. This is the major flight. The free-tails give a faint echo of the thunder of twenty years ago when perhaps 100 million tiny mammals squealed from the room in the rock wall and took to the night sky, an army of hearts, lungs, and fangs ranging out twenty, thirty, forty miles, beasts ripping the soft abdomens from moths, feasting in the dark hours.

A crescent moon hangs and the bats become fine lines etching the glowing face. In four minutes it is over. A flight that once took hours is now 240 seconds. The cave falls silent.

They are gone.

WHEN COCKRUM FINISHED his banding, 88,176 bats had been tagged. From this he plotted the colony's migration route from Arizona to Sonora and Sinaloa in Mexico. This helped him understand the dying.

When the bodies were examined back in the laboratory, the scientists found dieldrin, toxaphene, and DDT. The colony kept shrinking and Cockrum began to understand why. He had already noticed that bats had deserted Tucson. Once they had roosted in the old buildings of the university campus and were a common sight under the street lights. Then with the massive use of household pesticides they vanished.

He began tracking DDT sales in Arizona. Five hundred and forty thousand pounds were sold in 1965, and by 1966 the quantity had reached 107 million pounds. In 1967, 2.52 million pounds were poured onto the land. The agricultural district of the Gila Valley lies within easy reach of the bat cave and they fed heavily there.

That might be part of the answer.

When the United States ended the use of DDT in the late sixties, the colony did not repopulate. Below the border, the use of DDT continued, as it does to this day.

The bats acted as sensors for a world man created but ignored. They roamed the global skin where the insects fly and swallowed the parts per million and per billion that human beings measured and monitored. These chemicals were concentrated in the mother's milk and the young suckled lustily.

Cockrum thinks the tradeoff was reasonable. He likes bats and hates the idea of man causing the extinction of any creature. But, he hastens to add, he has worked in the Third World.

He puts it this way: would you rather die of a tropical disease in your twenties or perish in your sixties because of toxic chemicals? But of course, no one polls the bats on their views.

They simply die, humans live, the crops grow. It is part of this time in this century.

The dying goes like this. The young drink the milk laced with pesticides, the pesticides attack their central nervous systems. The small animals start to shake, then motor skills decline. Eventually the feet clinging to the mother or to the ceiling let go. They fall. The mass of beetle larvae move in. In thirty minutes the bones are clean, a fine wire of calcium across the dark guano in the warm cave.

The scream sounds far away at first, then nearer. We walk out the mouth of the cave. The howling continues, a screech, a long winding yowl as the cry of a big cat shreds the night stillness. We pan with the flashlight.

Twenty feet away two green eyes glow. We move toward the eyes, move instinctively and without hesitation. The cat bounds into the brush and is gone. We crash down the hillside through the thicket of mesquite and hackberry. The stream cools our legs. Bats skim the water sipping drinks. Now outside the warmth of the cave, the mites flee our bodies.

We eat dinner, have a drink of whiskey, and throw our bags down on the ground. Rocks fall from the nearby cliffs as bighorn sheep hop from ledge to ledge.

We are very excited by the memory of the bats brushing against our faces, by the roar of the evening flight, by the green glow of the mountain lion's eyes. Around midnight, the screaming returns. The cat moves around our camp howling. Scientists speculate that this behavior is territoriality, that the lion is staking out its share of the earth. We listen to the screams in the warm night and we do not wonder at what they mean. They say this is my ground, my place.

The sound pierces our half-sleep and then after fifteen or twenty minutes drifts down the canyon. Quiet returns and the screams persist only in our dreams.

Bats squeak overhead as they begin to hunt the poisoned skies and fields. They have few friends in the world of man. They are the demons of our dreams and their slow chemical death is not a matter of concern for many.

We lie under a roof of stars, wings rustling above our faces.

The lion does not return.

Speech Excerpt

From North Dakota Geological Conference

The following are excerpts from a speech titled "Geography, The Iron Reality Everyone Inhabits and Tries to Ignore," given in North Dakota at Bismarck State College on June 9, 2008, for the North Dakota Geographic Alliance. In his speech, Bowden describes the relationship humans have with geography and how our concepts of land use will eventually be antiquated from necessity. He speaks directly of his book published in 1977, *Killing the Hidden Waters,* which focused on the mining of water in arid lands and how this practice is unsustainable. These excerpts demonstrate the consistency, longevity, and breadth of Bowden's original message as it was first explored more than thirty years ago in *Killing the Hidden Waters.*

IN A MILD WAY, the Central Arizona Project is personal for me. Back in the mid-seventies I was working at a think tank at the University of Arizona when they got a federal contract to study the impact of human beings on groundwater. I toiled for months, turned in a bibliography that would choke to death a Ph.D. committee, and, as an act of kindness, kicked in a brief introduction that ran hundreds of pages in which I questioned the wisdom of giving new water, the Central Arizona Project, to a population dedicated to swimming pools, lush lawns, golf courses, and other thumbs in the eye of the desert. I was promptly fired—except universities don't really fire, they just don't renew contracts. As it happened, this manuscript floated around the republic without my knowledge and one day in 1977 I got a call from the University of Texas Press and they said they wanted to publish it. For the past thirty-one years it has been in print under the title *Killing the Hidden Waters*, and, yes, revenge can be sweet—I'm told it is used as a torture device in undergraduate courses. [. . .]

[. . .] LET ME END THIS with a little glimpse of the long term. Ten thousand years ago when the last ice age finally began to ebb, there were five million human beings on earth. That is a global population less than the current numbers in Arizona. Or look at it this way: the entire human race on earth ten thousand years ago was less than ten North Dakotas. Since then, we've invented agriculture, war (there is absolutely no record in Paleolithic art, not a single cave drawing, of violence between organized bands of human beings), the iPod, and of course, Red Bull.

It's been fun.

Now there are over six billion human beings on earth and in the last ten thousand years no human being has produced a single oil field, a single copper deposit, and except in rare instances of organic fervor, not much soil. We've basically mined the planet and called it *destiny*. Maybe all this happened because eight thousand years ago, we invented beer. I told a high school graduating class this spring that no sooner had the ice retreated than our ancestors felt the need to chill out.

Well, now we face the future and I'll bet my life on one notion: in the future, geography, meaning knowledge of where we live and the resources of where we live and how these resources were produced and how they can be husbanded, well, geography will become far more important to us all than television, YouTube, or talk radio. We've ignored geography by mining massive energy deposits and as they decline, we return to geography.

THE DAYS AND NIGHTS slash across the Covered Wells stick. This five- to six-foot piece of saguaro rib holds gouges and nicks. They are the marks of the Papago, a Piman people, and testify to their effort to discover what time and the Sonoran desert meant in their lives. The Papago, also known as the Papavi, the bean people, the desert O-otam, lived in and with one of the most arid stretches of North America. For centuries, they survived the land's heat, the land's rock, the land's three to ten inches of rainfall, the land's wild swings of want and abundance. Early in the nineteenth century they began notching the sticks, and history intruded into their minds with its love of the particular, the taste, the feel, the cost. The sticks would be handed down from man to man, generation to generation, with gouge and nick a clue to memory for what mattered among all things that had happened to the people.

The Covered Wells stick remembers when groundwater came to the people through the white man's pumps. It links a world based on renewable resources with a world based on mining nonrenewable resources. In arid lands groundwater is essentially like coal or oil: easy to exhaust, hard to replace. The story cut into the stick is an examination of what groundwater means to people and what it can do to their ways and means. The desert people knew that water from the earth was energy, and that like all forms of energy it must either be mastered or it will master. Water could never be just water in this place because here it determined both the amount and kind of life to be lived.

Most whites that hear the tales in the desert Indians' sticks are jarred by what they contain and by what they find beneath notice. Mainly, they find white people beneath notice. The Covered Wells stick does not recall the Mexican War. It has no mark for the gold rush of 1849, when tens of thousands of Americans on their way to the west coast traversed the lands of the Piman people. Sometimes the stick recalls nothing at all. Take 1845: "In that year nothing happened worthy of mention." Three years later there is silence on the Mexican and American contest for the Southwest and lengthy mention of a snowstorm. While half a million American boys go to their graves wearing blue and gray, the stick focuses on tribal games, gambling, the fact that two bachelor councilmen are given wives. Whites tend to make the stick because of their machines, and the machines rate a notch because they kill.

PLACE

The hunter, the farmer, the nomad can all find and know the arid lands. They can sense where they begin and end, and their lives become explanations of how arid lands differ from more temperate zones. Science has not been so fortunate. For decades it has wrestled with definitions that expand and contract such regions; various concepts of evaporation rates, minimum rainfall, rainfall spacing, vegetation types, and other yardsticks have been tossed around in fashioning criteria (Evenari, M., L. Shanan, and N. Tadmor, 1971; McGinnies, W. G., et al., 1968). Two belts of earth equidistant from the equator, the horse latitudes, are sectors of low rainfall. Depending upon the authority cited, anywhere from 15 to 20 percent of the globe's land mass is considered arid. Sometimes the poles are included because of their low precipitation rates.

The deserts and semi-arid rangelands are not so much occupied by unique humans, plants, and animals, as they are the home of forms of life that endure unique conditions. The plants are physically like those in wetter regions, and contrary to one's expectations they are often extravagant users of water. Their adaptation lies in the ability to survive long periods of want by going dormant. The animals, with few exceptions, show little more tolerance for heat than creatures of colder climates. They survive in the main by evading the hot days with deep burrows or rest, and by living their lives nocturnally. As for man, it seems the people of arid lands feel the pangs of thirst and the furnace blast of heat as much as other humans. The lore of the desert peoples is filled with testaments to the horrors of dehydration and heat prostration.

Modern industrialized communities in such places are oasis cultures living in the desert but not off it. With pumped groundwater, air conditioning, machines, and imported food, such centers have been able to remain ignorant of the environment just beyond the city pavement. About 150 years ago, a caravan of 2,000 humans and 1,800 camels died of thirst in the southern Sahara (Cloudsley-Thompson, J. L., 1965). During the summer of 1905, 35 humans died of thirst in Death Valley alone (McGee, W. J., 1906). When man leaves his modern cities and enters the desert, he is but a few hours from this world and short days from death if he fails to heed its presence. A day without moisture and he will chew anything for water; a few days without food and he will kill anything for sustenance.

"A poor devil on the Mohave desert," W. J. McGee relates in his classic paper on desert thirst, "reached a neglected water hole early in this stage [of dehydration]; creeping over debris in the twilight, he paid no attention to turgid toads and a sodden snake and the seething scum of drowned insects until a soggy, noisome mass turned under his weight and a half fleshed skeleton, still clad in flannel shirt and chaparejos, leered in his face with vacant sockets and fallen jaw; he fled . . ." (ibid.). His trail later showed that he spent the rest of his ordeal seeking again this same spot. When rescued he raved for days "of his folly in passing the 'last water.'" There are many such tales of men drinking their own urine, of Tom Newton who in 1905 went four days without water in Death Valley and was found "aimlessly 'leaping about in the sun like a frog . . . ,'" of a child who wandered into the Mohave and was found impaled on the hundred thorns of a cactus embraced in a terminal surge toward moisture (ibid.).

This is the core of aridity: the danger to biological life. It is a forgotten core, and the mummified caravans, the delirious prospectors, the ruins by the Tigris, the Euphrates, the Nile, the Salt, the Gila, the dead cities of the Iranian plateau, the vanquished communities of the Rajasthan desert—all these scraps of memory and fact are often regarded as a curiosity. The deserts that spawned religions, that drove men to rain songs, that resounded from singing sands with their twang like a monster harp, these places and things are little known or considered by modern systems of exploitation based on mining fossil fuels and fossil water. Blotted from consciousness, their reality seems to many more doubtful than the plenty of desert cities and irrigated farms. Humans have avoided the brunt of aridity by constructing microclimates with steel, electricity, fossil fuels, groundwater, pumps. But this shelter does not promise to be as enduring as the facts of aridity itself. The arid lands are reasserting themselves around the globe, and this process is now called desertification. It describes degradation of land to desertlike conditions because of human activities (Shercrooke, W., and P. Paylore, 1973). It is a message from the land.

A key problem facing man in the drylands is water, and the problem with the water is that it is largely sight unseen: groundwater. The surface supplies afforded by the few rivers and springs have long been exploited, and future expansion of human activity in the arid lands, indeed much of the current activity, depends on lifting water from the earth. Hydrology is in many ways the history of man's efforts to locate this buried water. Modern techniques and sensing devices have helped in this search, but they have not significantly changed the age-old problem that man looking for water underground largely looks blind. Expensive quests by scientists still sometimes result in dry holes, brackish or saline water.

In recent years a new machine has sought to minimize the hazards of this searching: the computer. Into its maw of printed circuits, massive piles of fact, graph, and notation are poured, then programmed and modeled into the closet drama of high technology simulation. As the pages of printout spew forth, aquifers can be drawn down, wells drilled, water qualities varied, decades of exploitation hypothesized in minutes. With aids like this machine, scholars believe that groundwater analysis has moved from a dowsing rod level to the credibility of a science. One survey of the field concluded that groundwater hydrology "is on the threshold of an important period of integration" (Simpson, E. S., 1967). By converting water, rock, soil, and human consumption to numbers and then rapidly digesting the numbers with the computer it is hoped that a way can be found to deal with the nature of groundwater in arid lands: that it is basically nonrenewable.

More data are sought for the machines on hydrogeologic mapping, the relationship between chemistry and aquifer properties, and the possibilities of artificial recharge (ibid.). Models have been constructed comparing rapid mining of an aquifer with steady-state use (Gisser, M., and A. Mercado, 1972). Water systems for regions can be simulated complete with reservoirs, canals, pumps, rivers, and rains. Under the title "Coping with Population Growth and a Limited Resource," Arizona's chronic overdraft of groundwater has been made a series of optimization and simulation models (Briggs, P., 1972). Sometimes the consequences of various water uses are projected, and, in one case, farmers are sacrificed to urban thirst (Kelso, M. M., W. E. Martin, and L. E. Mack, 1973). Irrigation districts are modeled, evaluated, planned (Heady, E. O., et al., 1971).

There are reasons for this. Many nations in the arid lands depend on groundwater. Tunisia's water supply is 95 percent subsurface. Morocco must pump 75 percent of its water. Israel is about the same. Saudi Arabia is based almost completely on groundwater. Wells are a major and growing source of water throughout North Africa, Western Australia, the American West, central Asia, India, Iraq, Afghanistan, Pakistan, and other nations (Cantor, L. M., 1967). The use and dependence upon groundwater are growing as population expands beyond the capacity of surface supplies. The United Nations has cautioned that "it is necessary to bear in mind that these natural resources (water and land) are permanent assets of every nation, in fact of humanity at large. These resources have to be used wisely and passed on unimpaired and, as far as possible, undiminished to the generations to follow" (FAO/UNESCO, 1973).

It is hard to fault these efforts to garner more information, simulate various futures, and wisely husband resources lest posterity be deprived of necessities. But when such inquiries are focused on groundwater in arid lands there is a limit to what can be done. If one accepts the hypothesis of those who argue against safe yield as a goal, little need be done since the society which exhausts its groundwater will in this very effort find the economic elements of a solution. On the other hand, any attempt to adhere to the United Nations advice about passing on water and land unimpaired and undiminished requires extremely limited use of groundwater. There simply is not much recharge to aquifers in arid lands because there is not much rain; to use such water sources in the manner typical of Western industrialized societies is to mine them. The information and the machines can help with speculations about how fast to use the water and where to use it. They cannot augment the supply. Or alter the region where it is found.

But the talk of turning the arid lands to account keeps pouring from the presses. Words of caution about the grotesque results of man's hand in such places (Sauer, C. O., 1969) and warnings about the creep of deserts into the croplands (Sherbrooke, W., and P. Paylore, 1973) are drowned by cadenzas of schemes and dreams.

Cheap energy, abundant water, and an army of studies have helped keep consciousness of the arid lands at bay. But this feat has been accomplished at a high cost in resources. As the water tables sink, as the price of a BTU increases, defenses against aridity will gradually decline. For the place has never really changed at all. It has merely been erased in small patches of the earth where humans have concentrated resources. Societies based on the rapid exhaustion of storages face the possibility of lasting just as long as those storages. That is why the place matters. The deserts and semi-arid rangelands are living off of the renewable solar flow of materials. They can wait outside the borders of human cities and farms. Ready to return.

PEOPLE

The woman remembers. She is fifty something, Papago. Her life has been spent in a village beneath Baboquivari Peak surrounded by kinsmen, desert, mud walls, personal things. Yes, she says, many used to farm, now not many. Her husband is one of the few tribesmen who has clung to the ancient O-otam way of wresting a crop from the Sonoran desert. This way is called *akchin:* arroyo mouth. It is very simple. In summer, due to tilt of earth and global swirl of air, the rains come to the Baboquivari Valley. Day after day the puff of cloud builds over land electric with the dry. Suddenly, release comes from the bondage of sunny skies: rain. The moisture strikes the land with violence and roars off the rock slopes of the mountains, savaging a route down the arroyos to the valley floor. Here, speed is lost, slope gives way to flat of floodplain, and the waters move as a sheet over the porous dirt, sinking in, making life possible. That is when the man plants.

Once the O-otam used a digging stick, then centuries ago a shovel was glimpsed in a European hand and the stick widened. A hundred years ago, Yankees came peddling metal tools. Finally, the iron plow and the horse were brought to the ancient fields. The tilled ground drinks the rain. Then, the man plops his seed in the mud and waits for the sprouting of corn, squash, melon, bean. He hopes for more rain, and the plants race the sun for the moisture in the alluvium. Sometimes he loses and the rains stay away from his part of the valley, and nothing gets planted or everything gets planted and everything dies. Sometimes he wins, and the seed planted in July with the rains becomes a plant guarded in the fall. The man works but a few acres. In the middle, a hut with mesquite beams, dirt floor, and walls of ocotillo ribs serves his needs. Here he sits in the heat of the day. Here in the fall he spends the night guarding his melons from raiding coyotes. This is the system called akchin: no fertilizer, no pumped groundwater, no insecticide, no herbicide. This way of growing food has all but vanished. In 1914 a federal survey found the Papago cultivating thousands of acres by floodwater farming (Clotts, H. V., 1915). Today, this enterprise is but a memory in the villages. Sometimes the remnants of former fields can be seen; sometimes nothing remains.

Since the 1930s this way of farming and the way of life based upon it have been driven from Papagueria. The old man with his field, his hut, his seeds, his wait for the July rains is a ghost on his own land, and when he dies and the other old men die in the next decade or so, akchin will be gone. It was a way of living in the desert without wells, without pumps, without electricity, without fossil fuels. These very forces have vanquished akchin by making it obsolete and futile in the eyes of the Papago. The young will have none of it and the old have mainly let it go. Here, in the struggle between akchin and the energy systems of the white man during the twenties and thirties, the Covered Wells stick ceases, as if to say that the need for history had passed and the past was no longer usable.

In 1915 the stick says:

Even while the well rigs were going, copious rains fell, making bounteous crops and feed for stock, thus proving the lack of necessity for wells and vindicating the judgment of the wise Indians in opposing the innovation (Kilcrease, A. T., 1939).

The record continues through the teens, noting the influenza epidemic, ignoring World War I. An aurora borealis lights the skies in 1921 and old Papagos say it is a portent. The rains fail for a year. The following year is marked by renewed faith in akchin:

The wise men decided that neglect to celebrate the rain feast was the cause of all these calamitous happenings and that it must be done this year. It was done and no more disasters have occurred (ibid.).

THE STICK PROCEEDS FOR A few years recording items of interest to the Papago. A road is built in 1928; a year later an automobile runs over an Indian. With the thirties, information from the nicks and gouges ends as the Bureau of Indian Affairs and federal work programs finally penetrate this desert world.

Perhaps this too is part of what the woman remembers. She has lived from the world of the stick into the world of today. Her life is a crazy quilt of different energy systems. The house is stucco-covered adobe surrounded by an eight-foot ocotillo fence. The fence is alive and it pulses green or brown with the rains. In summer, life is lived outside under the ramada of mesquite beams, saguaro ribs, dirt-packed roof. Two metal beds catch the night air. A dozen light blue Mexican pots hang; on the ground lies a stone metate for grinding corn. She is making tortillas; the ingredients are kept in two electric refrigerators. The work is done by hand. A metal sheet over a mesquite fire is the stove. The bag of flour on the table is federal surplus. The house nearby has electric lights, dirt floors. Across from the ramada is a chapel such as many Papagos have. Sometimes they contain *santos* centuries old next to crosses fashioned from plastic egg cartons. It is the heat of day and nothing stirs in the desert as the woman works. On the kitchen table is an alarm clock.

The woman knows the desert. On a walk she can show what plants are good to eat and when they should be picked. Like her husband's farming, this information will die with her. It no longer matters. Food comes in packages, energy from electric lines, water from wells.

The Papago today are much like their white neighbors an hour or so to the eastward. There, in the Santa Cruz Valley, three to four hundred thousand Americans live in a modern urban community. It is said to be the largest city in the United States based solely on groundwater. The streets are lined with trees, the yards lush with lawns. People with money build swimming pools. The largest single employer is the government. The inhabitants call their town the Old Pueblo. It is an outpost of money and resources from the east. Food comes from other states. Electric lines reach out almost five hundred miles seeking power. Water heaters run on natural gas from Texas. The homes, schools, stores, and automobiles are air-conditioned. The parks have artificial lakes. Local building codes have outlawed mud adobe construction. The Papago lands and the city touch.

This place called Tucson is a triumph of humans over the environment. A child in this city can flick a light switch and help make a power plant in another state burn 20 to 30 thousand tons of coal per day. Each human in this desert metropolis uses 175 gallons of water every 24 hours (Davidson, E. S., 1973). The community banks a river dry more than 300 days per year. It ignores this fact, like so much else, because it has access to abundant fossil energy from outside the desert. Water is pumped from the ground faster than it is replenished; in fact, the city leads its state in this activity. Each year the water table under the thriving city sinks several feet. Subsidence is expected by 1985 (ibid.). The inhabitants do not keep sticks.

These are two of the desert peoples of the region. Today they live roughly similar lives. They are consumers and what they consume are ancient storages of fuel, water, and soil. The Papago are considered poverty-stricken, which means they cannot devour goods at the rate they would like. The Americans are considered affluent, which means their enormous appetites are fed. But both are now aliens to the Sonoran desert itself with its natural flows of resources. Days long past pour from their faucets, feed their families, and power their worlds.

One thing separates them: what the woman remembers. Brief decades ago, almost until the start of the Second World War, the Papago lived in the world of the stick. Food came from wild plants and from the rains, and the rains came from rituals, and the rituals came from a past known only to myth. The O-otam way, now almost gone, dominated the people well into this century. As late as the 1930s one Papago was found innocent of the Gadsden Purchase and believed he still lived in a part of Mexico. The people were left to the land because whites did not want it. Finally, in 1916 a reservation was set up. The Papagos entered into the web of American life having never fought a war against the United States or given ground.

If one wishes to examine the impact of groundwater development, the O-otam offer a rare opportunity. Within the lifetime of humans still alive they have moved from a society perfectly adapted to aridity and absolutely independent of groundwater to a society independent of the desert and based on groundwater. For those interested in peace with nature, the Papago offer abundant clues to the price of such a peace. For those fascinated by development, they are an example of how it is done and what it does.

There is a debate going on about development itself. Humans are asking what past achievements mean, and what future plans should be. This debate continues under many guises, such as arguments about steady-state economies, pitches for green revolutions, alarms about the environment, concern over population growth—concern over growth, period. Groundwater leads one into this swirl of contention because it stimulates societies in arid regions it is by nature incapable of sustaining.

The history of the desert O-otam, and the Piman people in general, grants insights into this debate. They have lived its many aspects. It has not been a tidy journey, and the investigation of the move from renewable resources to nonrenewable resources demands a look at the culture of the humans who experienced such a change. To look away from deep wells and coal and oil and electricity is in this instance to peer into a world of dreams, sharing, rituals, akchin.

Snaketime

From *Wild Earth*, Summer/Fall 2003

SHE ARRIVED AT THE ranch house in May during a bad drought. I was living four or five miles from the Mexican border when one day a visitor found a coiled rattlesnake in the flowerbed by the porch. I walked over and looked down and was unnerved. The snake, well camouflaged, was all but invisible to me; in fact my visitor had been squatting to urinate—an effort to save water from the dying well—when she noticed it. I let the snake be. I was coming off a dark season and had outlawed all guns and all acts of violence from the ranch. The earth was burning from lack of rain and the brown range was beaten down. The snake stayed and eventually moved up on the porch where it would sleep all day near my chair. She was a western diamondback, the species credited with the most bites and deaths in the United States. I never could tell the snake's sex, but I named it Beulah for no particular reason.

IT'S ALMOST TEN YEARS later and I am in the Chiricahua Mountains near a blacktail rattlesnake, one of over a hundred in a study group that has been examined for 15 years. Part of what brings me here are nagging memories of Beulah and other moments from my collisions with rattlesnakes. I've been dropping by the study site for two years and in that time I never see the snake of my dreams and fears, the serpent moving like lightning with fangs extended. I have entered snaketime and in this time I never see one snake make a fast move.

For the snake a few feet from where I sit several things are obvious: I am large, and this is certain because of my footfall. She can hear the footfall of a mouse. I am rich in odor. She can pick up the faintest scents, identify them, and follow one single strand as clearly as if it were signed on an interstate highway system. I am clumsy, she can see that with her eyes, though she hardly relies on sight. And I am warm; she forms an image from her ability to pick up and analyze body heat thanks to the pits on her snout. I become a shape with a field of temperatures of different intensities, one so finely felt that she can perfectly target any part of my body. And I am irrelevant unless I get too close. She will ignore me if I stay six feet away. She will ignore me if I become motionless for 180 seconds. If I violate the rules of her culture, she will try to work through a sequence of four tactics. First, she will pretend to be invisible and hope I do not see her. If that fails, she will try to flee. If that fails, she will act aggressively in hopes of frightening me away. And finally, if I am completely ignorant of simple courtesy and get within a foot or so of her, she will attack me. I have failed at least a dozen times in my life in observing these boundaries—I've never been struck but I have caused alarming rattles. I am truly a barbarian.

She herself is cultured. In her lifetime, she will attack infrequently, a few dozen times at most. She will never attack any member of her own species. She will never be cruel. She is incapable of evil.

I never walk my ground without her being in my thoughts. I never make night moves on my desert without a hyper-alertness to her. She never wants to meet me. She never stalks me.

Sometimes I sit in the dark trying to imagine how I look to her. I can only brush against such powers of perception. I cannot hear the footfall of a mouse. My powers of catching scent are feeble in comparison. I can barely sense the presence of others through heat. I am almost always full of aggression barely kept in check.

I have always feared her. That is why I have come here.

WITH BEULAH, THINGS BEGAN slowly. First, I had to deal with my fear. I was in an addled state that spring and I had decided to erase boundaries in an effort to calm myself. For example, each evening I would put Miles Davis on the stereo, pour a glass of wine, and sit on a chaise lounge on the porch in my shorts. Clouds of bats would come to my hummingbird feeders, and they would hover all around my mostly naked body and brush my arms and legs and chest and face with their wings. When I arose to refill my glass, the cloud of bats would magically part and when I returned they would continue their exploration. Beulah became part of this careless web I was weaving. At the same time, deer would come near the house, twirl, and make their evening beds. I lived alone, made no fuss over anything, including the rattlesnake.

As the weeks went by, I began to notice little facts about Beulah. I would be out on the porch in the blazing heat of May and she would be curled by my chair as I read. I'd get up and go get another glass of water, and she would not stir. She was coiled but seemingly at peace.

I would rummage through my limited snake lore, the various myths that different cultures had employed to deal with serpents. I noticed they all had one common feature whether they saw snakes as good or evil: snakes possessed potential menace. Of course the Christian version with its Garden of Eden, serpent and apple, baffled me the most. I could see the loss of nakedness as a serious matter. But I could never understand how knowledge was part of any meaningful fall from grace.

With Beulah, I learned to move slowly out of courtesy. Once or twice visitors popped in unannounced and saw the snake on the porch. I offered no explanation. But then I was already considered eccentric for living out so far, living alone. Without a gun.

THEY ARE RIGHT OVER THERE in the shelter of the rock on this hillside on the eastern flank of the Chiricahua Mountains near the Arizona and New Mexico line. I am sitting on the ground six feet away. The two pregnant females are piled atop the other and this arrangement does not seem random. Each female has that section of her body, where the fertile eggs are lodged, exposed and gestating in the sun. The rest of their bodies cool in the shade. The sunlight will hasten gestation, just as having their bodies piled on each other will raise the temperature and accelerate the eventual live birth of the young.

I'm with Dave Hardy, who is busy making notes. He carries gear on his back for tracking the snakes in the study population, each of which has been surgically implanted with a transmitter and antenna. This means two simple things: the subjects can always be found by their individual signals and the subjects are almost never alarmed. In the almost 15 years of the study, the snakes have rarely displayed aggression except when they have been grabbed for battery changes, a maintenance task that must be done every eighteen months. So far Dave and his partner Harry Greene have amassed thousands of field observations of *Crotalus molossus,* blacktailed rattlesnakes. For thousands of years, human contact with rattlesnakes in the wild has gone like this: we collide with a rattlesnake or we have no contact with them at all. For our kind, rattlesnakes are coiled, tail vibrating, fangs at ready to poison us. It is as if we formed our entire knowledge of automobiles from head-on collisions.

What Dave and Harry have found is a separate nation. One thing stands out about how our nation sees their nation. We see rattlesnakes as menacing, as simple-minded eating machines. In 15 years, the study has witnessed one kill. It happened August 21, 1997. Dave was radio tracking a female, No. 21. She was an almost-three-foot-long adult and that day was coiled and in hunting alert when a cottontail came by. She struck it in the left shoulder. The rabbit jumped into the air and ran about 12 feet away, paused, and started making distress cries and spinning in circles. No. 21 returned to her hunting coil. Then the rabbit ran off about 20 more feet and the rattlesnake slowly began pursuit following the scent trail. For the next two hours, Hardy followed the snake as she followed the rabbit. Sometimes the snake would get within three feet of the rabbit before it would tear off again. When Hardy came back the next day, the snake had a bulge, undoubtedly from swallowing the cottontail. She stayed in place for 11 days, and then on September 1, 1997, moved about 30 feet to the east. The flash of the strike, and then the endless ribbon of languor that seems to be snaketime.

After about a half-hour, Dave and I stand and move off. He flips his radio receiver to another frequency and we go to visit with another rattlesnake. The two females are still, just as we found them, as if we had never existed or mattered to their world. When I look back I cannot even make them out on their rock ledge. They fit in a place I visit but do not know.

MY FEAR NEVER LEFT ME. I'd thought of snakes as things, and so Beulah, for a long time, remained for me some kind of robot that was fully programmed at birth and could unleash her toxins at any moment and poison me. I began to worry about her diet and would look closely at her each morning hoping to see a bulge from some kill made in the night. But the drought was a lean season for everything. I wondered at times why she was there. I would tick off the possible answers. A house is built by disturbing soil, and loose soil is good habitat for rats and thus draws snakes. The drought, I would think, might have something to do with it even though rattlesnakes have low moisture needs, and they hardly need to eat for that matter. But mainly, I did not think about it at all. There was a great horned owl along the wash that roosted each day by a trail I took. At first, the owl would break cover when I went by. Then slowly its reaction time narrowed and it would only take off at the last moment. Finally, it ignored my daily passage completely. I became like the owl. Leery, but slowly adapting to Beulah.

One day, someone came to the ranch I had not seen in years, an old buddy from high school. He'd gotten deep into Eastern religion and had just come back from a pilgrimage to India and Nepal. By that season the great horned owl had mated, built a huge nest just below the ranch house in a cottonwood along the wash, and now the two of them had a clutch of hatchlings to feed. For a week or two, I'd been going down to the nest with a drink in the late afternoon and sprawling out on the ground as I watched the owls. I sent my friend down there to see the birds and the nest while I stayed up at the house on the hill and cooked dinner. The owl instantly attacked him and knocked the hat off his head.

I realized he was a stranger to the owl.

That is how I began to relate to Beulah. She did seem to react to my presence. She was not a pet but somehow I was part of an accepted landscape. She coiled next to my chair as I read in the heat of the afternoon. I moved slowly so as not to alarm her. We seemed to learn each other's ways.

After a while, I began to notice something startling to me. Increasingly, when people came out to the ranch, Beulah disappeared. I would be sitting with her during the inferno of the afternoon—and one day it hit 117 degrees—and I would hear a car pull up, the clunk of the doors, and then arise to see who had come. When I came back, Beulah would be gone from her post by my chair. If no one came, she'd spend the afternoon out there with me. But if strangers descended, she seemed to hide.

I began to wonder if she could tell me from other people.

FOR A LONG TIME THE DESERT was nothing but snakes to me. When I slept on the ground in the desert, I thought they would come for me. When I walked the summer nights, I thought they were out there, coiled and ready to strike my flesh and fill me with poison. Once I crossed a dune and repeatedly put my foot down near coiled sidewinders half buried in the sand. Ribbons of snake tracks covered the swells. At dusk, I threw my bag down and slept, the sleep of surrender. I think that marked the turning point, the moment when I grasped two facts: that there was nothing I could do about the snakes and that there were no snakes in my desert hunting me because I was too big to swallow.

Later, random facts gave me further comfort. Some of the bites that come into local emergency rooms are dry, devoid of poison. Poison is expensive for the snakes to create and one possible assumption is that they are reluctant to waste it on the likes of me. I doubt this fine discrimination, but still there are these dry bites.

It is a June long ago, and the air runs 90 degrees as I stumble through the desert without a trail around midnight. My bare legs bleed from small scratches left by thorns and no matter how much I drink I am sinking into dehydration. My pack weighs a good 70 to 80 pounds. This is when I step on the rattlesnake. The sound of the rattle, the feel of the snake under my running shoe, my movement away—all this is one single memory. The snake does not strike and remains coiled. I sit down a few feet away and stare at it in the half-light of a world revealed by stars.

That's it. An anecdote that illustrates nothing except possibly the luck of fools.

I ceased to think of snakes as enemies. I started thinking of them as part of a web, something I dimly belonged to, a reality I shared. And this dim sense of kinship fed another sensation: otherness. They were not my friends, they were not my enemies. They were not like me; they simply were.

I lost interest in their mouths with the two long fangs that could inject venom into my tissues. I began to consider them another nation, one with a culture about which I had not a clue.

There are lines we are warned not to cross. Ethics teaches us we cannot consider other life forms as things. Science teaches us we cannot project our human natures onto other living things. I am from another place. I am not like the snake. But I am not below or above the snake. I lack any sense of hierarchy in the natural world regardless of the charts drilled into my head since boyhood of the odyssey of evolution. I don't see my species as the culmination of anything, nor do I look at a rattlesnake as a failed ancestor.

That night in the long-ago June heat, the air is dry in my nostrils, the snake stays coiled, I drink water, and the safe ground formed by the beliefs of my people erodes out from under me. I continue for years to move at night across the desert floor. A part of me is never relaxed, another part of me is always resigned.

I do not accept rattlesnakes. That attitude would have me assuming a power that is beyond my reach or my right. Rattlesnakes do not need my approval. Sometimes people ask me about problem snakes hanging around their houses and threatening their dogs and themselves. I tell them to live with them or kill them.

Some years back a woman was horseback riding near Phoenix when she fell on a rattlesnake, took a hit with massive venom, and died. That is just as likely to happen to me as to someone who hates every snake on Earth. There is no justice in this matter. Or malice. Or virtue. But there is this place without friend or foe, the place where rattlesnakes live with their internal drives and terrain and infrequent meals of rats. I am of that place. As dusk deepened at the ranch that spring and early summer, the roar of hummingbirds at my feeders on the porch would slacken. I had about ten species of hummingbirds and hundreds in the population. I would have exactly 64 at a time feeding and a mob swirling around them waiting in turn. Orioles would come also and I delighted in the clack of their bills as they devoured honeybees on the feeders. Beulah would be seemingly oblivious to this roar of life and appear to sleep through the day—though to my knowledge no one knows by any brainwave study if rattlesnakes really sleep.

But as the night came on, at that moment when I could still see but the sun was down, Beulah would uncoil and slowly slither across the porch, passing within inches of my foot, tongue flicking and body undulating. Once she actually crossed my bare foot. She would go down the steps and vanish into the wild grasses and then be gone from my view. When I arose in the morning, I would find her at first light by my chair. I never knew where or why she went—I assumed her expeditions were about hunting. But there was this part of her world locked off from me.

THE YEAR NEITHER BEGINS nor ends. There is no harvest moon, nor appointment calendar. Time is a ribbon, or perhaps time is a moment. There is a future tense, the snake coils by a game trail and waits for prey. So there is a future. The past is beyond our speculation. We simply cannot decide if a rattlesnake has a past. Except that there are clues: young eastern timber rattlers, born some distance away, have been observed following the trails of adults to winter dens. Is this learning? And if something is learned does it constitute a past?

Blacktail rattlesnakes have home ranges roughly 200 meters wide and 500 meters long in the study area. If they are transported several miles from their home range and released, they inevitably starve to death. If they are moved less than two miles, they return. This implies they know the resources of their home range, which in turn implies they learned them, which in turn implies that they have a remembered past. Snakes that are moved tend to keep cutting right angles, as if they were looking for some known geography, perhaps a horizon line.

They live in a world with little temperature variation. The winter dens run in the sixties and when outside they use sunlight or shade to keep their blood at a fairly constant heat. Calling them cold-blooded means that they cannot generate their own heat, not that they are cold. In the study group, each individual eats only a few wood rats and other small mammals a year. Given a life span of 20-plus years, this suggests that the strike—that image burned into human consciousness—is a minor part of a blacktail's life. The strike takes less than a second and happens only a few dozen times in a snake's life. This adds up to at most one minute of time in decades of life. The barnyards would rejoice if our appetites were this restrained.

Dave Hardy and Harry Greene are closing in on 4,000 field observations of their subjects and have seen precisely two strikes—one successful, one a miss. Mainly, they find the snakes moving slowly, or inert. The rattlesnakes have no conflict with the researchers, or with other snakes. Once they reach some size at age two or three, almost nothing tries to kill them (excepting people). They live a life with acute sensitivity to the world around them, slight food needs, almost no climatic stress, and huge swatches of time.

That is the brute life of a blacktail: sensation, time, lack of stress, scent, color, and light.

The partly overcast sky dapples the hillside above Silver Creek. I know No. 39, a female, is very near from the radio receiver beeping in Dave Hardy's hand but still I cannot see her. She is in the middle of the wash, clearly outlined by the gravel and sand and near a dark limestone rock when I finally make her out. She is coiled, rattles tucked out of view, head held slightly back, the classic hunting posture. No doubt she is by some game trail detected by her fine sense of smell. We know male snakes can figure out which way a female snake has gone by noticing the scent differences on each side of a blade of grass or a pebble where she has passed. A bug lands on her, she flinches ever so slightly, then goes still again in her camouflaged ambush posture. Rattlesnakes must wait for prey. They cannot run them down. Which raises an interesting question: how much time do they spend hunting?

They are normally coiled in order to save body heat and so to our eyes almost always in a hunting posture. They are often poised by a game trail but then they must be somewhere, so why not sit by one of the many strands marking the earth that rats have created? And they appear sleepy and yet alert. Harry Greene used to keep a bushmaster, a huge Central American viper, in his lab at Berkeley. He fed the snake every month or so. The snake never seemed to move; it was like a pet rock in its cage. And yet when Harry tossed in a mouse the bushmaster invariably caught it in mid-air. Imagine that state of rest and yet alertness. So far, we lack the words for such a state and, certainly, we lack any analogy in our own personal experience. And what does hunting mean to an animal that hardly eats? To an organism that can in hard times literally skip eating for a year or more.

No. 39, like all the snakes in the study, has a known and mapped home range, a winter den (and blacktails either winter alone, or with one or two others), a birthing den, and a known pattern of travel from each site to the creek where in August the rats are thick and the mating season occurs in what seems a little like a blacktail Woodstock. In the courtship season, males hungrily follow the scent trails of females, sometimes traveling 500 meters a day. Their testosterone levels also rise during the mating season. All but two of the snakes in the study have been captured and equipped with transmitters because of their attraction to females with transmitters during the mating season. In the case of females, they have been revealed by lusty males with transmitter implants seeking them out.

The famous combat of rattlesnakes where two males rise, intertwine, and fight for females is more like arm wrestling. The larger male invariably knocks down the smaller male and wins. Combat with no physical damage involved. Copulation can go on for a day or more—in the study group, Dave and Harry faltered and got tired of watching somewhere after the twentieth hour. The sperm is stored, the eggs fertilized the following spring, and young born live thereafter. The mother stays with the young until they shed their skins and can see—this takes about two weeks. This offers one of the tantalizing and rare examples of parental behavior observed in some reptiles. The litters are three or four young, and the females generally go two or three years between birthings. Apparently, almost none of the young survive, but then blacktails, with a 20-plus-year life span, require a very low replacement rate.

In the fall, the snakes migrate uphill in the valley to their winter dens and largely stay within them until spring. That is the year for a blacktail.

Few real enemies. No problem with food—the snakes in the study group are almost all of good flesh. A relatively constant temperature due to using natural shade or holes in the ground to even out the weather. As I mentioned, we do not know if they sleep, we are ignorant of how much stress they experience. But we do know this calendar and within it, there seems lots of time for things besides the struggle for survival.

We go down the hill to the creek and find No. 34, a female, basking in the sun. Three days ago she ate and the bulge is still clearly visible. Blacktails eat so infrequently that their stomachs shut down. After a kill, it takes three or four hours to reactivate their digestive juices so that they can absorb the fresh nutrition. We find No. 46, a male, about 15 feet from the female and gliding up and down the rocks of the creek bank apparently following her scent trail. No. 46 had surgery for his transmitter replacement ten days earlier. I sit on the ground and watch him and then decide to sprawl on my belly to better take the snake's view of things. He is a fat snake and as he glides he slowly moves his head from side to side, tongue flicking, searching for the scent of the female. The air is still, the silence so total a fly buzz seems the only sound. The male is maybe four or five feet from me gliding as I make notes.

He is alert and yet somehow relaxed as he wanders back and forth nosing out the scent trail. The female is 15 feet away basking and finally, after a good long spell, the male gets to within one or two feet of her and then coils on the opposite side of a log and rests. Later that afternoon, he is in the same position, and again the next morning. I have brushed against snaketime where even the imagined urgencies of mating follow protocols whose outlines we barely know. Fourteen days later, days spent together, often within a foot of each other, they finally mate.

FOR YEARS I LIVED WITH a desert tortoise named Lightning. Early each November, he went into his burrow and emerged the following spring. While he hibernated my yard seemed dead to me. For a spell, I worked by a floor-to-ceiling window and Lightning would come over, get on his hind feet, and stare at me. Once in a while, I put out plates of greens and vegetables. Eventually, I learned he had a savage hankering for bananas. But what I really realized was that he reacted to people differently. He'd follow me around like a dog as I worked the garden. He liked the electrician and would paddle around after him as he worked. He hated the plumber who always seemed to be digging up old pipes; Lightning would go underground for days once he appeared on his turf. In short, he could distinguish between people and this was a revelation to me since I initially thought of him as a pet rock. I never picked him up. I never made him into a pet. Once a cat got into his food and he seemed enraged and chased the cat around in circles for more than a minute. He was my first bridge into what is called cold blood. I hooked up with a woman and he repeatedly charged her on sight—possibly, as one visiting herpetologist offered, as part of a mating drive. The woman concluded the tortoise and I had a homoerotic bond.

Beulah was a deeper current for me because I was afraid of her. I have no illusions about rattlesnake venom—a bite will not likely kill a healthy adult but the ride will be very rough and a visit to the hospital can easily run 20 grand. And yet here I was whiling away days with a rattlesnake. I began to feel badly when company came and she disappeared, as if I were a bad host, or at least a thoughtless roommate.

I would slip into snaketime for hours, doing nothing as the snake beside me did nothing. But wait. It was not simply losing track of hours or days. It was diving deep into the moment and yet at the same time finding each moment immense and full. I had the bats and Miles Davis at night, but during the day, I had the frenetic pace of hummingbirds on the porch and Beulah, at rest and yet ready to spring in an instant, teaching me a different sense of time. I know now that in the study area, a snake basking in the sun and sitting out on a ledge, the common way people sometimes see snakes, takes up only about 5 percent of their schedule. The rest is this state of being I witnessed with Beulah each afternoon. And of course, we know so little. In the 15 years of the blacktail study, only two or three blacktails have entered the study area from outside the mapped home ranges. Does this mean the group in the little valley are some genetic pocket, a tribe perhaps? We don't know.

One June day about four A.M., I make coffee at the ranch, throw on a shirt, and paddle barefoot and bare assed onto the porch to see the death of the morning stars. I feel something under my foot, hear a rattle, and look down at Beulah stretched out as she is apparently on her way to the woodpile and a brief canvass for rats. I lift my foot and she slithers off.

I remember the alarm at the rattle, the heat and scent from the coffee rising in my face. I do not remember deep fear—I think it happened too fast for a rational response. But mainly I remember this: looking down and thinking, Beulah, I'm sorry, I didn't mean to step on you. I think I said something out loud to her about my clumsiness.

That afternoon she is back at her post by the chair as I sit and read as if nothing had happened.

I HAVE A PILE OF NOTES from Dave on the life histories of several blacktails. The snatches of behavior caught in the field form a kind of false history of months of calm punctuated by events—movement, denning, birthing, courting. Every time I string the notes together into a biography I get that false speed that is characteristic of nature films, the montage of eating and fornicating and darting here and there. This montage misses the state of grace that covers what we cannot understand or learn.

But of course, grace cannot be within the reach of snakes because it is a divine gift and they are beneath the cares of God. Nor can grace be possible for snakes because they are organisms with Latin names and locked within a logical schema we have created that bars God at the door. So I am left with the calm of the blacktails, the long silences and slow motion, the apparent lack of anxiety, the appetite that seems not linked to hunger as we know it, the courtship that is alien to our frenzied notions of love, the endless ribbons of time that seem a bower within which the snakes crawl and repose and live a peace we can never know. We are left with the fangs and venom and the strike, rare moments that reassure us of a kinship. We are left with these tiny seconds of violence to estrange us from our comfort zone.

In the end, two things remain. Our knowledge of blacktail rattlesnakes is very slight. And no matter how much we learn of them the fear never completely leaves. They do not hunt us, they have no apparent interest in us, they hardly ever harm us, certainly not nearly as much as we harm them. We can no more kill all of them than they can kill all of us. We are together in this thing called life.

Nothing makes a person completely safe in rattlesnake country. Nor does anything make a snake completely safe. Certainly not being the research subject of eminent herpetologists in the Chiricahua Mountains. Last year, a group of illegal Mexicans camped along the creek while awaiting their ride from a smuggler. Such bands of illegals had never visited the study area before but this year at least a dozen parties had descended on the out-of-the-way little valley. Apparently, the Mexicans stumbled upon No. 26. All Dave found was the transmitter with no remains. Harry speculates that they discovered the snake, killed it out of fear. And then ate it. This was the third human killing of an adult blacktail in the 15 years of the study. Years ago, No. 1 was killed with a shovel by two men who found it crossing a dirt road. No. 11 perished when it was accidentally run over. Most likely it was the first and last time No. 26 had a confrontation with a human in its life.

THE RAINS FINALLY CAME to the ranch in early July. The wash ran, the stock tanks filled, and the hills turned quickly green. At night thunder and lightning filled the valley and one evening huge bolts shattered oaks and mesquite near the house. Beulah disappeared and I never saw her again. I assume she moved out into a new and friendly country, possibly for the courtship rituals that come with the summer rains. A friend moved onto the ranch after I left. A rattlesnake, maybe Beulah for all I know, killed his dog near the house.

She could still be alive, patiently tasting the days and nights on the ranch. But mainly she lives inside my head, especially in the evening when I sit alone in the dark out in the yard and share the lessons she taught me of snaketime. She slithered away from my life leaving no track except for undulating strands across my mind.

Excerpt

From *Inferno*

A DAY OR TWO AGO I was sprawled by a creosote out on the edge of the Tule desert just south of Christmas Pass. The names do comfort us, no? And it was 1:00 P.M. and I looked up and saw a black-headed grosbeak riding the slender limb of the greasewood. The bird did not belong here, it should be in the oaks of the mountains or, better yet, coursing through the pines.

You are in the right place.

I flipped open a bird book just to make sure and yes, the grosbeak did not belong here, it said so right in the text. There were maps also marking winter and summer ranges. The book left no question about the bird being out of place. The beak was thick and heavy, a thing designed to crack sturdy seeds, a yellow beak that opens to devour pine seeds, cherries, blackberries, strawberries, elderberries, mistletoe berries, buds, beetles, codling moth caterpillars, cankerworms, grasshoppers, bees, wasps, flies, spiders. So what in the hell is it doing here?

They do not fear my kind. We have kept records so we know this one fact for sure. It is June 3, 1893, and S. F. Rathban is on the prod to get close to a grosbeak nest. He looks and ten feet above him, in the fork of a willow sapling, looms a nest, a messy thing of twigs. He shakes the sapling but the bird will not stir. Then he takes out his knife, cuts down the sapling, and slowly lowers it until the nest is right there before his face. The grosbeak stares at him a mere foot away. He reaches out with his free hand and finally the bird flies from the nest. But the grosbeak lands just a foot or two away. The man is fascinated, the bird not. The bird knew its place. But then that time, more than a century ago, it was in the right place, on ground where streams wandered and trees clogged the path and fruit beckoned its fat strong beak. But here, it is a lost soul, as am I. As that grosbeak clung to the slender limb of the greasewood, the orange on the body flamed out in the midday heat and the mouth opened as the grosbeak panted. And then in a flicker of time, the bird took off and was on its way. I felt a kinship. I sensed it too came here before it was born.

I got up and walked into the desert and in about fifty yards came upon a fresh badger hole, one dug with violence and force as the badger pursued some dream of rats. I love badgers because of the surliness of their hungers. They fear nothing and move like oxen on meth. They are seen by some as eating machines. Their hair bristles and dogs perish swiftly in their jaws. Here, they live without water and slake their thirst with blood. We place them in the same group as skunks and weasels, but I lack the courage to tell them of this fact. A friend of mine once had a badger at dusk amble up to him, sniff, and then move on. Another man I once met had a badger attack the tire of his truck. He stayed in the cab, of course. I once slept by a badger hole and the opening was encircled with a bracelet made from the heads of rats. They fuck in the summer but do not give birth until the following spring. A white stripe wanders down their backs but this can vary and no one knows why. Here, where I stare at the fresh hole near the greasewood where the grosbeak briefly landed, the stripe is quite different from a specimen collected in the rock mountain just across the valley of the Tule desert. Scientists puzzle out these matters as they wade through the bones and hides of their collections within the deep calm of the universities. I approve of this activity and yet scorn it.

I thirst for knowledge, just as my brother the badger thirsts for rat blood, but still a part of me is leery of the knowledge, suspicious that it is easy and is based on things my kind can measure and count and does not touch some central thing, some level of knowing, that is the floor under all the good moments. And the good moments usually entail women and smell and taste and the black peace of night. I am better when I see less and feel more. I understand this desire to organize, measure, and tote up the score. It is all driven by our fear of death, of disappearance, by our dream of stopping the clocks and being here forever and forever. We must measure all things so that we can be the measure of all things. I am no different in my appetite, but I am not of this belief. I have given it up. I have been here before I was born and so I know I am not long for here and that like the grosbeak I do not belong here. This last thing we cannot question; after all, I just looked it up in my official bird book.

On the other side of the planet, as I examine the badger hole, savor the rake marks left by its claws, experts in Germany work to save the musical manuscripts of Johann Sebastian Bach. The rare compositions, thousands of pages of his flowing notes as music poured from his fat head onto the cloth sheets, are disappearing even though they are kept under lock and key. The ink has mutinied over time, and now sulfuric acid eats at it and each day the markings fade and go away. A project has been launched to salvage the manuscripts and I have no doubt it will succeed for a while. Of course, the task is unnecessary, we have many copies of the works and can in the twinkling of an eye print out millions more. But that is not the point: music is not the point, scores are not the point, time is the point, resisting time, beating time, killing time.

We fear going to the place we visited before we were born because if we do, then we stumble and fall into the fact that we come and go and it matters not at all, that nothing stays, except the sense of being here. We are fascinated by this thing we call nature because of our fear of death and we believe that within nature is a harmony and a balance that can be applied like a salve to this fear. But of course, this thing we label nature is about death and all its jaws and fangs and maws create death everywhere and every time and by that act, make death meaningless and absolute. We cannot escape, there is no balance or harmony, and that is why the pipe organ must be played and the sounds comfort us and yet haunt us even in our bunkers of lust.

The Germans, incidentally, say that their tricky plan for saving the manuscripts is very difficult. They compare the task to open heart surgery. The scheme is a holding action, I am sure of this fact, just a holding action, and it is holding out against what now surrounds me. Not barbarism, not ecology, not natural wonders, but something we fling names at and these names do not stick, they cling very briefly and fall away and are blown by the wind. The thing I try to reach when the spinning comes, the thing I lie about when I talk about resources and preserves. The ultimate Goldberg Variations that Bach sensed and, I suspect, he shuddered at this knowing and suddenly shut down his massive organ, left the church, and went home to the solace and deadening digestion of a fat roasted goose.

We are here, we have been here before, we will not be here. And we cannot seem to belong. We invent lies like reincarnation or lies like natural cycles or lies like religion. They do not answer the force of this sensation. We reach out in panic to grab hold of this wheel spinning before our eyes, this mandala of life, there, spinning, quick grab a spoke and be saved from the fact of your bones, those bones, rolling and tumbling down the green felt, bouncing off walls in the alley, crapping out, those bones singing, and then with time, the flesh falls away, the sun eats and whitens, the bones grow light, and slowly find their way to dust, but never, not for a second do they stop singing and we hear these choruses before we are born, after we are born, after we die, and at all the moments in between, ah, the bones, to be a bonesman, skull and bones, bones on the jolly roger, spinning, the black flag snapping in the sea breeze, the bones are the making of us and our final instrument. And we will do anything to try and stop this spinning, we will sit at our pipe organs and contemplate the variations, we will pull out all the stops, press all the pedals, peal out our fear, toss around words like *immortal,* mask our dreads with dreams and choirs, and still we are back where we began and this is a very good place to be, we must believe this fact, because it is the only place we can ever be.

There are dead men in my desert that I miss but when I am in the desert sometimes they are with me but usually, and this is the fine part, the blade slicing my mind and cutting so close to the bone, usually I am with them. But we feel this thing, like a breath on our necks, and we yearn for this thing, the sense of our senses. I think the badgers know this each time the blood trickles down their throats and ever so briefly slakes their thirst. They also do not belong here, but here they are. There is no explaining the grosbeak, the maps clearly show it is off course.

You do not belong here.

I MUST TELL YOU OF THE coffee in my tiny cup. It is a pious brew, the beans come from shade-grown plants in Central America, fields where the trees have been left so that birds can have a home. A friend of mine roasts the coffee and he too fails to appear in his place on the appropriate maps. He came from back east and wound up in a gulch living in a teepee. He became a smuggler and sold illegal things to give us good dreams. He made a lot of money and naturally spent it. Once he ran up a hotel bill in New York City of over ten thousand dollars, a cost he contends was inflated by room service orders for his dogs. Now he is legal and roasts coffee. He has named his blend of espresso after the famous opera house in Venice, and he delights in this fact.

One night I walked by that very opera house. It was closed for repairs after a fire but the Venetians, true to our kind, were restoring it even as their crumbling city slowly sinks beneath the waves. As I strolled past I could smell the stench off the canals and study the generous hips of the women as they scurried past on the dark footpaths of the city. Venice with its canals and lapping of waves and dank odors has the zest and joys of a swamp or a vagina. Venice is a city you wish to lick.

So I sit here and sip coffee and a flood of birds and opera houses and rising seas course over my tongue. There is a bundle of sensation in my small cup, not counting the snuffling of the badgers out there in the dark seeking a spot of blood for their tea time. I am not there yet, not at my destination, but I am making advances. My appetites are growing and I feel them chewing on my ideas, I am all but gagging on them, and spitting them out onto the ground. If I am patient, my appetites will make an end to my ideas.

There are irritants slowing my progress. I am wired into the planet. A few hours ago, words I had written were fed into a computer and the computer fed them to a microwave antenna and the antenna flung them at a satellite over France which in turn fed them to a warren of computers in Seattle where various trolls pummeled my words into submission and then put them up on a website for all the world to ponder. All this magic is paid for by a corporation in the hopes of peddling goods. And the words I fed into this process, the words on the website, are about the need for a park, the categorical imperative of saving ground, creating sanctuaries, walking lightly on the good planet earth. I want to believe every goddamn word I wrote and then pasted on the satellite hunkered over France. But they remain just words to me, like the sentences that roll off our tongues when we are pulled over, open our window, and talk to a cop all puffed up and clutching his book of tickets and greeting us with his grim mouth. Here, now, with the espresso still bitter on my tongue, I see something else in the blackness. I see a shrinking world and I also see a growing life. I am on an island of the wild and communicating with high-tech folk huddled around glowing cathode tubes. But I am also on the slippery slope leading down the gullet of a badger who is thirsting for blood. The notes are vanishing in Germany, the acid you know is eating them away, and yet here on this island in a crowded planet I absolutely believe that I am in the future, just as I came here before I was born, and I know the notes will vanish, the pipe organs crumble into dust and rust and rot and yet the thirst will continue. The thirst right now is my salvation, just as the thigh of a woman so often saves me in the nick of time. I always sleep on the ground so that the snakes can come to me. I am always open for business. It is my way, whether here in the summer blast of the desert night, or at 1:00 A.M. in the bar when the eyes hunt in desperation against the gong of closing.

Part II

The rest of my time was spent with another nature, the one we call, by common consent, deviate or marginal or unnatural.

FROM *TORCH SONG*

One Thing in Common: Sadness

The View from Both Sides

From the *Tucson Citizen*, August 19, 1983

I've never been in a real strike before. This is a real strike.

A STRIKER

I put in 24 hours a day. I'm not out here 24 hours a day, but my mind never quits work.

CARL FORSTROM OF THE AJO WORKS

THEY WERE FEW. Nineteen strike supporters faced seven squad cars at the dawn of shift change. The convoy swept into the mill gate at 6:45 a.m. A striker yelled, "Good morning, scab."

The town still slept. The strike seems a trifle act twice a day as the 12-hour shifts roll in and out of the works.

The sunrise crawled through the sky of gray.

HE HAS LIVED HERE ALL HIS LIFE—he's in his 40s, he's got more than 20 years in the mine, he's in a craft union.

He's on strike.

His brother is going in. He has friends who go in. He will not go in.

He has lots of reasons, and as he sat in his yard sipping a can of Pepsi they tripped easily from his tongue. If he goes in, he said, he will be blackballed by his union everywhere in the United States. If he goes in, he will have to face living here after the strike.

"I work with some pretty rough boys," he said. "I have to live with these people." So he's put it all on the line.

He talked to his boss just the other day. His boss told him to come on in; his boss told him he couldn't hold his job much longer, that the slots were filling up.

His brother said, "Come in! Come in!"

But he can't. He voted against the strike. Back then, he argued with his union brothers.

"I stood there and talked to the guys until I was blue in the face, and they'd say I was a chicken," he said. "I told people 10 years ago something is going to have to give here. I'd say, 'When I get ready to retire, I'm going to be making $500 a day at the rate we're going.'"

His eyes are sharp and move quickly. He is the smart guy, the one who figures things out.

"I don't believe Phelps Dodge is lying," he said. "I believe they're hurting. And when I saw the package offered by the company before the strike, I was shocked by how good it was."

He said he believes the strike is probably lost. The company, he explained, has the law on its side.

But he stays on strike.

He has his reasons, his deep reasons, and as he talked, he worked his way toward them.

CARL FORSTROM HAS WORKED every day since the middle of May. The mine now has 235 people crossing the picket line to do the work that normally requires 550. He hires security, leases helicopters, leases vans, terminates strikers, puts people out of their company-owned houses.

So he works. The mill's capacity is 28,000 tons a day. In July, the operation averaged 27,640 tons a day.

"I tell you," he said, "I'd like to go to a two-hour day. . . . I'd go to Gila Bend right now if I could to relax. I've got a cabin in Alpine. What I usually do is go up there and read—read those easy-reading novels."

HE HAD A SIMPLE DREAM before the strike. "My daddy said, 'If you want to go to college, I'll send you.' I said, 'If PD's good enough for you, it's good enough for me.'"

He figured he would work the mine for 30 years and retire by age 50. By then, he would own land in the White Mountains for the summer and land in Ajo for the winter. He would get jobs from his union a couple months a year.

Now the dream is going away.

"I've got guys I went to school with," he said, sighing, "guys I drank with, guys I sat up with all night around a campfire, and now they see me on the street and they turn their heads. They're ashamed they went in. They've got wives, families—they had no choice."

That's ruined part of the dream. Violence will take even more. He asked what people think will happen when a guy realizes that the only way to get his job back is to get rid of the man who took it.

First, he said, there will be threats, then rocks through the window, then maybe a rattlesnake left on the car seat.

Then, shotgun blasts through the door.

"I hate violence," he said. "I'm not going to hurt anyone to protect my job."

But he knows his town.

"There's going to be violence. There will be violence for 10 or 20 years after this. PD has the law. There's nothing the union can use to keep people from crossing that picket line except violence."

But he still won't cross it. His brother does, his friends do.

But he won't.

Some things run deep.

THE TOWN IS FULL OF DECISIONS. One bar won't serve non-strikers, period. A man on the picket line is leaving after 26 years in the mine. He's taking a Civil Service exam Sept. 3.

"This town ain't fit to live in anymore," he said.

The company reviews videotapes of strikers. When they spot something they feel is "strike-related" misconduct, they fire the person.

The local teachers meet and discuss how to deal with the strike in the classroom. There are rumors that students must sign notes not to harass other students over the strike.

Decisions.

HE TRIED TO EXPLAIN WHY he won't cross that invisible line drawn at the mill gate.

"PD says, 'Where are you going to find a job this good?' They are right. But these guys come down from Phoenix looking for jobs and they say, 'Look what you got!'

"And we say, 'How do you think we got it? We fought for 25 years.'"

That's part of it. He sipped his Pepsi and calmly dissected modern unionism. He was quick and he made short work of it.

But his roots run deep, and so do the memories.

"My daddy was an old coal miner," he said. "When I was born, he was working for $2.50 a day. My daddy told me about a time a man got his finger cut off, and he wanted to go to the hospital and the foreman told him to wrap the stub with a bandage and go back to work.

"Then John L. Lewis came along.

"I'm a union man."

He let that memory drift across the yard.

THEY WERE FEW. Fifty strike supporters faced nine squad cars and two ambulances at the evening shift change.

Carlos Camarillo, steward of the Operating Engineers, was on the line. Last week when violence broke out, he collapsed at the union hall. They thought it was a heart attack.

He said the doctors tell him it was angina pectoris. He has a bottle of nitroglycerine tablets.

Who's winning?

The men answered, "Who's got the law on their side? The power? The governor? The National Guard?"

Seventy-one vehicles filed out from the mill filled with non-strikers. The people on the line shouted "scab."

And then it was over for another 12 hours.

Lt. D. A. Starr of the Pima County Sheriff's Department surveyed the scene. He said, "There are contingency plans out all over the state. Everything depends on PD—which way they move."

He paused and then continued: "The talks are the only things holding the lid on all this."

Excerpt from "Using Our Children for Sex"

From the *Tucson Citizen*, April 17, 1983

We can't afford to block out the ugly.

The polite expression is the sexual molestation of children.

The boy was small and the father admitted to mutual masturbation.

The University Medical Center ran some cultures. The boy had gonorrhea of the mouth.

The polite expression is the sexual molestation of children.

THEY HAPPEN EVERY DAY, in the home and out of the home. The Tucson Police Sexual Exploitation of Minors Unit investigates 60 cases a month of what it calls out-of-home molest. This means the child was sexually used by a non–family member.

Most of these cases fall apart. Sometimes the police cannot assemble enough evidence for an arrest, or they make an arrest but the case proves too fragile for trial. Often the children cannot handle the pressure of court, or the courts cannot handle the efforts of children to tell their stories. So the violations go out of the justice system and into a wilderness of private hurt.

The numbers look like a bad dream. Statistics on child molesting can be of whatever scale a person can stomach. Sometimes they can look small. Those cases that make it all the way to trial are very strong. For 122 of the victims last year, the unit made 158 arrests, and achieved a 100 percent conviction rate.

That is the small number.

The Sex Crimes Unit of the department handles in-home molests—the violation of the child by the father, mother, stepfather, brother. Last year, the Tucson police detail on in-home molests handled 114 cases that they took to the prosecutor.

That is another small number.

But these numbers deceive. Again, most cases never make it to court because a child is a weak witness by legal standards. Also, a heavy rape load in September, October, and November meant the six-person staff of the Sex Crimes Unit could spend no time on child abuse. One sign of the size of the problem is that last year the police were tipped by Child Protective Services alone to more than 2,000 reports of abuse.

Most sexual crimes against children are never reported. Even when they catch an offender, they may never fully know the list of victims. Out-of-home molests are usually the work of pedophiles: adults who focus on children as objects of love and sex. A New York state study of 238 offenders found they averaged 68.3 victims apiece.

The local police think that out-of-home molests, for example, are at least 10 times the reported rate. That would be 600 victims a month, 7,200 a year in Tucson. The detail working in-home molests handles basically the same case load, 50 to 60 a month, and also believes this is maybe 10 percent of the actual molests.

That adds up to at least 40 molests a day, just in the city limits.

Every day.

The numbers do not matter. The attacks on children are many. What all the numbers mean is this: the attacks will touch you.

It will happen down the block. It will happen to your friends.

It will knock at your door.

Rape

From the *Tucson Citizen,* April 6, 1984

The subject is rape.

The rule at the Citizen *is that sexual assaults will not be described in detail. This time the rule will be broken. If the use of plain language in discussing these crimes disturbs you, this account is not for you.*

Mainly, this story will consider the experiences of one woman and what happened to her. She does not have the solution to the problem of rape in the city but she has questions.

Questions she wants us to answer.

LEAVING THE NIGHT BEHIND

The woman puts a match to a Kool Light and the smoke curls toward the acoustical tile ceiling. The walls have no windows and the street lies nine floors below. This is the Victim Witness program in the Superior Courts building where the county hires people and marshals volunteers to calm the husband and wife quarrels, handle the child molests, the burglaries, the murders. And the rapes. This is where the defeated come, the people who have been translated by one act from citizens to victims.

I ask a favor. Can I ride with counselors when they answer a rape call?

The woman is unsure. She says we are very protective of our clients and if a stranger were at the crime scene, well, it might be a terrible invasion of privacy.

She wears brown slacks, her eyes are very clear and the voice flows smoothly and with confidence. The cigarette sits like a delicate wand between her fingers.

I press the point. I find it difficult to state logically why I want to be there and I stumble in trying to explain my need to capture a certain feeling, a sense of detail. It is important to be there, to feel, to see, to hear. Secondhand is not good enough.

She knows, she knows, but it is a sensitive matter.

An industrial vacuum opens up with a roar in the hallway. The sound fills the ninth floor and the woman speaks through it without a pause. She wants to help, she says, but the request is unusual. She will have to see.

Then the noise of the vacuum cleaner is ripped open by a woman's voice coming through the wall from another room. She does not sound too old. Words tumble out powered by sparks of hysteria.

The voice shrieks that he came in through the window and I was in the bathroom and he made me take off my clothes.

The vacuum cleaner is relentless in its quest for dirt. The machine rises and falls in walls of roaring sound. The voice smothers under this sonic load and then breaks through again.

The voice cannot stop its account. He told me to turn around. And bend over.

The words shred and the voice says, I feel so dirty.

The woman sitting in her ninth floor office with no windows continues explaining her concerns about having me along on a rape call. Smoke rolls from her mouth.

"Is that a voice on a tape?" I ask.

"No," she replies.

THE YOUNGEST IN 1983 was a 10-year-old, the oldest was 81. Rape can be converted to numbers. The Tucson Rape Crisis Center last year saw 497 clients, 91.9 percent of them female. Of these women, 267 had been raped, either that year or in the past. These numbers break down neatly into racial portions: 55.1 percent Caucasian, 10.2 percent Hispanic, 2.2 percent black, 1.4 percent American Indian, .2 percent Indochinese, and more than 30 percent unknown origins.

More than half knew their attackers. Another third were assaulted by perfect strangers. Most dealt with one individual, and 10.4 percent faced a group of men.

Weapons were a matter of differing tastes. For 27.1 percent of the victims the weapon remained a mystery. Guns confronted 5.2 percent, knives 8.6 percent.

But for 44.6 percent no weapon was involved.

Location also offered many choices. The public buildings swallowed up 2.6 percent, the motels 2 percent, the party or bar 2.6 percent, and hitchhiking .2 percent. For 13.2 percent the bad time came in the assailant's home.

But for 30.9 percent, the violation came in their own home, the place that was once called a person's castle.

The police have different numbers and report 253 rapes last year.

Such numbers are very flexible because no one knows how many women are raped in the community. We just know more women are attacked than ever make it into the tables of statistics. Some segments of the population notoriously don't report or under-report, and some reports are false.

There is only one thing about the numbers of which we are confident: They are enough to make every female in this community stand in fear. For them the night is another country filled with dangerous parking lots, sounds outside the window, streets not safe to walk, parks lush with threat, whistles and hoots pouring from passing cars, and footsteps coming up from behind that could mean trouble.

People have varied reactions to these numbers. A few say the women who are raped ask for it, or do some subtle thing that invites it. Or deserve it. Most will not say these things out loud anymore.

But many think these thoughts.

And some say there seems nothing to be done. Rape is a crime difficult to throw police at. It occurs anywhere, at any time. Banks stay put and can be guarded. Human beings move about.

Mostly people say nothing at all. Rape has become a kind of background noise that they no longer hear. The reports are buried in the newspaper as sexual assaults. The addresses are blurred, the names erased. Readers stumble over them, glance, and get on with their lives.

These acts have moved beyond our notice.

THE SIGN IN THE downtown hotel lobby admonishes:

NO VISITORS
TO ANY ROOM
AT ANY TIME

Some people are not much on rules.

She said he entered her room during the night and stayed three, four, five hours. Apparently, she put up a bit of fight. He insisted on vaginal intercourse and oral intercourse. And then toward dawn it ended.

A woman lay in the next room during those three, four, five hours, too old to intervene, too terrified to act. So she kept very still.

The woman who resisted had her ankle wrenched pretty badly but at the end she was alive.

She was 77 years old.

The story ran in the newspaper, a couple of inches buried way back, and then it went away.

The night that the 77-year-old woman survived has elements of the past and the present.

At her hotel, they dish up the past. I ask a woman there about the rape. And she looks kind of puzzled and says what rape? Her? She wasn't raped and if she was, she probably enjoyed it. The woman's hair is gray, her smile kindly and she knows, she says, she knows.

The rest of us are the present. We glance at the incident and pass on. We do not really remember. Twenty years ago, 15 years ago, perhaps 10 years, we might have been struck by a 77-year-old woman attacked for hours in a hotel room. We are past that now. It is not that we do not feel. We have been hammered.

We either know someone who has been raped or we will. We have accepted rape as part of the fabric of our life. We do not admit this fact. But we live it.

THIS CITY HAS FIVE COPS to track hundreds of rapes. The County Attorney's Office offers the Victim Witness program to help the casualties through the initial experience and give them counseling and therapy. The Tucson Rape Crisis Center has six full-time employees, two part-time, and 50 volunteers doing similar work.

If you are a woman in this city and are raped, there is a system of care for you.

If you are a woman in this city and have not yet been raped, no one knows what to do to protect you.

There is advice about locks, secure windows. Warnings are given about hitchhiking, about accepting rides from strangers after an evening in a saloon. But what protects a woman from the man who breaks into her home, who grabs her in a public place?

Some information exists about rapists. About 70 or 80 percent of the people sentenced and caged for rape have been abused, either sexually or physically or both, as children. Therapists believe some abused children grow up into adults with deep angers and act these angers out.

Rape is no longer considered an act of sexual appetite. It is a crime of violence where the woman becomes an object and the object is beaten, violated, humiliated, perhaps killed.

We are struggling to provide therapy for abused children but there are such numbers of them and many, many are missed. We are providing therapy in some prisons for men who rape but we are not sure how well the therapy works.

None of these efforts have paid off on the street. We have not learned how to prevent rape. Instead we have created an industry of care based upon its existence. This industry comforts us by telling us we are doing something, by convincing us we do care.

The number of rapes keeps growing and nothing we do seems to touch that fact.

So we grow weary and turn the page. As a nation we are not too good at problems that require the long haul.

Some find our frustration and silence unacceptable.

NEWSPAPERS DON'T PRINT the names of sexual assault victims. They blur locations, smother the details. This is done to protect the victims.

Not from their attackers but from the rest of us. From our judgments, our condemnation, our obscene phone calls, our threats. Our silent but overwhelming contempt.

Maggie is one of these victims. Her real name is not Maggie but she is not a composite. She is not a typical case either. There is no typical case. She is simply a person who has been violated and she despises our silence.

She is 62 years old and vigorous. When she speaks she stabs her finger forward for emphasis and she does not shy away from an argument. Her eyes are brilliant and her mind constantly darts from idea to idea. She is good company.

Once, this bright and smiling surface was not a surface. It was her. But that has changed. Now she lives in what must be called the world of rape.

When she talks of such matters her vivacity disappears and the world suddenly becomes flat, colorless, and cold. She does not like this fact and has tried very hard to put this world of violence, humiliation, and fear behind her.

But she cannot.

She can forgive us almost anything but one fact.

Our silence.

She wants to shatter that silence.

And she has decided that the only way to move us to speak and act and think is to tell us a few basic facts. It has taken her months and months to decide to do this thing.

Having made the decision, she does not wish to spare us any unpleasant details. She wants us to listen and listen hard.

THE JULY NIGHT IS VELVET with the soft darkness of summer as the ambulance rolls from Sells to Tucson. Maggie sits in the back monitoring the IVs on the patient. She nurses five days a week in Sells and keeps an apartment there. Weekends mean her small house in town.

The ambulance left Sells around 10 and she knows it will be midnight or later before the patient is fully admitted to Kino Community Hospital. She will stay in town for the night.

Night roads are no strangers to her. She has spent years nursing in mining camps and Indian reservations, or walking the dark streets of slums with her black medical bag. She is 60.

Maggie is a Scot, and in the past the road slicing across the hard desert of the Papago lands is one spot that has triggered her yearnings for home. Once she was driving from Ajo to Tucson and suddenly the rock mountains and lean desert brought tears to her eyes. Scotland. Green, cold, distant Scotland flooding her mind. She began to make up a song:

I want to walk your rugged shore,
Listen to the ocean roar,
Pick blue bells in the glen . . .

The words possessed her and she sang out mile after mile as the tires whirred on the hot asphalt road.

Walk in rainy, misty days,
Laugh at funny Scottish ways . . .

Deep hunger gnawed at her as a childhood of picking flowers in the green swales, walking through the roar of blooming heather at Inverness, as all these particles of home ambushed her on the long desert drive.

Maggie thought, "I must get to Scotland before they change you."

And then it passed. There was no going home to Scotland. She was home.

Years before, she had taken up citizenship. It had not been an easy decision. Her first experience with Americans had been seeing brash soldiers in Britain during World War II. Hollywood movies had convinced her this was a money-mad nation.

"The turning point," Maggie feels, "was having a sense of history. I said to myself, there is no nation in the world that has done as much for ordinary man, no nation. And I said, Yes, I want to be an American."

That was long ago, and tonight Maggie does not have homesick thoughts for Scotland. She tends her patient, decides to stay in town, and listens to the ambulance knife through the warm fabric of a July night.

The tasks at the hospital take until 1 A.M., then the ambulance drivers bring her home. The house is small and old and divided into cozy rooms. There is a back porch, a small kitchen, a living room that Ls into a dining alcove. Off the front room is a guest bedroom and in back is a larger one Maggie uses. Beige walls form the backdrop for a collection of Indian baskets acquired through years of reservation work, and there are books, everywhere books. Maggie says she is a "fiend for reading." Here and there, always present, never highlighted, are the signs of the faith, madonnas surveying the peace of this small house with cozy rooms.

She invites the drivers in for a cup of tea, some sandwiches, cold cuts. Maggie shows them her house and the new security windows just installed. Around a quarter to two they leave and she sits on the burnt orange sofa in the living room and watches the late news. The night is warm, very warm, and the cooler roars and a fan blows.

Maggie is tired. She has been on her feet since 3:30 P.M. She finishes her tea and goes to bed in the back room. For a while, she lies there and reads, as is her custom. Then sleep begins to take her and at precisely 2 A.M. she reaches over and winds the alarm clock. She puts her hand on the light to flip it off and notices a curtain is open by the window. She thinks she should get up and close the curtain but then the sleep is so powerful and the window itself is shut and locked.

She snaps out the light and falls into her dreams.

She awakens with a person lying on top of her. His hand covers her mouth and a knife presses against her neck.

The man says, "Don't move, you bitch, or I'll kill you."

Maggie struggles through the remaining mists of sleep. She thinks she is dreaming and that this is a nightmare.

Then the man says, "Don't look or I'll really kill you."

He rolls her over facedown on the bed. The light goes on and a pillow is pulled out from under Maggie. Then she hears tearing noises. He asks if she has any panty hose.

Maggie says "I don't wear them but there's a pair in the dressing table drawer."

She hears him fumbling with the dresser.

Then he is back. He ties her hands and feet and asks for money, jewelry, silver, and guns.

Maggie says there is money in her purse.

How much?

She thinks perhaps $20 or $25.

He wants things, he wants jewelry or money or silver or a gun.

"I don't have any jewelry," Maggie explains, "except costume jewelry and no silver and I've never known the need to have a gun."

Then the sound of drawers being opened and rummaged through returns. Maggie starts to pray. She is a spiritual person and her faith is a living thing.

She says out loud, "Dear Lord protect me, Dear Lord and all you angels of God, come to my aid. Mother of God help me."

The man says, "Shut up, you bitch."

Maggie keeps on praying. She floats in a place where everything is clear and yet nothing seems real. Thoughts flash through her mind, images focus and then blur and still there is this quality of a dream gone bad, of something that she will awaken from.

Then she thinks this is really happening. Now.

He cannot find the purse. She moves and feels it under her arm and tells him. He pushes her aside and repeats that he will kill her if she looks. She feels the bonds on her wrists and has her hands pushed up against her eyes.

The purse yields only $15.

"You lied to me," the man snaps.

Maggie says, no, no, I stopped and bought gasoline—I forgot about the gasoline.

He asks if anyone else lives in the house. She realizes he has prowled round her home and found the other bedroom.

Yes, she lies, and her friend will call soon and if the phone is not answered the friend will know something is amiss.

How did you get in? Maggie asks.

"That's my business," he says, "I was watching you through the window. And now I'm going to rape you."

A feeling like death sweeps through Maggie. She lies bound hand and foot on the bed and she thinks now it is only a matter of time.

Scotland flashes in her mind. Her brothers and sisters and friends, all of them move across her consciousness. How terrible this will be, she thinks, to have me found this way and the ordeal of the mess and the funeral.

She prays to God, "Be kind, dear Lord, to my family and friends. Don't let them be too bitter against America that this way of life could be tolerated here."

This kind of death has never occurred to her. Her thoughts on the dignity of marriage and the sanctity of sexuality, all these beliefs bob through her mind. She realizes that she will fight and that fight will be the end of her.

Still, she cannot grasp that this is happening to her. She has lived in so many different countries and never before this moment has she truly known fear. She has spent her life grateful for the gift of courage instilled by her family. These things come to her mind.

He still wants money.

She suggests writing a check. Maggie says, look you can guide my hand and I'll sign it for you. There's about $320 in the account and you can have it.

"What are you trying to pull?" he asks. "I want satisfaction. I'm going to rape you."

"Do you want that added to your sins against humanity?" she cries out. "What do you want a 60-year-old woman for when I'm sure you'd rather have a relationship with a person who wants you?"

She feels his hands go along her legs and up her thighs. Her body becomes rigid.

"Look," she says, "I'm a nurse, I've had a long shift. I've given my life to taking care of the sick and the poor and I don't know why you're here when I have to get up in the morning and go to work. I want you out of here."

He says, "Do you want to die, lady?"

Maggie again feels the knife at her neck.

She says, "If this is how God means for me to die, so be it."

The sensations come now. She anticipates the horror of the violation of her body. She is not dreaming and she knows it. She thinks, "Not this Lord, not this."

Her mind races and images suddenly tumble out from the early independence of the Belgian Congo when convents were sacked and nuns raped. Maggie reproaches herself:

Who do you think you are? What makes you so special?

Her mind gropes toward some kind of understanding.

She decides, "I don't know why you're allowing this to happen, Lord, but who am I to be so righteous and pompous and say it shouldn't happen to me? Thy will be done."

Then the man says something very strange: "Lady, I don't want to hurt you."

That is when Maggie becomes alive again.

She whispers, "Thank You, Lord—there's something I've said that has gotten through to him."

She knows there is a presence in the room, a thing palpable and uplifting. She senses a battle in this room between good and evil and the two sides are not ideas, they are forces she can feel. A kind of peace fills Maggie.

He pulls her off the bed to the side and she sits there waiting and wondering what is next. Her mind scrambles trying to find clues, reviewing all the literature she has read on these crimes and these men and the tactics of violent confrontation. She reaches deep inside her memory for some scrap of fact to guide her. The light is out now.

He moves to the window and looks out.

Then the man says, "If you won't give me satisfaction one way, you'll do it another."

He unzips his pants and takes out his penis. He places her hand on it.

He pushes his penis down her throat.

Maggie starts to choke and feels a wave of nausea. She pulls away.

The man says, "Don't try anything or I'll kill you."

"I think," she tells him, "I'm going to be sick."

"Haven't you ever done this before?"

"Never."

The man says, "You'll get to like it."

His hand begins to move up and down his penis, he rams it down her throat and ejaculates.

And then she begins to think, really think about the matters that fill police reports. She tries to forge some kind of order out of what is happening to her. She realizes she must know more about him, assemble some kind of a description. If she should live through this, she decides, she should be able to give his height. Something.

She feels his pelvic bone and tries to visualize how far his hip is from the floor. Her mind concludes he is 5 feet, 8 or 9 inches tall. A quick glance upward in the night suggests to her he has clipped hair, not long hair, and that the face is thin and angular. The features are lost to darkness.

Suddenly he pushes her back onto the bed, facedown on the pillow. What now, she wonders. Is this where she dies?

The sound of a door opening snaps her alert. She looks off to the side and sees the lamp has been turned on again and has fallen against the bedside table.

I must lift that, she thinks, I must set it aright before the bulb burns the wood.

She lies there quietly, listening, listening, listening. The silence overwhelms her but still she does not move. She continues to pray and remains frozen, facedown on the bed.

This kind of trance goes on five, maybe ten minutes. The bulb burning into the wood continues to trouble her. Nothing, absolutely nothing can be heard in the house.

Did he leave? Is he really gone?

She reaches over and puts out the light. She falls back and remains quiet on the bed with every fiber of her body electric with tension. Perhaps he is just looking in the other room? Maybe he is trying to find jewelry? A gun?

Maggie rolls onto the floor, still bound hand and foot. She must do something, she thinks. She crawls forward from the bedroom to the living room. Then she waits, listens, wonders if he is around, still coming back for her.

She decides he must have left.

She picks up the phone and realizes she does not know the emergency number. In Great Britain it is 999. She dials and somehow gets through to the correct number, 911.

A voice comes on the line and Maggie blurts out that she needs help, she's been assaulted and tied up.

The voice asks for a description and Maggie says, "All I know is he was a black man."

She remembers his speech and it sounded black, and she remembers when he reached for her purse—a glimpse of his black arm. The voice asks for more detail and Maggie snaps. "Just send the police" and she hangs up.

She crawls across the living room to the front door, grabs the handle and pulls herself up. She eases open the door, flips on the porch light and begins to fear again. What if he is still out there and now he comes back?

The police arrive very quickly and she moves back from the door, still bound, and falls. A cop steps inside and says, "I'll untie you." He cuts her free with a knife.

Suddenly she is on the couch. For an instant there, she must have passed out. She cannot tell. The police are very kind and their questions are gently cushioned. She takes great comfort from their manner.

Crews arrive to take prints and photos. The University police come, then Victim Witness from the prosecutor's office. Everything is brightly lit and there are people in all the rooms, on the porch, outside in the yard. The house throbs with life and activity.

Do you want anything, the people ask, can we get you anything?

Tea, she thinks, tea with a spot of Scotch in it.

She sips the cup and answers the questions, the endless, detailed questions. The police have her check the kitchen knives to see if any are missing. Maggie cannot tell. They ask her to scan the house for missing objects.

The television, she says. Yes, the television.

They show her where the man entered through a window on the back porch. It was the one place she didn't install a security window.

Maggie looks up at the clock: 10 minutes to 3. Only 50 minutes have passed since she wound her alarm clock and dropped off to sleep.

Then she hears the police on their radios saying, "Why don't you bring it over."

The door pops open and somebody puts her television down on the floor. She asks where they got it and they say nothing. She asks again.

Have they caught him so soon, she wonders.

A policeman had been riding his bicycle home after finishing his shift. He saw a man walking down the street with a television and pulled up beside him, flashed his badge and asked his name. The man heaved the television, caught the cop broadside and knocked him to the ground. Then the man took off running.

He got away. It happened a block and a half from Maggie's house. The cop did not know of the rape call.

That is the story Maggie hears.

The police want her to call a friend but she resists. She cannot face waking someone from a sound sleep and telling them what has happened to her. She asks for her medicine. The man spilled her purse on the bed and the medication is part of a heap being examined for fingerprints.

The police ask, medicine?

Yes, she says, for my angina.

The police become upset.

She stands there thinking about the man. She says, "I am alive, alive and he is out there running along the back lanes like a hunted animal with no one to talk to."

A cop interrupts her with, "Do you realize this is violence, a crime of violence? He is a criminal."

And Maggie knows the policeman is right but still she thinks of him. What she had seen in the war did not shake her belief in others the way this night does.

"That another human being," she reflects, "could do this for no reason, do this when I was asleep in my bed after a good day's work."

She recalls Robert Burns.

"Man's inhumanity to man makes countless thousands mourn."

She had learned that poem as a schoolgirl but this night she finally understands it. Then, she begins to make the calls. Her sister is a nun in a healing order in London.

"Not you," she says, "Oh, not you."

Maggie asks, "Why not me?"

The other calls produce the same response: not you, not you. Friends come over. The shift begins to another day.

At 6 A.M. she calls the monsignor from her parish and he comes. She kneels on the floor by her dining room table and takes Communion. As the bread becomes flesh and wine blood, she feels some renewal of spirit.

She asks him to bless her house. She wants him to say "that peace will come to all in this home and all that come into this home."

He moves from room to room with the holy water and this makes Maggie feel better.

He says he will now go to give the early Mass for her and offer up the prayers of the church. This matters. She is hungry for the comforts of her faith.

Now she sits down on the sofa with friends watching over her and she remembers the Victim Witness team leaving an hour before.

As they went out the door one man said, "It won't be long, the dawn is coming up."

The black night began to ebb before their eyes.

And Maggie thought, "A new day and I'm still alive. Thank you."

A FRIEND CALLED FROM Albuquerque and said, "I want you up here, I want you to get on a plane."

Maggie said yes.

The day after the attack Maggie said yes to a lot as she floated through the hours and the phone calls and the police interviews. Her home was now a haunted house and she could not bear to be there. The fear, the fear, Maggie explained.

She slept at friends'.

The bedroom was no longer part of her home. She did not enter. She did not want to look there. She never slept in it again.

People were kind. Friends rearranged the furniture and moved her bed to another room. Victim Witness called on her.

She was used to a network of friends. Normally, laughter came easily to her and she was a gifted mimic, a woman always ready with a tale. Her bottle was always half full, not half empty, and the past was not her country.

Now something had been taken away from her. Now she was someone else.

At the airport she waited for her flight to Albuquerque and a black man sat down by her. She froze. She was appalled at her reaction but she could not control it. Then she boarded the plane and a black steward greeted her.

She stopped dead in the passageway. Finally, she moved toward her assigned seat and found a black man there.

She thought, "Oh, my God," and then a stewardess came up and said, "Can we help you?"

The black man looked up at her.

Maggie fled to the restroom and cried and cried. When she came out, the stewardess gave her some tea. She finally went to her seat by the black man. He was very polite.

She apologized for her reaction, for the expression that had flared across her face.

"I'm sorry I seemed so upset," she offered, "but I've had a very bad experience."

The man said, "I'm very sorry, I'm very sorry."

And then she was all right and they talked. Maggie thought to herself, "That was a dirty trick, Lord. I just wasn't ready." But she felt a shred of peace.

Her friend met her at the Albuquerque airport and they did not speak. They got in the car and drove and still they did not speak.

After a few days, Maggie went on and visited a friend in Cuba, New Mexico. She began to stumble over changes in herself. Things that previously meant nothing now gripped her mind. She remembered that a black family had once stayed next door and they had been visitors in her home. Suddenly remarks made, tiny facts remembered, all these things grew to sinister proportions. She called the police in Tucson to relay her suspicions.

Then she recalled that the night of the attack the neighbor's dog had not barked. Usually he howled if she so much as stepped into her backyard. What had happened? What?

And the sleep would not come. Night after night she could get no relief. The house in Cuba was like an old acquaintance and she had stayed there many times. Now she was afraid. Both she and her friend knew this but they did not speak of it. At night, she had to keep the light on in her room.

"I became angry lying there trying to fall asleep," Maggie says, "and afraid to fall asleep. I thought, he's taken my security, he's taken my sense of trust away. That is the biggest scar.

"Fear.

"I didn't know what fear was before. Now I know it."

So she lay there in the night under the burning light bulb and assessed the damage to herself. She was 500 miles from the place of her attack, in a home where she had known much happiness. And she could not sleep. She could not face the darkness.

The next day she decided to go back.

"I have to start picking up the pieces," she thought, "I have to go back. There are a lot more tragedies in the world than just mine. My friends can't live my life for me. There are sick to tend in the hospital."

She flew back. A friend suggested she house-sit for her. Maggie could not because she feared the strange night sounds of a different house, the creaks and drips and moans unlike those of her home. But she could not stay at her own home because she feared, simply feared. She feared the day, she feared the night, she feared the memories. She feared he might return.

For a few days she became a kind of vagabond staying with friends.

Security dominated her mind. She had her home equipped with new doors, locks, various gadgets to keep her from harm's way. An Indian friend who was an electrician came over to install outside lights to chase the night from her home. He sized up Maggie's condition and took her home to stay with his family until the job was done.

Then the police suggested bars be placed on the porch where the man had gained entry.

"This had a horrible effect on me," Maggie says. "The day I have to put bars on my window I will not stay in America. I will not stay anyplace I have to make a prison of my own home. That I cannot do.

"I just felt so bad.

"Bars would just keep reminding me that there is a terrible world out there *and I don't believe it's a terrible world.*

"No bars! No bars!"

The world of work, the world of helping the sick, laughing with friends, enjoying a bit of Scotch in the tea, sharing in the comforts of religion—this world that had been her life now moved out of reach. Maggie had prided herself on being tough, independent, confident. She had delivered babies in rough slums, worked isolated mining camps in the Canadian bush, traveled the back roads of the Hopi, the Navajo, and the Papago alone. Now she feared to step out into her own yard. Now she feared each sunset.

People became strangers to her. She did not like to talk about that night and yet she sensed some people were afraid she might mention it. In a way she could hardly understand, she had become a threat to some people. She was a voyager returned from a world they wished to deny.

She was sinking and she knew it and she watched her own decline.

One day she got up and simply sat on the couch.

"I was looking at the walls," she says. "I hadn't yet made my cup of tea, which I dearly love.

"I didn't want to make a cup of tea.

"I didn't want to dress.

"I didn't want to shower.

"I didn't want to eat.

"I just wanted to look at the walls.

"And I was saying to myself, 'What's happening to you, Maggie? This is not you. You come from better stock than that. We Scots have a great heritage.'"

Friends from work would call. The cops on patrol would pop in from time to time. Victim Witness kept in touch. Maggie floundered in a world of help that could not reach her wound.

One day she sat down and began the journey back. She wrote on a piece of paper, "WHO IS HE?"

Who is he that stalks the night with evil in his heart?

Who is it that waits and watches while the world goes by?

Who is it that lives in a world apart from the joy of living, of loving and helping others?

Who is he?

She paused. For weeks she had explored only the empire of her depression. The words became a way to act.

Who is it that preys on helpless women with actions so vile that even the elements revolt?

Who is it that strikes terror and fear in the hearts, minds and bodies that only wish to love and serve mankind?

He was not born that way, although evil taints us all.

Surely, he knew some love, some caring, some pride in decent living, as he learned to walk the road of life.

Where, how, why did he fall into the black depth of Hell that made him what he is today?

These are the questions that race through my mind, as I recall the break-in that night as I awoke with a knife at my throat, a hand pressed against my mouth, the threat of death and rape from that voice, that threatening void.

Who is he that could stoop to such inhuman behavior for $15 and a television, and leave scars that I hope family, friends and God, in time, will heal?

Sleep still did not come. Finally, she called her doctor and he explained that being awakened and attacked in the night often robbed the victim of the security of sleep. Maggie took comfort in his words. This was something she could cling to, something that connected with her training and nursing mind.

He prescribed sleeping pills, something which she found "much against my will, against my nature." But she tried them for two nights. They made her tense, hyper.

She decided to work this out on her own. Pills couldn't put her back together, friends couldn't, Victim Witness counseling couldn't.

Only she could.

But the act required more than will. Something had been taken from her spirit that night and she knew it.

The calls kept coming from work and the voices said, come back, come back. But she could not. The thought of facing people, of the questions, stopped her.

The evenings kept her a prisoner of her fears. One night she heard a noise outside the bedroom window and she froze. The sound continued, a kind of scraping. She got out of bed and listened. Then she thought, I must get a hold of myself. She went back to bed.

The sound began again.

"I could not stand it any longer," she recalls. "I called the police and as I was waiting I thought about what had happened to me: I resented that he had taken my courage and left me fear."

The police saw a dog run from the driveway as they pulled in. Maggie thought with relief, "Now I know it was a dog munching on a bone."

Another night she heard a thump on the roof. She froze again and wondered, "What is that?" For the rest of the night, she waited, tense and alone.

Two days later a neighbor came over and told her a side of her roof cooler had fallen off.

Thump.

Maggie realized what was happening to her. Every sound now had menace.

A phone call came and Maggie answered and there was silence. She asked, Who is it? Who is it? No one spoke but she could sense someone on the line. She hung up.

The call chilled her. The next day the same thing happened. And then it happened again and again.

Maggie called Victim Witness and asked, What can I do? Soon the phone company sent a form asking for her permission to monitor all her calls.

The anger rose in her.

Her friends said sign it, let it be done. The man knows your house—it could be him. But she could not sign it.

It was one more intrusion, one more violation of her life. Everything reminded her of how much she had lost and yet she could not control her feelings. When a repairman from the phone company came out one day, she demanded to see his identification. She had never done anything like that before in her life.

As a child, Maggie had been a gifted mimic and at one time she wanted to go into theater as a career. She could do Marlene Dietrich, the haughty tones of the gentry, whatever. Now she retrieved this talent.

She decided that when she answered the phone, she would lower her voice like, say, Lauren Bacall and sound like a man. Should someone ask for Maggie, why, she would say in a very deep voice, "Just a moment," and come back on the line as herself.

She called up her sister in Canada and tried out the ruse. It worked.

She knew then her life was poisoned. Even the telephone represented a breach in her security system.

She was deep inside the world of rape.

She kept trying and trying to make order out of her life and get the past filed away. Maggie wrote a letter to the police commending the three officers, Sgt. A. Chesser, Sgt. K. Magoch, and Sgt. R. Hardyman, for the way they had treated her.

A month after the attack, she went back to work. During the week at Sells, she slept fine. On the weekends in town, the lights were kept on inside and out and she avoided going out at night because she feared coming home after dark.

A month or two later, Victim Witness invited her again to attend therapy classes.

She said no. She wanted to make it on her own. The thought of sitting around with other women recounting painful experiences repelled her.

Maggie thought, "I trusted You, Lord, before it happened, I trusted You when it was happening—help me trust You now."

Victim Witness kept calling and five or six months after the rape she gave in. The group held seven or eight women, and Maggie listened to what had happened to each and realized her experience could have been much worse. The women told of boyfriends, husbands, family that resented and condemned them for being raped. Maggie found this hard to understand. Such an idea had not occurred to her.

On her drive back to Sells after the class, she cried all the way.

Her anger swelled.

"What fools we are," she thought. "One day the world is our oyster and then the world turns upside down."

She went back for another class and the instructor told them to write out how their feelings had changed since their attacks. Maggie put fear at the top of her list—the fear of strangers, of telephone calls, the dread that overtook her every time she left her car in a huge parking lot or returned to it.

The group talked about their lists and the leader chalked them on the board. They all pretty much agreed until Maggie wanted to ask one thing: "Where is the Christian community? Where are the good people? Why are they allowing this wonderful town to become like a jungle?

"Where are the good people?

"The churches?

"The religious organizations?

"Why are they silent?"

No one else in the group agreed with this point. They said religion and such concerns were a private matter.

Maggie never came back.

She began to think she must leave Tucson. Nothing was getting better, the fear wrapped around her like a shroud. She applied and got a job in Albuquerque, flew up and inspected the new clinic, looked for a house. Two days later the clinic burned to the ground before it ever opened and her job was gone.

Maggie gave up. She took the destruction of the clinic as a sign from God.

She decided she would stay in Tucson and do something about the rape of women.

Maggie felt driven by God. She felt a sharp spiritual pain and this troubled her far more than the physical and emotional pain she had been through.

She began to confront her church.

She went to a priest and demanded to know why the church remained silent about the violence against women in this community. And the priest led her to a lay organization in the church. And they suggested the bishop.

And she asked each in turn, Why? Why? Why?

She went to Bishop Manuel Moreno. They talked. She gave him the poem she had written and he read it.

The bishop said that earlier another person had come to see him with the same problem but he had not known how to pursue it, what to do.

Maggie exploded.

"You won't do that to me," she said. "I don't think God will allow that. If something had been done about this other person, maybe I would not have been attacked."

And so the rape of July 1982 began to surface from her depression as a mandate, as a charge to her to do something. She could not believe that nothing could be done and she refused to believe that this pain in her life was meaningless, just a police report and four inches of boilerplate in the newspaper.

She told the bishop, "I wouldn't want to be in the shoes of the Christian leaders when Our Lord asks them, 'What did you do to help our women who were being violated?'"

Maggie was past the point of being reasonable, she had no time for reasons. She did not care about theories explaining why women were beaten and raped. She did not care about cries of manpower shortages from the police. She did not care about anything but stopping it.

Day by day she would read her newspaper and weep for the women raped.

She had reached the point of action, some vague, instinctive action. But action. And she began to talk with others who felt the same way.

She moved from Sells to Tucson so she would have more time to devote to the work. She wanted to find some peace of mind and spirit. And she felt she owed this country and she wanted to pay it back.

She said, "I owe it to women and I owe it to Tucson and I owe it to America. When I took out my citizenship, it was because I believed in this country, and if I felt this were happening in Scotland, I would speak out.

"Why am I silent here?

"I am a private person and I value my privacy, but I feel I have to go through with this."

Eighteen months had passed since her rape and she was still not restored as a person. After a lifetime of faith, she found it difficult to trust God. What took less than 50 minutes one July night still had not ended for her.

Maggie lived in a valley filled with half a million people and felt alone.

Now she demanded some satisfaction.

SOMETIMES RAPE IS NOT someone else's story. Sometimes it is closer to home. This was years ago but I can reach out and it is still there nearby.

The call from a relative came after midnight and the voice was very calm and flat. We talked for perhaps a moment and you would have thought we were speaking of the time and temperature. I said, yes, I will come down.

The light glared in the hospital waiting room. Tension snapped through her body but her manner was very controlled. Only the eyes gave her away as they hunted through the chairs, tables, lamps, ashtrays, walls, and ceilings for some scrap of information that would steady her.

The man was rigid and the color had left his face. He and his wife tried to talk of other matters. They kept propping up each other's spirits.

Then suddenly his head fell into his hands and he cried, "My baby girl, my baby girl."

Their daughter was in her early twenties and I'd known her for years. Now she lay on the operating table maybe 50 feet away. She had gone to visit a friend and when she got out of the car, a man forced her back in. They drove around and wound up in the foothills. The man was a stranger to her and he had a gun. He pistol-whipped her, raped her, shot her, and left her for dead. She crawled through the desert to a house with a light on.

The surgeons were busy tracking a bullet that had wandered through her guts toward her heart. They had to cut the hair off her head to cleanse and stitch the gashes and lacerations.

The face I knew from countless jokes and talks and dinners was gone. And what I saw in the recovery room was a message from another country, a violent country. I can't recall her features that night. But the rest is in perfect focus, the close cropped hairs on her shaved scalp, her voice trying to be brave, the tubes pumping life into her veins. Just not the face, bashed here and there by the metal of a gun.

For days and weeks afterward wherever I drove, I was looking into the faces of other drivers and wondering: are you the one? I had no idea what I was searching for; it could be anyone, they said. But whenever I went about the city, I thought, he is out there, perhaps behind me in the checkout line or sitting on the next bar stool.

Men would express their outrage to me and tell me what they would do to the rapist and what weapon they would use and how long and painful they would make his remaining time on earth. I would listen and nod, but this talk passed me by.

I did not feel any anger. I did not care about the rapist. On that level my feelings became dead.

Mainly I felt a kind of guilt I could not understand. I felt guilt over movies I had seen, over magazines I had read, over jokes I had told.

I felt guilty over being a man. None of this made any sense to me. I detested censorship, I enjoyed rough humor, I had never struck a woman, much less raped one. But the feeling was real and deep and lasted a long, long time and never completely left me.

I had learned something but I could do nothing with my knowledge.

MAGGIE IS BACK IN THE world but something is missing for her. She enjoys her job, she tends the sick, dines with friends, goes to club meetings. But she is terrified of the thought that she might be raped again. She is certain that the next time she will resist and when she resists she will die.

And her spiritual peace is slow in coming back, and for Maggie that is a major matter.

Once she nursed a woman who because of marital complications had been denied the sacraments of the church for almost 30 years, and Maggie was touched by her plight. She promised her she would look into the matter. And then the rush of life's little moments caused her to put off the task. She was at Mass one day and when she took the wafer into her mouth, she could not swallow it. A voice spoke to her and said what about that woman you promised? What about her?

This happened twice.

Maggie feels a little odd telling this story because she knows the kind of world she lives in. But it happened, not once but twice, and it ended her peace. She had to do something and began the long odyssey from rectory to rectory looking for a priest or monsignor or a bishop who would attend to the woman.

Finally, in one office she broke down and shouted that her soul was not at peace because of this matter and that this was a serious thing for her and she would never relent until something was done and she got some peace.

And something was done.

That is the way Maggie feels now. Since her rape, she had tried to leave Tucson; she could not. When she tried to bury herself in her work, she could not. When she tried to take therapy and put the pain behind her, she could not.

She finally decided there would be no peace for her until she did something about these crimes against women. She began to talk to friends and friends of friends and form links with others who shared her feelings. They talked about what could be done.

She and her friends want to end the silence about rape, to end the sense of helplessness, the kind of communal shrug that this city gives to the question of preventing rape. They want to force people to talk about it, think about it, do something about it.

The Chamber of Commerce and other boosters of the community send out literature celebrating this city and inviting people to move their companies, their meetings, their families, and their vacations here.

Maggie and her friends talk of sending letters to the same people advising them that if they choose to come here, they should realize they may be raped.

The resort hotels host conventions of people from all over the country who come here to lie in the sun and drop money at local restaurants.

Maggie and her friends talk of putting leaflets on the windshields of such visitors advising them that during their stay in Tucson they should be careful, very careful, lest they be raped.

They think the leaders of this community will pay attention to this matter if it begins to cost them money. So they want to make sure it costs them money.

Maggie loves Tucson and she has ambitions for her city. She says this community must become like a beacon, a light for other cities and states. She says this place must show other places that a caring community can bring back the night. Before she was raped, she always believed most people were good, truly good. And she still holds this belief. She cannot understand how a small number of criminals can dominate the lives of a large number of good people.

The theories and explanations of violence in modern urban life tell her nothing. She does not want to learn how to accept life as it is. She wants to change things, she wants to change this city.

Maggie always returns to one simple point: most of the people in Tucson are good people. And given this fact, it is almost a sin for them to believe they do not determine what kind of community this city will be.

Maggie and her friends want more attention paid to the rights of victims. They want a tougher attitude toward offenders.

But they do not have a magic bullet that will end rape, a simple program that will abolish the problem. They are not that pompous or foolish.

They do not claim to know all the answers.

But they think we have to talk. They think we have to cease accepting that these things will happen in a big city in the booming Sun Belt.

They want the silence to end.

WE'RE HAVING COFFEE AND the woman is angry, very angry. She despises the way rapists are portrayed in films and much fiction. The silhouette at the door, the giant shadow, the silent, hulking form with heavy breathing rasping over the soundtrack—the deadly stranger that enters our humdrum lives at will and then leaves ruin behind.

She says, look, I've counseled lots of rapists in prisons and they're not like that, they're not big, tough, macho guys. They're jerks. They're losers, nobodies, wimps.

And she rolls on and on that she is tired of all this crap about rapists and somebody ought to tear down these fantasies and explain to people that these are not heavy dudes, these guys are whiners, are greasy hair, are people you don't notice except to spit at.

So tell them that, she snaps.

The cops see rapists this way: these guys, they say, don't care, don't feel, it's like they just brushed their teeth. For them it's a 20-minute thing, for the woman it's at least five years.

But the woman cannot do much with her anger and the cops cannot do much with their contempt. Because they are talking about us and these fantasies we entertain about rape and rapists and they are saying we don't know and we don't seem to want to know.

We prefer to stay with our fantasies and leave the streets to the rapists.

WE ALWAYS RETURN TO THE same place: we are helpless, we can do nothing. We cannot take back the night and now we are losing the day.

Last year according to police figures, 253 women were raped in this town.

That is what we are helpless about.

What if last year 253 men had been raped? What if 253 times a man was taken down in his home, or seized in a parking lot, or grabbed while walking, or dragged off from a morning run? What if 253 times a man was overpowered and told to bend over?

And then was sodomized.

What would we say then?

What ideas and acts would enter our minds then?

What if these victims and other men stormed the police station or City Hall and demanded some action? What if the cops kept a squad of manhunters, relentless trackers half bloodhound and half computer, stalkers who would be released when an attack occurred and told not to return until they found the offender? What if every time a rape happened the culprit would know someone would be on his trail the rest of his life?

Of course this is just fantasy. This has not happened.

And we all seem to agree there is little to be done about rape.

I FINISH A SEVEN-MILE RUN and turn the corner toward home. She is walking down the sidewalk, a working woman dressed in the uniform of a fast-food franchise. It is about 11 A.M., the sun is brilliant, and the day promises to be good, very good.

He pulls up beside her in a beat-up old car. It has been a spell since he has attended to his basic grooming. As she walks, the car creeps. He leans out the window and starts saying things.

I cannot hear him but I know every word.

The woman stiffens and walks faster. Her body becomes a thing in a block of ice and she keeps her eyes fixed straight ahead.

He does not let up. The words keep coming and a big smile crosses his face.

I jog up the street and he sees me and drives off.

The woman keeps walking.

We all go our separate ways and never speak of this matter.

This report was written by Tucson Citizen *staff writer Charles Bowden.*

In his two and a half years with the Citizen, *Bowden has written on child molestation, illegal immigration, and Arizona's copper strike.*

They are the "big stories" but they start with something small: A human voice.

To Maggie, and others like her, Bowden acknowledges a debt.

Torch Song

At the Peripheries of Violence and Desire

From *Harper's*, August 1998

I CAN'T TELL MUCH from her silhouette. She's sitting off to one side, her shoulders hunched, and toward the front is the box with the teddy bears. Or at least I think they're teddy bears. Almost twenty years have passed, and I've avoided thinking about it. There are some things that float pretty free of time, chronology, the book of history, and the lies of the experts. In the early eighties I went to a funeral as part of my entry into a world, a kind of border crossing.

It started as the gold light of afternoon poured through the high, slit windows of the newsroom. I had no background in the business and I'd lied to get the job. I was the fluff writer, the guy brought on to spin something out of nothing for the soft features and the easy pages about how people fucked up their marriages or made a quiche or found the strength to go on with their lives because of God, diet, or a new self-help book. Sometimes they wrote the book, sometimes they just believed the book. I interviewed Santa

Claus, and he told me of the pain and awkwardness of having held a child on his fat lap in Florida as ants crawled up his legs and bit him. One afternoon the newsroom was empty, and the city desk looked out and beckoned me. I was told to go to a motel and see if I could find anything to say.

The rooms faced a courtyard on the old desert highway that came into town and were part of a strip of unhappy inns left to die after the interstate lanced Tucson's flank. When I was twelve this belt still flourished, and my first night in this city was spent in a neighboring motel with a small pool. I remember swimming until late at night, intoxicated with the idea of warm air, cool water, and palm trees. My sister was fourteen, and the son of the owners, a couple from the East with the whiff of Mafia about them, dated her; later, I read a newspaper story that cited him as a local purveyor of pornography. But the row of motels had since lost prosperous travelers to other venues and drifted into new gambits, most renting by the day, week, or month, as old cars full of unemployed people lurched into town and parked next to sad rooms where the adults scanned the classifieds for a hint of employment. The children always had dirty faces and anxious eyes. The motel I was sent to was a hot-sheet joint, with rooms by the hour or day, and featured water beds (WA WA BEDS, in the language of the sign), in-room pornographic movies, and a flock of men and women jousting through nooners.

The man at the desk had a weasel face and the small frame of the angry, smiling rats that inhabit the byways of America; the wife was a woman of some heft, with polyester pants and short-cropped hair. They seemed almost delighted to have a reporter appear, and after a few murmured words in the office, where I took in the posters for the featured films of cock-sucking, butt-fucking, and love, ushered me across the courtyard, with its unkempt grass, to the room. As we entered, she apologized and said she was still cleaning up. The linoleum floor looked cool, and the small chamber offered a tiny kitchenette and a small lavatory with shower, the old plastic curtain stained by years of hard water. The water bed, stripped of its sheets, bulged like a blue whale, and as the woman and I talked—he was quiet, she seemed nice, they didn't cause any fuss, the kid was a charmer—a dirty movie played soundlessly on the screen hanging off the wall and confronting the bed. I seem to remember a mirror of cheap streaked tiles on the ceiling.

I walked around aimlessly and popped open the door of the old refrigerator—shelves empty—and then the little door to the freezer, where two bottles of Budweiser, frozen solid, nestled as if someone with a powerful thirst had placed them to chill in a hurry and then been distracted. I heard the woman's voice in my ear explaining how the mother had gone to work—she danced at a strip joint, one of the new gentlemen's clubs that featured college-looking girls instead of aging women with bad habits—and so was gone when it happened. I nodded, purred soothing words, closed the freezer door, and strolled back by the water bed; the blue of its plastic had the gaiety of a flower in the tired room. I looked at a big splotch on the cinderblock wall, and she said, "I haven't had time to clean that off yet."

That's where the head had hit, the skull of the toddler just shy of two years, as the man most likely held him by the legs and swung him like a baseball bat. He probably killed the kid out of boredom or frustration with the demands of a small child, or because he'd been bopped around himself as a child, or God knows why. The man had taken off, then been caught by the cops, and was sitting in jail as they figured out what level of murder he'd scored. The dancer they'd found wandering in the desert, and they'd flung some kind of charges at her. As I stared at the block wall, the proprietress bubbled up in my ear again and said, with that small, cooing voice American women sometimes favor when indicating feeling, "We kind of made a collection and customers chipped in and we bought him an outfit for the burial." She told me they got the clothes at Kmart. I drove back to the paper, wrote an impressionistic piece pivoting on the frozen bottles and all the hopes and basic desires found in a beer chilling for a thirsty throat, and then phones started ringing at the city desk and I was hurled at the funeral.

So I sit through the service studying the mother's profile. She has fine hair, a kind of faint red. I once knew a woman with hair like that, and as I stare I can smell this other woman and feel my hands tracing a path through the slender strands. I can smell the soap, the scent of the other woman; the small smile and fine bones and clean, even teeth. In my memory the coffin is open, the boy's small face very pale and blank, and he is surrounded by donated teddy bears that came from a town that told itself these things are not supposed to happen, and if such things do happen they're not supposed to happen in our town.

Just before the service ends, I have a hunch that the cops are going to take the mother out the back so that the press cannot snap her image and I cannot scan her face. So I get up and leave the chapel of the cheap mortuary and go to the back, and, sure enough, suddenly the metal door opens and two cops burst through with the lap dancer handcuffed and sagging between their grip. The light is brilliant at 1:15 P.M. and merciless as it glares off the woman. Her face is small, with tiny bones, and her age is no longer possible to peg—somewhere between nineteen and one thousand. She is wearing tight pants on slender, girlish hips and a black leather vest over her blouse. The waist is small, the hair falls to her shoulders, the lips are very thin. A moan comes off her, a deep moan, and I sense that she is unaware of the sound she is making, just as she is unaware of what has happened to her.

The only thing she knows is what I know. There is a toddler in a box with teddy bears, and the box sits in a room full of strangers from this town where she has bagged a job dancing for other strangers.

The cops look at me with anger, drag her slumping form away, and toss her into the back of a squad car. I stand still, make no notes. Then I go back to the newsroom and write up the funeral. That is when it begins. The toddler's death probably didn't have anything to do with child molestation, but for me this child became the entry point to rape and other categories of abuse. For the next three years I live in a world where the desire of people, almost always men, to touch and have their way with others makes them criminals. Gradually I began to lose the distinction between the desires of criminals and the desires of the rest of us. I am told I can't get off this kind of beat, because most reporters won't do it. This may be true, I don't really know, because those three years are the only ones I ever spent working for a newspaper and practically the only ones I ever spent working for anyone besides myself. I would quit the paper twice, break down more often than I can remember, and have to go away for a week or two and kill, through violent exercise, the things that roamed my mind. It was during this period that I began taking one-hundred- or two-hundred-mile walks in the desert far from trails. I would write up these flights from myself, and people began to talk about me as a nature writer. The rest of my time was spent with another nature, the one we call, by common consent, deviate or marginal or unnatural.

I can still see the woman coming through the metal door, slumping between the paws of the cops. I am standing northwest of her and about twenty feet away. It is 1:15 P.M., the glare of the sun makes her squint, her hips are bound in impossible pants, her face has never seen anything brighter than the dim lights of a strip joint, and her wrists, in the chrome gleam of cuffs, are tiny. I can remember this with photographic detail, only I can't remember what became of her or her lover. Just the boy, the splotch on the wall, the blue water bed, and the frozen Budweiser.

Until this moment, I've avoided remembering what became of me.

NIGHT, THE WARM NIGHT OF EARLY FALL, and they form up in the park, the women and their supporters, with candles and flashlights, banners and the will to take back the night. The green pocket of trees and grass hugs the road. They go a few blocks and swing down one of the city's main thoroughfares. Safety in numbers, group solidarity, sisterhood is powerful, protest, demands, anger, laughter, high spirits.

They find her later in a narrow slot between two buildings, more a gap in the strip of commercial facades than a planned path or walkway, the kind of slot that sees hard sun a few minutes a day and then returns to shadow. She is seven and dead. While the march to take back the night was passing through here, she apparently left her neighbor's yard nearby and came over to see the spectacle. The police and press keep back one detail: she has been eviscerated. That is part of what a newsroom feeds off, the secret facts that others do not know or cannot be told, the sense of being where the action is and where the knowing people gather. So we say to one another: opened up from stem to stern that night.

I come in the next morning ignorant of all this and am called into a meeting. The city editor, the managing editor, and the publisher are agitated. They have children; they want to do something, but they don't know what. I'm told to make a difference in the slaughter of our children. I nod and say, You'll have to give me time. The exchange is very short; this paper has no long meetings. I go back to my desk and remember another night long ago: the man crying. And when I remember, I don't want to take this assignment, but I do.

HE SPEAKS IN A SMALL VOICE as his hands cradle his face in the hospital waiting room, and he says, "My baby girl, my baby girl." His wife looks on stoically. The call came in the middle of the night, and when I arrive there is the cool of fluorescent lights, the sterile scent of linoleum floors, and the memory of her going down the corridor on a gurney with her face pulverized into raw flesh. She had gone to visit a friend near campus and stepped out of her car onto the quiet street.

That is when he took her. He forced her back into her car, and they drove out of town into the open ground. He raped her, pistol-whipped her, pumped two rounds into her, and then left her for dead. She saw a house light and crawled toward it. The people inside feared her pounding in the night and did not want to open up. Somehow an ambulance came, and now she is in surgery as I sit with her weeping father and stoical mother. At the time, I am related by marriage. But that does not help. I am a man, but that does not help. I am not a rapist, and that does not help at all. Nothing really helps—not words, not anger, not reflection. For days afterward, as the hospital reports come in, as the visits to the room present a bandaged and shaved head, as the unthinkable becomes normal for all of us, nothing really helps. We have stepped over a line into a place we refuse to acknowledge, a place of violence and danger, where the sexual impulses that course through our veins have created carnage.

I was in my late twenties then, and I remember my male friends all coming to me with visions of violence, scripts about what should be done to the rapist, what they would do to him, how these instances should be handled. I would nod and say very little.

I'm over at a house where friends live, the kind of male dormitory that has a dirty skillet festering on the stove, clothes tossed here and there, and empty beer bottles on the coffee table giving off stale breath. It is precisely 10:00 A.M., and one guy is just getting up from the mattress on the floor of his room. He is a Nam vet with a cluster of medals and has two interests after his war: hunting and women. A stack of skin magazines two feet high towers over the mattress, and a fine .270 with a polished walnut stock leans in the corner. He tells me they should take those guys out and cut their dicks off, and then he staggers down the hall with his hangover to take a piss. I feel that I am watching something happening on a screen but that I am not really here.

Eventually, a red-faced detective comes by to placate the victim's family and express his sense of urgency as we sit in the quiet kitchen. He explains all the things being done, but he convinces no one. How do you find a rapist when half the population is suspect? This is when I first hear the police read on rape: "Fifteen minutes for the guy, five years for the woman."

I had a vegetable garden then, and this was the only place where things made sense and fell into some kind of order. So I sit on the dirt amid the rows of bell peppers, tomatoes, eggplant, marigolds, and squash, sip red wine, and let my mind flow. I wonder if there is a monster lurking in all of us. I never cease, I realize, scanning faces when I prowl the city, and what I wonder is, Are you the one? I look over at the other cars when I am at a stop-light. This becomes an unconscious habit. Sometimes I think I have adopted the consciousness of a woman. Now I think like prey.

Later, a year or two later, a guy goes to a party near the campus, drinks and whoops it up, and leaves with a woman he meets there. He takes her out and rapes her and tries to kill her. Turns out he is the one, and they send him off to prison. By then, it hardly matters to me. I know he will be back and he will be older, and that that will be the only change. I bury the memories and go on pretty much as if nothing had ever happened. As does the woman who was raped, pistol-whipped, shot, and left for dead. You can know some things and the knowing seems to help you not at all.

"My baby girl, my baby girl." These memories resurface as I leave the editorial meeting with my instructions to figure out something for the paper to do about the slaughter of a seven-year-old girl during a march to take back the night. I sit at my gray desk and stare at the clock on the east wall. It is early in the morning, 7:00 or 8:00 A.M. I have no delusions that I will magically crack the case. But I decide to look into the world where such acts come from, though I do not consciously know what such a desire means in practical terms. I have no plan, just this sensation of powerlessness and corruption and violation and grief. I can feel my eyes welling with tears, and I know instantly that this feeling will do nothing for me or anyone else.

After that I follow my instincts, which is what the predators do also.

THERE ARE FIVE THINGS I KNOW to be true. These rules come to me out of my explorations.

No one can handle the children.

Get out after two years.

Always walk a woman to her car, regardless of the hour of the day or the night.

Don't talk about it; no one wants to hear these things.

No one can handle the children.

The fourth lesson is the iron law. We lie about sex crimes because we lie about sex. We lie about sex because we fear what we feel within ourselves and recoil when others act out our feelings. American society has always been more candid about murder ("I felt like killing him," we can say out loud) than about the designs we have on each other's bodies. What destroys people who have to deal with sex crimes is very simple: you lose the ability to lie to yourself about your feelings, and if you are not careful you fail to lie appropriately to others. When we are in bed with each other we find it difficult to say what we want, and when we brush up against sex crimes we find it difficult to stomach what we see and even more difficult to acknowledge the tug of our fantasies. In the core of our being live impulses, and these impulses are not all bright and not all as comfortable as an old shoe.

Soon after I embark on this assignment, I am at the home of a friend, a very learned man who is elderly. When we sit and drink he is open to any topic—the machinations of the Federal Reserve, the mutilation of young girls in Africa, male menopause, or the guilt/innocence of Alger Hiss. I have just written a story for the newspaper on child molestation that runs four solid pages without one advertisement because no merchant wants products next to such a story. I vaguely remember the lead. I must do this from memory, because regardless of the passage of years, with their gentle soothing effect, I cannot look at the clips yet: "The polite term is child molestation. The father said he had done nothing but fondle his son. The boy had gonorrhea of the mouth. The polite term is child molestation."

As I sit with my friend and we ponder the intricacies of the world and swap lifetimes of reading, he suddenly turns to me and says, "I want you to know I didn't read your story. I don't read things like that."

I am not surprised. After the story hits the press, women at the newspaper come up to me for soft conversations and want to have lunch or drinks. They murmur that they are part of the sisterhood or secret society of the maimed. The men avoid me, and I can sense their displeasure with what I have written and the endless and relentless nature of the piece. I realize that if I had not written it, I would avoid reading it, too.

Another revelation comes from having drinks with a retired cop. We are kind of friends: cops and reporters are natural adversaries and yet, in some matters, have no one else to talk with (see rule number four). I ask him how the local police handled rape during his time.

He says, "Well, the first thing we'd do is take the suspect out of the house and into the carport, and then we'd beat the shit out of him with our saps. Then we'd take him downtown and book him for assault." He does not read the piece either.

Then there is the woman who is passionately into nonviolence and vegetarianism and speaks softly as if she embodies a state of grace. She comes to my door one night after a couple of my stories have run, and we make love on the cement floor. Afterward, she tells me that when she was a girl her father, who was rich and successful, would sit around with his male friends and they would take turns fucking her in the ass. I walk her to her car.

I AM SITTING ON THE NORTH END of a back row facing the west wall. The room is institutional and full of therapists, counselors, and other merchants of grief who have gathered to share their experiences treating victims of sex crimes. I scan the crowd, mainly women without makeup wearing sensible shoes. I listen for hours as they outline play therapy, describe predators (with children, usually someone close and accepted by the family; with rape, often as not the mysterious stranger), call for a heightened public consciousness about the size of this plague. Their statistics vary but basically suggest that everyone is either a victim of a sexual crime or the perpetrator of a sexual crime or a therapist treating sexual crimes. They all agree that children do not lie and that more attention must be paid.

Late in the day a woman walks to the podium. I have been noticing her for hours, because she does not fit in with the group. Her lips are lacquered, her hair perfect, and she wears a tasteful lavender dress—one I sense she has bought just for this occasion—and high heels. She is the only woman wearing high heels. She speaks with a Southern accent and tells the group that she is not a professional person. She is a mother, and a neighbor molested her daughter, her very young daughter. And she wants something done about it. In her case, she continues, nothing was done. The neighbor still lives a few doors down, and her daughter still lives in terror—they have had to seal her window with duct tape so "he can't look in."

The woman at the podium is on fire and very angry. Her words slap the audience in the face. She has no theory, she says, and no program. She simply wants her government, her police, and her city to pay attention to the problem. And she will not rest. She reads her words off sheets of yellow legal paper, and her articulation is harsh, as if she were drumming her fingers on a Formica kitchen table.

Afterward, I cut through the crowd and find her. I say I am a reporter and would like to talk more. She is flustered. She is not used to talking to audiences and not used to talking to the press. She gives me her number, and we agree to meet. I notice her eye makeup and the sensual nature of her lips.

When I turn, another woman comes up to me. I vaguely noticed her enter when the woman whose child was molested was speaking. She is about thirty and wears leather pants and a motorcycle jacket. Her eyes are very intelligent, and she tells me she is a therapist. Her smile is generous. We walk out and go to a nearby cafe, which is empty and half-lit in the late afternoon, and sit at a round table with a dark top. We both sip longnecks.

Her life has not been simple lately. She is distancing herself, she explains, from a bad relationship. She has been living with a man, and he is very successful. He came home a few days ago and they made love. He told her she was the sixth woman he had had that day but that he liked her the best. He never comes, she says; anything else, but he never comes. He withholds, don't you see? she asks.

When I go to her place she is in shorts and a shirt and is roller-skating in her driveway. She tells me she wanted me to see her that way, free and skating with delight. We lie on the floor. She says, "Squeeze my nipples hard, squeeze my titties as hard as you can." Later, we are in the bathroom, because she wants to watch us in the mirror. We go back to the bedroom and she rolls over on her stomach.

She says very softly, "Yes."

Somewhere in those hours my second marriage ends. I know why. I, too, tend to say yes. The marriage ends because I do not want to live with her anymore, because she is a good and proper person and this now feels like a cage. I do not want to leave my work at the office. I do not want to leave my work at all. I have entered a world that is black, sordid, vicious. And actual. And I do not care what price I must pay to be in this world.

The therapist has a lot of patients who are fat women, and they fascinate her. She herself has not an extra ounce of fat; she is all curves and muscle, her calves look like sculpture, her stomach is flat, her features are cute. She is very limber. Once at a party, she casually picked up one of her legs while talking to a couple and touched her ear with her foot. She was not wearing panties when she performed this feat. She runs daily, has been part of a female rock and roll band, takes showers three or four times a day, and is proudly bisexual. She tells me one of her best tactics for keeping boyfriends is to seduce and fuck their girlfriends. She smiles relentlessly.

What fascinates her about the fat women is their behavior. Not the eating. She cannot even fathom the eating part, since she never gains weight and eats whatever she wishes. Her place is always cluttered with bowls of macadamia nuts for guests. No, it's their sexual lives she is interested in. Their sexual lives are very simple: they will do anything. That, she tells me, is why men like fat women. They will do anything; name your fantasy, try out your imagined humiliation.

She tells me how she became a therapist. She went to visit her own therapist once and he questioned her openness, and she wound up doing golden showers in his office. After that she fled to an analytic center on the West Coast and studied very hard. No, she says, she is not bitter about it. She learned he was right; she was not open enough.

I find her smile addictive. We sit in her kitchen and she makes a Greek salad. She becomes a blur cutting up the feta cheese and dicing olives. And then we go to the bedroom. She tells me I have green blood and smiles with the promise that she will make it red.

Here is how play therapy goes. You look through one-way glass at very small children on the floor. The child holds anatomically correct dolls, ones with actual sexual organs, and acts out what has happened in the past. It is something to see. The dolls look like Raggedy Ann. And do pretty much exactly what adults do with each other. My guide in this place is a gray-haired woman who is very well-spoken and has the quiet calm of a Quaker lady. She used to work in a ward with terminally ill children. She tells me this work is harder. Ah, now the child is moving the two dolls. We talk for twenty-two hours. Not all at once, no one can do that, but for very long stretches at a time. That is how the lady in the lavender dress with the hard words, the lady who stunned the seminar audience, begins. With talk.

We sit across from each other with the coffee table and a patch of rug between our chairs. She is cautious. This is her story and, like most people, she wishes to tell her story but only to the right person—the person who listens. I have no tape recorder, just a pen and a notebook, and we begin spiraling into the tale. It is night, her daughter is in the tub, she mentions pain and points. The mother hides her alarm, asks gentle questions, and it slowly comes out as the minutes crawl past. He is the older man, the pal of neighborhood kids. Always a smile, perfectly normal, you never would have guessed.

As she talks, her daughter, so very young and small, plays out in the yard, and from time to time I catch a glimpse of her as I look up from my notepad or glance away from the woman, her monologue flowing from her full lips.

The child is in sunlight, gamboling about without a worry in the world. For a second, none of it ever happened. I see this apparition through the sliding glass doors, and then the woman's words pull me back to the night, the aftermath, the weeks and now months of coaxing the child back first from terror and then from a sense of betraying her special friend by telling—and, of course, she was warned not to tell, they always make sure to stress this warning.

When I am with the woman I enter, as she does, a kind of trance.

When I am away the trance still holds to a degree, and I talk with no one about what I am doing. I make a point of filing other stories to disguise the hours I spend listening. I live in worlds within worlds, since the child's identity must not be revealed, and so for me things become generic and universal and yet at the same time, looking into one woman's face and taking down one woman's words, specific, exact, and full of color, scent, and feel.

I write the story in one long fury, and the print-out runs about twenty feet. I crawl along my floor, reading it and making changes. Sometimes my therapist roller skater drops by and finds me crawling on the floor with my felt pen, and she does not approve of this act. It is too involved, not suitable for things that should be done at a desk with a good lamp and a sound chair. I sense I am failing her by falling into myself, and our sex grows more heated and yet more empty. This goes on for weeks. I don't know what to do with the story, and then finally I turn it in and they print it.

Fifty subscribers cancel in less than an hour, I am told.

I prowl through the police blotter, savoring the rapes of the night: The woman who leaves the bar at 1:00 A.M. with the stranger. No, can't sell her. The woman who decides at 3:00 A.M. to take a walk in short shorts and a halter to the all-night market for a pack of cigarettes and then gets bagged. She's out, too. The girl who goes into the men's room with her boyfriend to give him head and then his friends follow and gangbang her. No sale. I course through the dull sheets of pain, hunting for the right one—the one I can sell, the one to which readers cannot say, "Well, that could never happen to me," the one they can't run away from so easily.

A woman rides the freights into town and then hooks up with two guys at a cafe, and they say if you need a place to crash come with us. She does. She decides she needs a shower, and they say go ahead. When she comes out of what she calls "the rain closet" they're on her. She later goes to the cops, describes herself as a motorcycle mechanic, and tells them of the rape. The paper takes one look at my story and says forget it. And, of course, they're right. Rape, like many things, is kind of a class matter. You have to not deserve it for the world to care even a little bit. This I learn.

Sometimes for a break I drop in on a small bookstore where a heavy woman with a British accent sells used volumes. A gray cat is always nestled inside, and the place has the feel of afternoon tea in someone's living room. Then she is attacked and held hostage in her home one night. The store closes; I don't know what happens to the cat. Eventually, she leaves town and settles in a somewhat distant city. Finally, I hear she kills herself.

I keep hunting, talking with fewer and fewer people. Except for those who live in this world or at least understand its dimensions. I'll be somewhere, maybe kicking back, feet up on the coffee table, glass of wine in hand, and someone will play, say, the Stones' "Midnight Rambler," and my mood will sink and go black. Best not to visit people.

THE DAYS OF THE WEEK CEASE to have meaning, as do the weeks of the month and the months of the year. My life went by clocks and dates and deadlines, but the order implied in paychecks, withholding taxes, dinner at six, and Sunday-morning brunch vanished with my consent. I did not lose control of my life; I gave up the pretense of normal life, and followed crime and appetite. I learned things on the run and without intention. Knowledge came like stab wounds, and pleasure came with the surprise of a downpour from a blue sky in the desert. I remember sitting with some women who had been raped after I wrote a profile of the rapist. Turns out all the guy's co-workers, mainly women, found him to be a polite, nice person.

One woman looked at me and said flatly, "He wasn't that way when I was with him."

Stab wounds.

I have become furious, but mainly with myself. Certain protocols in writing about such matters anger me. I decide never to write the phrase "child molestation" or "sexual assault" except in a context of deliberate mockery. I am angry at the pain I witness and listen to each day as I make my appointed rounds, and I am angry at the hypocrisy of it all. We want to believe that the intersection between sex and crime happens only in an alien country, one that does not touch our lives or feelings or lusts of the midnight hours.

A woman is at the door and she has three balls on a string she wishes to insert in my ass, and then she will pull the string at the moment of orgasm.

A woman is at the door and she says she has cuffs.

A woman is at the door late at night and we make love, and as she leaves she says she can't see me again because she is getting married in the morning.

Two women are at the door . . .

We like to call things that disturb us a jungle, to wall them off from our sense of order and self. But we all inhabit that forest, a dense thicket of desire and dread, both burning bright. We want to categorize: victims or studs, seduced or seducers. And we can hardly look at people who we agree are criminals and admit we feel some of their passions and fantasies within ourselves. My life in those days erased boundaries and paid no attention to whether I was a predator or a victim or a newspaper savior with a byline. I was attractive to women because what I knew made me somehow safe. Ruined people were telling me things they never told anyone else, and the women dealing with ruined people were sharing secrets as well, and some of those secrets were fantasies they wished to act out. There is a way to go so deep into the secrets and hungers of your culture that you live without concern for the mores and with a keen sense of your own needs. I have seen this state most often in the old, who finally realize that the rules of conduct are optional and read what they wish, say what they think, and live in sin without a qualm. I didn't feel guilt. Then or now. I didn't feel love. I didn't seek a cure. Getting in bed with women was a pleasure but not the center of my life. The center of my life was crime. And sex was also an attempt to redeem or exorcise what I saw. As the crimes piled up and corroded my energy and will, I ceased to find even cold comfort in women, and everything in my life became perfunctory except for the crimes. I have hard memories of my life then but not bad memories. But of the work, I still have nightmares. I still drive by commonplace haunts and see weeping women, bodies, a terrified child, an eviscerated girl. There are accepted ways of dealing with such experiences: the secular renunciation of a clinical visit to all the Betty Ford centers out there, the religious rebirth of being born again. I did neither. I simply continued plowing my way into that night.

She sits up in bed and asks, "Aren't my breasts beautiful? Aren't they the best you've ever seen?"

I nuzzle her hair. Time has passed, the story long gone, the woman in the lavender dress with the hard words and the maimed child is now the woman here.

She tells me her husband has been suspicious of me. I ask her what she told him.

"Don't worry." She smiles. "I told him you were a queer." Then she slides over, gets up, and rolls a joint. The rapes are bad but not that bad. The mind is protected from what adults do to adults. There is a squeamishness about the rapes, an embarrassment among the men who investigate them, and an anger among the women who treat the casualties. But the rapes can be handled to a degree. Of course, it's not as easy as homicide; people stay in homicide forever and never lose pleasure in their work. Sex crimes generally cycle people out in two years. And it is the kids who do it. No one can handle the kids. But then the highway patrol always dreads the car wreck with kids. It goes against nature as we know it.

Once I was helping a guy move—him, his wife, their two young daughters—and a box I was carrying out broke open and small paperbacks spilled to the ground in the bright sunshine. I gathered them up and then idly flipped through one, and then another and another. They were all cheap things from no-name presses about men—daddies, uncles, whoever—fucking kids. I was stunned and did not know what to do. I felt oddly violated, like it was wrong for me to have to know this. So I put them back in the box and put the box in the truck and said nothing and did nothing.

That is part of what I feel as I enter the gray police station and go to the offices where the sex-crimes unit works. They've got a treasure trove of child pornography seized from perps, and in my memory the stack rises six or seven feet. They leave me at a table with it, and what they want is for me to look at it and come out with an article recommending that people who possess such materials go to prison.

The collection mainly features boys, seven, eight, nine from the looks of them, and they are sucking off men, taking it in the ass, being perfect pals about everything. I am struck not by what I feel but by how little I feel. It is like handling the treasured and sacred icons of a dead religion. I have careful constitutional qualms filed in my mind—basically, that to think something is not a crime. Fucking kids and taking pictures—that is already against the law. So I stand firmly on the Constitution of the United States and look at photographs I do not believe should exist made by and for people I do not believe should exist. I look for hours and still feel nothing. I am in a place beyond the power of empathy.

A few months later I get a thick packet of fifty or sixty typed pages. The writer is facing a long prison sentence for having had sex with Scouts, as I recall. He writes with courtesy, clarity, and an almost obsessive sense of detail. Essentially, nothing ever happened except that he tried to comfort and love his charges. I doubt him on his details but come to sense that he means his general thesis about love. He loves children, totally, and locks on them with the same feeling I have for adult women.

That is what I take away from the photos the police want outlawed and the autobiography of the man they eventually send away to be raped and possibly murdered by fellow convicts for being a child molester. A crime is being committed by people who see themselves as the perfect friend. Other things are being committed by people who see themselves as lovers. And, of course, a lot of things are being done by people who have no romantic delusions about their desires but are full of hate, who drag women off into the bushes or a corner because they hate them and are going to get even by causing pain, humiliation, and, at times, death. Cycles of abuse, the role of pornography, the denigration of women by Hollywood and glossy magazines—there is no single, simple explanation for sex crimes. But in the case of the men who use children for sex there is often this fixation, this sense of love, which always leads them to betray the very idea of love itself by using children for their own selfish ends.

During this period of my life my musical taste changes and slowly, without my awareness, starts sliding backward through the decades. One day I decide to look up a style of music I've been listening to in a big Merriam-Webster dictionary. Torch song: from the phrase "to carry a torch for" (to be in love); first appeared in 1930; a popular sentimental song of unrequited love.

The walls are block, humming fluorescent lights replace windows, and we sit in rows forming a semicircle as the woman teaching the class speaks. She is very nicely done up in a sedate professional suit, tasteful hair, low-key makeup; she has a serious and clear voice. The prisoners mark time as I go through rape therapy in the joint. I am not here because of a story. I've come to find something beneath the stories or deep within myself. The boundaries between normal, accepted sexual appetite and crime are blurring for me. People get an erotic charge out of playing with consent—holding each other down, tying each other up—indulging in ritualized dominance. Rape is an eerie parody of accepted life, an experience using the same wardrobe but scratching the word "consent" from the script. I am obeying the law and the rules of consent, but I am losing a sense of distance between my obedient self and those who break the law. When I listen to women tell of the horrors they've experienced, the acts they recount are usually familiar to me, and what they recount as true terror, the sense of powerlessness, strikes chords within me also. I can't abide being in the joint even for this class. I can't take the bars, guards, walls.

The men, struggling to earn good time, feign attention. They answer questions appropriately and wear masks of serious thought. I don't believe them for an instant, and I think that this class is a farce and that nothing will deter my colleagues from their appointed rounds when they leave this place. The woman herself, from a good family and with sound religious values, has been attacked—"I am part of the sisterhood," she once told me shyly, and she has brought me here so that I will see hope and share her hope. So I sit with the current crop of convicted rapists. "There are no first-time offenders," a cop once snarled at me, "just sons of bitches that finally get caught"—and feel no hope. Of course, prison is rape culture—"just need a bunk and a punk," one local heroin dealer offered in explaining his lack of concern about doing time.

The session finally ends, and we bleed out the door of the room into the prison corridor. I am ambling along in a throng of convicts, the woman walking just ahead in her prim suit with her skirt snug on her hips. The guy next to me is singing some kind of blues about what he's gonna do to that bad bitch. I've blotted out the actual song. I can remember the corridor (we are strolling east), see her up ahead, hear him singing next to me, his lips barely moving as he floats his protest against the class and her fucking control and all that shit, but not the lyrics themselves. They're gone, erased by my mind, I suspect in self-defense. Afterward, she and I go to a truck stop and eat apple pie, and I can still see the whiteness of her teeth as she smiles and speaks brightly about her work.

Later, I taste child-molestation therapy, a regimen where men who have fucked their own children sit in a circle and talk while their wives run the show. It's either show up at such sessions or the joint—so attendance is rather good. Afterward, I go off with the boys and we have beers. In recounting his lapse from accepted behavior, each and every one of them describes the act itself as fondling. Apparently, there are hordes of diligently caressed children out there. I nurse my beer and say little, pretending to try to understand. But I understand nothing at all. I have seen the end result of fondling, and it does not look at all like fondling to me. I cannot put myself in their place. I cannot see children as sexual objects, it does not seem to be in me. I fixate, I realize, on women. And my fixation is sanctioned, as long as I toe the line. Such thoughts lead to a place without clear light. We all share a biology and deep drives, and what we have created—civilization, courtesy, decency—is a mesh that comes from these drives and also contains and tames them. Whatever feels good is not necessarily good. But what I learn is that whatever is bad is not necessarily alien to me. Or to you.

She loves pornography. It's around midnight, and she is standing in the motel room clutching a bottle of champagne against her black garter belt and peering intently into the screen of the television as fornicating couples, powered by the handyman of American fantasy, the telephone man, frolic. This is one of the seedy motels that cultivate hourly rates, water beds, and hard-core cinema, a place much like the room where my life in this world began with the splotch on the wall left by the toddler's head. She is a counselor, one of the many I now deal with, and she likes sex and is fascinated by pornography. This is not unusual; another woman, a professional woman I deal with, has several hundred pornographic tapes. But the interests of the woman in the black garter belt are kept off the table at her work and left to the night hours and random bouts with me. Days are for the maimed—in her case, children with cigarette burns and sore orifices. Some nights are like this.

I glance at her naked ass, see the serene concentration of her face as she tracks the movie, and I am empty. She and I share the same country, and there is a big hole in us, so we come here. We live in a place past the moral strictures of sin and lust; we run on empty. For us, sex has been drained of its usual charge, delight is beyond our reach. This is a fact. As the months roll past, I feel this slippage within me. I will have lunch or dinner or a drink or coffee with someone and wind up in a place like this. Romance is not a consideration. There is seldom anyone to talk with, and when there is someone, a person like the woman in the black garter belt watching the porn movie, a person stumbling across the same terrain, there is nothing to say, since we both know. So we come here. A proper distance from our appetites has been denied us, so we seek moments of obliteration. I have never regretted those moments or fully understood them. I just knew then, and know now, that they come with the territory.

But the slippage bothers me. I seem to drift, and the drift is downward. Not into sin and the pit but into that emptiness. I am losing all desire and mechanically go through the motions of life. Food also does not tempt me. I flee into the wild country with my backpack, flee again and again for days and days, but increasingly this tactic does not work. Once I am lying by a water hole in July and it is 104 degrees at 1:00 A.M. (I get up with my flashlight and check my thermometer.) I am crawling with crabs. When I go back I buy twelve bottles of the recommended cure and for a day have coffee or drinks with a succession of women, handing each a bottle. I take this in stride, as do they. One woman is briefly anxious because she fears I have called her only to deliver the medicine, but this feeling passes when I assure her that this is not true, that I really wanted to see her. I think we then go to bed. It turns out that this mini-epidemic has come from the therapist who showers three or four times a day. She also is quite calm about it and prefers to talk about her new favorite movie, something entitled *Little Oral Annie*. She tells me she resents the smirks of the male clerks when she rents it at the video store, and I politely sympathize.

The moments of my impotence increase. I am not alarmed by this fact but clinically engaged. I sense that I am walling off everything, all appetites, and have room for nothing but this torrent of pain and squalor that pours through me from the daily and weekly harvest of rapes and killings and molestations. I remember once reading a statement allegedly made by Sophocles in his old age, when sexual desire had left his loins; he said he was glad to be free of the mad master. So I am becoming classic and care not at all. I repeatedly try to leave the work, but the city desk always wins because a part of me feels bound to the crimes. So I protest, and then return. I tell myself it is a duty, but what I feel is the desire to run out my string, to see how much I can stomach and learn. And yet then, and now, I cannot really say what this knowing entails. I can just feel its burden as I lie with caring women in countless cheap motels, the movies rolling on the screen.

The end begins in the bright light of afternoon on a quiet street lined with safe houses. One moment an eight-year-old girl is riding her bicycle on the sidewalk near her home; the next moment the bicycle is lying on the ground and the girl is gone with no one the wiser.

This one is my torch song. The rudiments are simple. The alleged perpetrator is a man in his twenties from a very good home in another city, a man whose life has been a torment of drugs, molestation of himself by others and of others by himself, a man who has slipped from his station in life into dissipation and wound up roaming the skid rows of our nation. None of this concerns me, and I leave ruin in my wake. I fly to that distant city, talk my way through a stout door, and gut his mother like a fish. When I leave she is a wreck, and later that night her husband goes to the hospital for perturbations of his heart. I get into files—legal, psychiatric—that I should not have had access to, and I print them fulsomely. The child favored a certain doll, and I buy one and prowl the city with it on the truck seat beside me, a touchstone. I am standing in the backyard as the mother of the missing girl makes a plea to whoever took her daughter to bring her home safe and sound. The woman's face is grief made flesh, and I note its every tic and sag. It turns out that the alleged perpetrator stayed for a time with a couple in a trailer court. I visit; the man is facing child molestation charges himself, the woman is a hooker with a coke habit. "Do I have to tell you that?" she whines. I remember leaving them, driving to a saloon, setting my small computer on the bar, and begging a phone for the modem. I sip my drink and write in one quick take. The story flits through the wires and descends into the next edition. The following night a local PTA meeting takes a recess, walks over to the trailer, and then it goes up in flames.

My temper is short, my blood cold. A young mother who works in the newsroom comes over to my desk and asks me what I think the chances are of the girl being alive. I snap, "Fucked, strangled, and rotting out there." And keep typing. The sheriff leaps into the public wound and starts leading marches of citizens holding candles and decrying violence and the rape of children. It is much like the time so long ago when things began for me with a seven-year-old eviscerated while people marched to take back the night. I pay no notice to these marches; they are for others. The reporters on the story all speculate about the girl—even when the arrest comes and still the girl is missing. I do not. I know. Bones bleach out there. It is months and months before her remains turn up, but this hardly matters to me. I know. This is my country.

It ends several times, but at last it finally ends. The city desk asks my help to find a woman whose son, a famous local rapist, has just escaped. I leave, chat up some neighbors, and within an hour I am in a state office, a bullpen of women toiling over desks and processing forms. She has done everything she can—changed her name, told no one of her son, gone on and tried to fashion a life. I approach her desk and tell her my errand. She pleads with me, Don't do this to me. She leans forward and whispers that no one typing away at the other desks, none of them knows anything about this. Leave me in peace, she says. I look into her careworn eyes and I say yes. I tell her I will now leave and she will never read a word of my visit in the newspaper. Nor will I tell anyone of her identity.

When I enter the newsroom, the editor comes over and asks, "Did you find her?"

I say, "Yes."

"When can I have the story?"

"I'm never writing the story."

He looks at me, says nothing, then turns and walks away.

That is when one part of me is finished. I know I must quit. I cannot take the money and decide what goes into the newspaper. I do not believe in myself as censor and gatekeeper. And yet I know I will never write this story, because I have hit some kind of limit in pain. The phone rings. It is a woman's voice. She says, "Thanks to you she has had to go to the hospital. I hope you are happy."

I tell her I am not writing the story. I tell her I told the mother I would not write the story. She does not believe me. This does not matter to me. My hands are cold, and I know from past experience this means I can take no more. I am righteously empty.

The other ending is more important, because it does not involve the work, the little credos and dos and don'ts of journalism. It involves myself. It happens the night the arrests come down for the missing eight-year-old snatched off her bicycle on that safe side street. Around three in the morning, I wrap the story and reach into my desk drawer, where I stashed a fifth of Jack Daniel's bought earlier in the day. I do not drink hard liquor, and I bought the bottle without questioning myself and without conscious intent. So I finish the story, open the drawer, take the bottle, and go home. I sit in my backyard in the dark of the night, those absolutely lonely hours before dawn. I drink, the bite of the whiskey snapping against my tongue, and drink in the blackness.

After a while I feel a wetness and realize that I am weeping, weeping silently and unconsciously, weeping for reasons I do not understand. I know this is a sign that I am breaking down, this weeping without a moan or a sound. I feel the tears trickle, and step outside myself and watch myself clinically in a whiskey-soaked out-of-body experience. That is the other ending.

I quit the paper, never again set foot in a newsroom, and go into the mountains off and on for months and write a book about them. That helps but not enough. I sit down and in twenty-one days write another book about the land, the people, and the city. That helps, but although I barely touch on the world of sex and crimes in this book, it broods beneath the sentences about Indians and antelope and bats and city streets. Nothing really helps.

That is what I am trying to say. Theories don't help, therapies don't help, knowing doesn't help. The experts say they have therapies that are cutting recidivism, and maybe they do, but I doubt it. I live with what I am and what I saw and what I felt—a residue that will linger to the end of my days in the cells of my body. I have never been in an adult bookstore. Two years ago I was at a bachelor party in a lap-dancing place and lasted fifteen minutes before I hailed a cab and fled. This is not a virtue or a position. I have no desire to outlaw pornography, strip joints, blue movies, or much of anything my fellow citizens find entertaining. Nor have I led an orderly life since my time in sex crimes. I write for men's magazines and pass over without comment their leering tone and arch expressions about the flesh. I am not a reformer. So what am I?

A man who has visited a country where impulses we all feel become horrible things. A man who can bury such knowledge but not disown it, and a man who can no longer so glibly talk of perverts or rapists or cretins or scum. A man who knows there is a line within each of us that we cannot accurately define, that shifts with the hour and the mood but is still real. And if we cross that line we betray ourselves and everyone else and become outcasts from our own souls. A man who can be an animal but can no longer be a voyeur. A man weeping silently in the backyard with a bottle of whiskey who knows he must leave and go to another country and yet never forget what he has seen and felt. Just keep under control. And try not to lie too much.

Just before I quit, I am in a bar in a distant city with a district attorney. He shouts to the barkeep, "Hey, give this guy a drink. One of our perverts whacked a kid in his town."

The bartender pours and says, "Way to go."

And I drink without a word. Nobody wants to hear these things.

Part III

Mexican civilization existed before the American people were even a thought. Americans have come to the game very recently, and like so many new arrivals believe they possess all the answers. At the moment, human beings are moving all over the planet to save their hides. Things have been upended, the moon rises at a strange hour, it is blood red, and dripping with hunger.

FROM *EXODUS*

Excerpt

From the 2008 Photography Exhibit "The History of the Future"

Bowden wrote "The History of the Future" for a December 2008 photography exhibit in Santa Fe, New Mexico, displaying the works of Julián Cardona and Michael Berman. Cardona's work is featured in the books *Exodus* and *Juárez: Laboratory of Our Future,* and Berman's work is featured in *Inferno* and *Trinity.*

I NEVER WALK THE LINE, I cross it. And I've been ignoring borders for most of my life. I share this trait with the plants and animals that surround me, also the soils that blow through in the storms. The border is now the official American laboratory for stopping change, a place with twenty thousand armed agents on the U.S. side plus walls, car barriers, electronic towers to stare off into the cauldron of life, and checkpoints on the public roads complete with drug sniffing dogs. I have lost track of the number of times I have crossed the Mexican border on foot and as an outlaw. I can remember huddling under a mesquite as a chopper stalked me and failed. I can remember pulling odd little things out of the soil, ground sensors, and pitching them. Of course, now my behavior is a commonplace as a million of my fellow human beings trudge through the line on their way to El Dorados in Chicago or Kentucky or Kansas or North Carolina or Florida—to thirty-eight states being busily colonized by Mexicans fleeing poverty.

Since I don't respect boundaries on the ground, I hardly pay heed to them on the wall. I have no patience with the genres of photography—landscape, photojournalism, art photography, and so forth. There is one world, period, and an image either captures it or fails. So I have only two categories of photographs, good and bad. Or, depending on my mood, true or false.

The past cannot lie, it is already done, a final thing beyond alteration. Of course, we have stuffed our public offices and institutions with professionals who lie about the past, but still, I believe the truth will win out in the end. The present lies like a horse thief. The future is always in play. This history of the future stares deep into the past and rides on ancient pollens and lances and climates and tribes. This history is about fantasies of power and leads, inevitably, to a mushroom cloud in the New Mexican desert just before a rainy dawn in July of 1945.

NO ONE HAS EVER SUSTAINED POWER in the region now called the U.S./Mexico border. And it has for ten thousand years been a kind of border in the biological world, a set of jaws between a tropical south and a temperate north, and these jaws grind up cultures and nations, spit out migratory beasts and invading plants. That is why I fell in love with the place at age twelve. I could sense that the lies stopped here. My ground is a boothill for both Manifest Destiny and babble about La Raza.

So much of what I think depends on a woolly mammoth killed in what is at the moment the Mexican state of Puebla about twenty thousand years ago. The beast was brought down by human beings. At that time mammoths ranged from the glacial north into central Mexico and they seemed to have respected no borders beyond those of climate and forage. The very zone that birthed the atomic bomb is also a burying ground for mammoths murdered by our ancestors. I dream of the virtual border and the armed border of agents facing down some woolly mammoths.

But I've learned even more from hummingbirds, one of the most aggressive creatures on earth. The average, mild-mannered hummingbird spends 20 percent of its waking moments in combat. But what I've learned from hummingbirds is not about violence—my fellow human beings have provided an ample education in that area—but movement. The young make their first migration southward with no help from the adults. They just take off and they probe my hemisphere in hopes of finding their world. The Rufous, for example, winters in Central America and summers in Alaska. They pass through my border world in the spring and fall and it is like having a group of Hell's Angels pass through my plodding life.

But they go anywhere—they've been seen storming off the west coast and flying straight out into the Pacific, perhaps with dreams of sushi dancing in their tiny heads. Many of these young birds find death because they go to places where they cannot survive. Migrations in hummingbirds and humans are about the same thing—exploiting pockets of resources that fail to exist where one is born. Rufous traditionally migrate along a Pacific flyway, but they turn up each year on the east coast and along the Gulf Coast. This profligate scattering of life into hopeless channels is the hope. Every Rufous is a Christopher Columbus and some of them find new worlds for their kin. Two days ago, a Rufous turned up at my feeder near the line during the first week of July, weeks ahead of their normal southward migration. On the same day, I saw ten Border Patrol agents standing in a circle around a mesquite tree. Under the tree were two Mexican men and a woman in a summer dress. I have no doubt who is going to win in the end.

The future is migration. As human numbers swell and the trees and streams and plants and animals and soils disappear into the maw of our species, everything moves into play. Climate change simply accelerates this process. My ground, the border, is simply the point where the obvious is registered. Here the lies of our culture meet the facts on the ground and the facts are people and animals and plants in motion in an effort to survive. The lies are that resources are limitless and that some magic show called the global economy perfectly distributes these resources and that some voodoo called markets perfectly maintains the health of the planet.

These photographs are about this ancient new world where no human group has ever been able to dominate for long. They capture the eternal in the click of a camera. The grasslands that have flourished since the end of the last ice age, those floating islands of green that splash across the line, are now being destroyed in a frenzy of growing biofuels. The migrants streaking through the deserts and mountains are now being hunted by an army larger than the U.S. forces at the launch of the Mexican War. The rains are staying away. For about ten years, experts said the region was experiencing a drought. Now the experts say the region is experiencing the future. The Rio Grande no longer flows to the sea. The Colorado River storage called Lake Mead will be empty in thirteen years.

I have spent my life on the line waiting for the other shoe to drop, and now the thud of it hitting the ground is music to my ears. The future is in my face. Here is the deal: you can pretend that the human migration is manageable and you can pretend that the world of rock and soil and plants and animals will be preserved without any constraint on human appetites and without any regulation of human markets. Or you can really look at these images. And if you really look, you will learn a simple fact. This ground will be destroyed before you die unless you act. These human beings fleeing north will never stop coming unless their world is made whole.

I live in a beautiful and terrible world.

We can love it or be erased by it.

But we can no longer ignore it.

When I was a boy, my favorite poem was by Carl Sandburg and the lines I remember said:

> When Abraham Lincoln was shoveled into the tombs, he forgot the copperheads and the assassin . . . in the dust, in the cool tombs.
>
> And Ulysses Grant lost all thought of con men and Wall Street, cash and collateral turned ashes . . . in the dust, in the cool tombs.
>
> Pocahontas' body, lovely as poplar, sweet as a red haw in November or a pawpaw in May, did she wonder? does she remember? . . . in the dust, in the cool tombs?

Take any streetful of people buying clothes and groceries, cheering a hero or throwing confetti and blowing tin horns . . . tell me if the lovers are losers . . . tell me if any get more than the lovers . . . in the dust . . . in the cool tombs.

While You Were Sleeping

In Juárez, Mexico, Photographers Expose the Violent Realities of Free Trade

From *Harper's*, December 1996

THE WHITE EYE OF THE blank screen waits in the dark room. A few moments earlier, Jaime Bailleres was nuzzling his thirteen-month-old child and walking around in the calm of his apartment. His wife, Graciela, puttered in the kitchen, and soft words and laughter floated through the serenity of their home. A copy of a work on semiotics lay on the coffee table, and the rooms whispered of culture and civility and the joy of ideas. Outside, the city of Juárez, Mexico, waited with sharp teeth and bloody hungers. Now the lights are off as Jaime Bailleres dances through a carousel of slides.

I am here because of a seventeen-year-old girl named Adriana Avila Gress. The whole thing started very simply. I was drinking black coffee and reading a Juárez newspaper, and there, tucked away in the back pages, where the small crimes of the city bleed for a few inches, I saw her face. She was smiling at me and wore a strapless gown riding on breasts powered by an uplift bra, and a pair of fancy gloves reached above her elbows almost to her armpits. The story said she'd disappeared, all 1.6 meters of her. I turned to a friend I was having breakfast with and said, "What's this about?" He replied matter-of-factly, "Oh, they disappear all the time. Guys kidnap them, rape them, and kill them." "Them?" "Oh," he continued, "you know, the young girls who work in the maquiladoras, the foreign-owned factories, the ones who have to leave for work when it is still dark." Of course, I knew that violence is normal weather in Juárez. As a local fruit vendor told an American daily, "Even the devil is scared of living here."

That's when it started for me. The photographers, like Jaime showing me his slides, are the next logical step to understanding the world in which beaming seventeen-year-old girls suddenly vanish. The cities of Ciudad Juárez and El Paso, Texas, constitute the largest border community on earth, but hardly anyone seems to admit that the Mexican side exists. Within this forgotten urban maze stalk some of the boldest photographers still roaming the streets with 35-mm cameras. Over the past two years I have become a student of their work, because I think they are capturing something: the look of the future. This future is based on the rich getting richer, the poor getting poorer, and industrial growth producing poverty faster than it distributes wealth. We have these models in our heads about growth, development, infrastructure. Juárez doesn't look like any of these images, and so our ability to see this city comes and goes, mainly goes. A nation that has never hosted a jury trial, that has been dominated by one party for most of this century, that is carpeted with corruption and poverty and pockmarked with billionaires is perceived as an emerging democracy marching toward First World standing. The snippets of fact that once in a great while percolate up through the Mexican press are ignored by the U.S. government and its citizens. Mexico may be the last great drug experience for the American people, one in which reality gives way to pretty colors. These photographs literally give people a picture of an economic world they cannot comprehend. Juárez is not a backwater but the new City on the Hill, beckoning us all to a grisly state of things.

I've got my feet propped up on a coffee table, a glass of wine in my hand, and as far as the half-dozen photographers present for the slide show are concerned this is my first day of school and they're not sure if I've got what it takes to be a good student. After all, no one comes here if he has a choice, and absolutely no one comes to view their work. The photographers of Juárez once put on an exhibition. No one in El Paso, separated from Mexico by thirty feet of river, was interested in hanging their work, so they found a small room in Juárez and hung big prints they could not really afford to make. They called their show *Nada Que Ver,* "Nothing to See."

Beginning in the early 1980s, photographers began to show up with university degrees and tattered copies of the work of New York's famous street shooter, Weegee (Arthur Fellig). A tradition of gritty, unsentimental, and loving street shooting that has all but perished in the United States was reborn in Juárez, in part because the papers offered a market but mostly because the streets could not be denied. The street shooters of Juárez are mainly young and almost always broke. Pay at the half-dozen newspapers runs from fifty to eighty dollars a week, and they must provide their own cameras. Film is rationed by their employers. "We are like firemen," Jaime Bailleres explains, "only here we fight fires with our bare hands."

The slide presentation clicks away. A child of seven is pinned under a massive beam. He and his father were tearing apart a building for its old bricks when the ceiling collapsed. Jaime says that the child is whimpering and saying he is afraid of death. He lasted a few minutes more. Alfredo Carrillo stares intently at the images as Jaime gives him tips on how to frame different scenes. A hand reaches out from under a blanket—a cop cut down by AK-47s in front of a mansion owned by Amado Carrillo Fuentes. Carrillo is a local businessman. U.S. authorities calculate that he moves more than 100 tons of cocaine a year across the Rio Grande and into El Paso. He is estimated to be grossing $200 million a week, and to the joy of economists, this business is hard currency and cash-and-carry. To my untrained eye the dimensions of the dope business are simple: without it the Mexican economy would totally collapse.[1] A gold ring gleams on the cop's dead hand; for Bailleres it is a study in the ways of power. Alfredo says, "All these young kids dream of being Amado Carrillo."

The competition is rough. Yesterday, Juan Manuel Bueno Dueñas, twenty-three, got into a dispute with a drug dealer. Juan belonged to Los Harpys. Today at 4:30 P.M. he was buried in the municipal cemetery by his fellow gang members. The *campo santo* was crowded with people, the afterflow of the Day of the Dead observance. Carloads of guys from Barrio Chico, rivals of Los Harpys, opened fire on the procession. No one is certain how many people were wounded. The gangs of Juárez, *los pandillas,* kill at least 200 people a year. Accepting such realities is possible; thinking about them is not. Survival in Juárez is based on alcohol, friendships, and laughter, much laughter. But this happens in private. The streets are full of people wearing masks.

In this city of sleepwalkers, elementary facts, such as the population, are given scant attention. No one knows how many people live now in Juárez, but the ballpark figure is 2 million. Since December 1994 Mexico's currency has lost over half its value, prices have more than doubled, and jobs have disappeared wholesale. Real numbers hardly exist—for example, in Mexico you are counted as employed if you work one hour a week. In 1994, millions of poor Mexicans walked away from their dying earth and headed north. About one million managed to cross into the United States. The rest slammed up against the fence in places like Juárez. Since then this exodus has increased. Juárez is part of the Mexican gulag, the place for the people no one wants.

Adriana Avila Gress was found about a week after her disappearance in a desert tract embracing the city's southern edge, a place called the Lote Bravo. Adriana worked six days a week in a foreign-owned factory making turn signals for cars like the one you drive. She took home about five dollars a day. In a photo of her body that I saw in the newspaper morgue, her panties were down around her ankles as the police circled her still form. At least 150 girls disappeared in the city during 1995, and the government said that most ran off with boys. When more bodies were found, the police blamed an American serial killer and handily arrested a suspect. But girls continued to disappear.

JAIME BAILLERES HAS PROJECTED a beautiful black carved mask on the screen. The head is tilted and the face is smooth with craftsmanship. The hair is long and black. It takes a moment for me to get past this beauty and realize that the face is not a mask. She is a sixteen-year-old girl with a forgotten name. She was found in the park by a bridge linking Juárez to El Paso; the park on both sides of the Rio Grande is dedicated to friendship between the two nations. The girl's skin has blackened in the sun, and the face contracted as it mummified. She was kidnapped, raped, murdered. Jaime explains that the newspaper refused to publish this photograph. The reason for this decision is very loud. The lips of the girl pull back, revealing her clean white teeth. Sound pours forth from her mouth. She is screaming and screaming and screaming.

"We don't give a damn about the editors," Jaime snaps. "We can educate people. To look. To watch. We work in a jungle."

The face floats on the screen as music purrs through the stereo speakers. No one will ever publish this photograph, Jaime tells me. I start to argue with him but soon give up. I can't deny one jolting quality of the image: it is deafening.

It is after midnight when Jaime's photo show breaks up, and I head downtown. A wind whips across Juárez. The city often sprawls under moving walls of dust since so little of it is paved. The whores are out, sixteen- and seventeen-year-olds. There is no way to tell if they are full-time prostitutes or factory workers making an extra buck. The peso has lost another chunk of its value in the last day or so.

"How much?" I ask.

She leans into the car window and says the equivalent of fourteen dollars.

"How long?" I say.

"How long can you resist me?" she asks with a laugh.

There are ways to measure the deep movements of an economy that are more accurate and timely than the bond market and this girl with her mask of thick makeup is one of them.

"JUÁREZ," PHOTOGRAPHER Julián Cardona explains, "is a sandwich. The bread is the First World and the Third World. We are the baloney." Julián, about thirty, is a tall, long-legged, thin man with a deep voice. On the street they call him El Compás, the compass. He laughs easily and always seems to be watching. One night at the newspaper, as I plowed through a thick stack of negatives, he watched me like a hanging judge. Finally, I plucked a negative of a cop holding up the shoe of a dead girl found in the desert. Cardona looked at it and for the first time allowed himself a small smile. "This is a good image," he said, almost with relief.

Like all the shooters in Juárez, Julián is keenly aware of the seasons. In November and December, there is a bumper crop of drug murders as the merchandise moves north and accounts are settled. Then around Christmas and New Year's people hang themselves. The first few months of the new year bring fires and gas explosions as the poor try to stay warm. Spring means battles between neighborhoods (or colonias) over ground for building shacks as well as outbreaks of disease in a city largely lacking sewage treatment. Summer brings water problems to a head (Juárez will run completely out of water within five years unless something is done), more disease, and batches of murders by the street gangs. The cool days of fall open a new season of battles between colonias, and then, with the holidays, the photographers return to the drug killings and the Christmas suicides. As Manuel Saenz, the photo editor of the morning paper, puts it, "Anything can happen here at any time. It can blow at any second." That is the inside of the sandwich.

Julián, like many of the street shooters, sees his work as a mission. Juárez is the fourth-largest city in Mexico and is historically famous for vice and violence. Since the end of World War I, it has been a place that draws Americans for women and dope. Since 1991 the homicide rate has increased by at least 100 percent (given crooked cops and crooked government, solid numbers are hard to come by). What is happening in the city is often dismissed by simply saying that many cities are violent, that gangs occur in the United States as well, that strife and dislocation are just the normal growing pains of a society industrializing, and so forth. All of these statements make a lot of sense, and all of them are lies. The photographers of Juárez know they are lies and believe body and soul that their work will state the truth. They say their cameras are more deadly than AK-47s.

Julián Cardona is on his way home at 7:00 A.M. after twelve hours of prowling for the blood of the city's night. He glimpses a small crowd and pulls over. A man has been stabbed thirty times, and the arms are frozen in rigor mortis. A police technician is crouched over the chest, photographing forensic evidence. Julián shoots a few frames.

SNAPSHOTS BRIEFLY MAKE JUÁREZ stand still. You can run from photographs but you can't really hide. This fact seems to keep the photographers going. A shooter is desperate to get the shot of a man who has cut off his own genitals. But by the time the photographer arrives, the mutilated man is in an ambulance and the doors are closed. So the shooter pops open the back doors and clambers in. The man lying there is in shock, his crotch a pool of gore. He raises his head just as the photographer leans forward and goes click. The photographer is no fool; he knows this picture will never be printed.

His name is Jaime Murrieta, and he is thirty-five years old. He never turns off his police scanner. He beats the cops to many crime scenes and once got a medal for rescuing someone from a blaze when he arrived ahead of the firemen. He has photographed over 500 murders. Once he crouched over the bloated body of a girl who had been raped and murdered just as it burst. He sighs when he thinks of the Pentax he used. It never worked again.

Now we are in a car moving through downtown Juárez at about sixty miles an hour. The streets are clogged with people, and we miss hitting them by inches. I feel like I am in a long dolly shot from an Indiana Jones movie. It is 5:07 in the afternoon, and Murrieta has just heard of a shooting in Colonia Juárez down near the river. He is exploding with sheer joy. "I love violence," he tells me.

The other night around eleven, two women and a twelve-year-old girl drove a Dodge Ram Charger down the streets of Juárez. Each was shot in the head with a .45, a caliber favored by the federal police. Murrieta got some nice shots of them slumped in their car seats. This morning he covered their funeral and was beaten by the women's relatives, who were *narcotraficantes.* He keeps changing vehicles so that the gangs don't recognize what he is driving. Recently, seven rounds ripped through his car and somehow missed him.

"Yes, I am afraid," he admits. "But I love my work. I am on a mission, and everything has its risk. God helps me." He has this dream of his death.

Someone is coming at him with a gun or a knife, and there is nowhere to run. As they fire at him or shove in the blade, he raises his camera and gets the ultimate murder photograph. "I will die happy," he insists. At the moment, he's been warned that a contract killer is looking for him. He is not that easy to find. It has taken me days to rendezvous with him because he comes and goes from the newspaper without warning, and probably lives more in his car than under any other roof.

In Colonia Juárez, the body we have come to see sprawls in front of the doorway of a corner grocery store. Three rounds from a .38 Special went through the head, and five tore up the chest. That was twelve minutes ago. The victim, El Pelón, is also known as Francisco Javier Hernández. According to optimistic police figures, he is murder number 250 this year in Juárez. At 5:00 P.M. he was twenty years old. He was a junkie, and he also sold drugs. He belonged to the *pandilla* called K-13, a group noted for its arsenal of guns. A crowd of his fellow gang members stands silently in the street. Jaime Murrieta leaps out of the car and hits the street running. At first the police keep him back, but then I offer the captain a pack of Lucky Strikes and the officer's face brightens. I light one for him—there are moments when I love Mexico. While the captain and I savor Kentucky tobacco, Murrieta scurries to the crime scene. His face is absolutely serene as he crouches over the body. Hernández wears trousers and boots, but his coat is almost off and the wound in his chest is visible in the good light that all photographers pray for. A pool of brilliant red blood frames his head like a halo. The storefront is pure white, with a painting of Mickey Mouse. A sign over the doorway says *Siempre Coke*. Across the street is a pink house where drugs are sold. A fat girl smiles at the body. Her T-shirt says KISS ME, I'M YOURS. There was a killing at this very corner four months ago.

El Pelón's mother stands a few feet from his corpse. Her hair is gray and she cradles her face in her hands. She is angry at her son. Only a week before, Los Harpys tried to kill him and still he did not take precautions. "This happened," she says, "because he is a *pendejo,* a fool."

A twelve-year-old girl strolls down the sidewalk, drawn by the possibility of excitement. She has dyed red hair and the smooth, serene face of a child. She pushes through the crowd and sees the body. It is her brother. The contours of her face disintegrate as if she were a plate-glass window through which a rock has suddenly been hurled. Two girls take her arms and hold her up as she slumps toward the ground.

Murrieta stops shooting. He is out of rationed film, but he got what he wanted.

Murrieta is a legend among the other street shooters. They love to tell a story about him. He is in bed with a woman, and his police scanner is on.

Murrieta is just about to climax when he hears a murder report crackle on the radio. He gets up and starts to dress.

The woman asks, "What are you doing?"

"I must go," he answers. "It is an obligation."

"You're not going to finish?"

"No."

IN A SIMPLE SENSE THE photographs come from cameras, but there is a deeper point of origin. The floor under the gore of Juárez is an economy of factories owned by foreigners, mainly Americans. I keep having the same experience when I talk with Americans about the foreign-owned factories in Mexico. I'll tell them the wages—three, four, or five dollars a day—and they'll nod knowingly, and then a few minutes later I will realize that they have unconsciously translated this daily rate into an hourly rate. When I practically drill the actual wages into someone's head, he or she will counter by saying that the cost of living is much cheaper in Mexico. This is not true. Along the border, Mexican prices on average run at 90 percent of U.S. prices. Basically, the only cheap thing in Mexico is flesh, human bodies you can fornicate with or work to death. What is happening in Mexico betrays our notion of progress, and for that reason we insist that each ugly little statistic is an exception or temporary or untrue. For example, in the past two years wages[2] in the maquiladoras have risen 50 percent. Fine and good. But inflation in that period was well over 100 percent.

Juárez is an exhibit of the fabled New World Order in which capital moves easily and labor is trapped by borders. There are a total of 350 foreign-owned factories in Juárez, the highest concentration in all of Mexico, and they employ 150,000 workers. The twin plant system—in Spanish, *maquiladoras*—was created by the United States and Mexico in 1965 so that Americans could exploit cheap Mexican labor and yet not pay high Mexican tariffs. Although the products that come from the factories are counted as exports (and thus figured into GDP), economists figure that only 2 percent of material inputs used in maquila production come from Mexican suppliers. All the parts are shipped to Mexico from the United States and other countries, then the Mexicans assemble them and ship them back. Two or three thousand American managers commute back and forth from El Paso every day. Juárez is in your home when you turn on the microwave, watch television, take in an old film on the VCR, slide into a new pair of blue jeans, make toast in the kitchen, enjoy your kid playing with that new toy truck on Christmas morning.

Politicians and economists speculate about a global economy fueled by free trade. Their speculations are not necessary. In Juárez the future is thirty years old, and there are no questions about its nature that cannot be answered here. The maquilas have caused millions of poor people to move to the border. Most of the workers are women and most of the women are young. By the late twenties or early thirties the body slows and cannot keep up the pace of the work. Then, like any used-up thing, the people are junked. Turnover in the maquilas runs anywhere from 50 to 150 percent a year. It is common for workers to leave for work at 4:00 A.M. and spend one or two hours navigating the dark city to their jobs. Sometimes they wind up in the Lote Bravo. The companies carefully screen the girls to make sure they are not pregnant. Workers at one plant complain of a company rule requiring new female hires to present bloody tampons for three consecutive months. The work week is six days. After work some of the girls go downtown to sell their bodies for money or food. At least 40 percent of Mexicans now live off the underground economy, which means they stand in the street and try to sell things, including themselves.

Workers who lose their jobs receive essentially no benefits beyond severance pay. Mexico has no safety net. Independent, worker-controlled unions barely exist, and anyone trying to organize one is fired, or murdered.[3] It is almost impossible to get ahead working in the maquilas. Real wages have been falling since the 1970s. And since wages are just a hair above starvation level, maquilas contribute practically nothing toward forging a consumer society. Of course, as maquiladora owners and managers point out, if wages are raised, the factories will move to other countries with a cheaper labor force.

And so industry is thriving. Half a million cargo-laden trucks move from Juárez to El Paso each year. Boxcars rumble over the railroad bridge. New industrial parks are opening up. Labor is virtually limitless, as tens of thousands of poverty-stricken people pour into the city each year. There are few environmental controls and little enforcement of those that do exist. El Paso/Juárez is one of the most polluted spots in North America. And yet it is a success story. In Juárez the economic growth in 1994 was 6 percent, and last year it registered 12 percent. According to Lucinda Vargas, the Federal Reserve economist who tracks Mexico's economy, Juárez is a "mature" economy. This is as good as it gets. With the passage of NAFTA, *narcotraficantes* began buying maquiladoras in Juárez. They didn't want to miss out on the advantages of free trade.

The street shooters are seldom allowed to take photographs inside the factories. And yet it is impossible to take a photograph in Juárez of anything without capturing the consequences of the maquiladoras. The factory workers have created a new school of architecture that is not seriously studied by scholars. They build homes out of odd material—cardboard, old tires, pallets stolen from loading docks. The structures are held together with nails driven through bottle caps—a cheap bolt. The designs flow unhampered by building codes. No school of aesthetics scolds, no committee votes, no zoning oppresses. Like the fabled Pilgrims, the people of the shantytowns have largely escaped the notice of their rulers. Electricity is stolen from power lines. (Jaime Bailleres once took a photo of a man up a power pole illegally clamping into a high-voltage line. The man was inept. As Bailleres took his picture the man was electrocuted.) Water is more difficult to acquire, and in many of the shanty communities it must be bought off trucks. Land for housing is also scarce and is often stolen. Gabriel Cardona, another Juárez photographer, has recorded a land invasion. It begins when a woman notices that her portrait of Christ is weeping. Soon her colonia has built a shrine out of scavenged wood, and the painting is surrounded by hundreds of votive candles. This miraculous painting inspires the local people to invade some vacant land and throw up huts. The next photo is of a man returning from a maquiladora to his home. It has been bulldozed by the police, and he stares at his bed and a bucket and a few other items piled up on the scraped earth.

The two daily newspapers in El Paso, the city of half a million that squats thirty feet from Juárez, can go days without a single story about the millions of people living in grinding poverty right before everyone's eyes. A recent killing sums up this attitude. Someone slaughtered a retired Juárez cop, José Muñoz Rubalcava, and two of his sons. They tied them with yellow rope and made a yellow bow. Then they put them in the trunk of a car, drove to the midpoint of a bridge between El Paso and Juárez, and abandoned the vehicle so that it straddled the boundary line. The plan worked. Neither country would accept the responsibility for investigating what had happened.

THERE IS A HESITATION WHEN the street shooters of Juárez mention La Pantera, the Panther. Once he was one of them. Then he took up the video camera and went to work for a television station. But it is his dedication to his work that gives the street shooters pause. They feel that he has gone too far, that he cannot survive living as he does.

Rafael Cora, better known as La Pantera, works twelve hours a day, seven days a week. He has not missed a tour of his appointed rounds in eight years. He works only at night, and his name comes from his eerie ability to get to murders before the police do. Sometimes he videotapes things the police do not wish to have publicized. He is thirty-two years old and has a quiet and reserved manner. His camera has stared at 800 murders. Five times the police have beaten him and destroyed his equipment. *Narcotraficantes* also view him with disfavor. La Pantera wears a bulletproof vest. Although his face has never appeared on television, he is said to have one of the highest-rated programs in the city.[4] His day begins with darkness and ends with light, and in between he roams alone in an old black pickup truck, a police scanner always plugged into his left ear. He shoots murders, car accidents, suicides, gang fights—all the violence of the night.

For several years he rode with an assistant, and then they fell in love and married. She continued riding with him, and one night when she was nine months' pregnant the labor pains came and La Pantera made a brief pit stop at the hospital so that their daughter could be born. For his eighty-four-hour workweek he is paid $100. He cannot live on this, so during the day he is a part-time fumigator. His daughter is now four, and sometimes she rides with him "so she will learn reality."

La Pantera is convinced that if he shows people what their city is like, then they will change their city. That is why he left newspapers and still photography: television, he believed, would reach more people with more force. He worries about being killed, but he cannot seem to stop. Being around him has the quality of visiting someone on death row. In your heart, you know he can't possibly make it. Once he came upon Jaime Murrieta being pounded by *narcotraficantes* in a bar. La Pantera leapt in to help him, and they both were beaten almost to death. "I can keep doing this forever," he insists quietly to me. "This is a mission for justice." In his spare time, he and his wife work with the Red Cross. People come to him for help in finding the missing. He is a faceless legend. He refuses to appear on the air because he does not want his personality to get in the way of the stories, the montages of horror he constructs every night. "I like to take the tragedies," he explains, "and make people feel them."

He is very proud of his work, and shelf after shelf in the station sags with the results of his nocturnal labor. He plucks a cassette and insists that I watch. A man is being beaten, blood coursing down his face, the soft voice of La Pantera narrating.

La Pantera silently watches his tape with the calm pleasure of a connoisseur. He fast-forwards the tape, and the people shouting and crying sound like cartoon characters. Then he slows the tape and the camera pans a suicide. The man is quite young and wearing a bulky blue sweater. By his feet is a five-gallon bucket. The rope around his neck is tied to a small tree in a city park. His neck is bent, but the rope is straight and taut. The camera frames the man and the tree, then zooms in to peruse his body, and quickly does a 180-degree pan around to his back. Then the camera zooms in again to one of his feet. It is touching the ground. During the hours he spent hanging here alone, the man's neck stretched and now he is firmly planted on the earth again.

When I leave the station, La Pantera walks me out into the 2:00 A.M. street. He touches my shoulder and says, "Be careful. This is a very dangerous city. Do not stop at any stop signs. They will leap out and take the car."

Every morning at 7:45 A.M. La Pantera's program runs as a special eight- to ten-minute part of the morning news. The segment is called "While You Were Sleeping."

IN 1991, NICHOLAS SCHEELE, the head of the Ford Motor Company in Mexico, said in admiration of the government's control, "But is there any other country in the world where the working class . . . took a hit in their purchasing power in excess of 50 percent over an eight-year period and you didn't have a social revolution?" Maybe you get something you don't have to define as a revolution. There are over 200 gangs in Juárez. They, not the police, define the borders of the city. They, not the government, represent authority to the human beings in the colonias. They provide work selling narcotics. And they kill and steal all the time to protect their spheres of power. They are not a progressive force; they are simply the force that grows when a society offers no progress. They have blossomed over the last three years as several factors made them inevitable: the slow decomposition of the Mexican government created a vacuum; the explosive growth of the drug industry created a livelihood; the death of the main bulwark of Mexican culture, the family, created a need. For the women, the assembly plants are sometimes liberating, but more marriages and families collapse. Mexico had to create one million jobs last year for young people entering the economy. Instead, the country lost one million jobs. And most importantly, the fabled pull of the border brought hordes of almost Neolithic peasant families to a city where their skills were worthless. In Juárez you face Stone Age parents staring helplessly at Computer Age children. Nothing the adults know or can provide has much value, and the fabric that has held families and Mexico together tears right before your eyes. You can actually hear the tearing. I'll be standing at a murder scene, the shooters will be feeding on a fresh corpse, and as I make notes I can hear the gang kids murmuring about me. When I look up I see very hard eyes, and I know everyone but me is packing. There is nothing to be done about this. I am like everyone else here: I simply go about my business as if death were not a few feet away disguised as some twelve- or thirteen-year-old with a gun and eyes older than I can ever hope to be.

This new world makes stabs at beauty. Juárez historically is a cultural cauldron where folk Mexico confronts and fabricates life out of the high technology of its American neighbor. In the 1940s, pachuco culture with its zoot suits exploded out of Juárez. Black velvet painting also started here. The *pandillas*, like many U.S. gangs, at first spray-painted signs on walls and then started doing full figure paintings. Otto Campbell, a noted Juárez artist, became interested in their work and offered to teach them. And so he did.

Julián Cardona holds a large photograph of a mural painted by the *pandilleros* on the Puente Negro, the black railroad bridge linking El Paso and Juárez. The image is taken from the Mexican side. American officials have erected massive sliding doors on the bridge to stop people from crossing, and the *pandilleros* have painted these doors in the style of the old masters from the revolution. Peasants are marching along the bottom of the mural. Above them are the girders and machines of modern industrial life, and blood is spilling from this future.

In the photograph take by Jamie Bailleres, the doors are opening as two U.S. Customs officials push them apart to permit a train to enter Mexico. The locomotive is blue and huge and with its white beam stares out like a Cyclops. It looks like the train will move forward and kill the peasants any second. Cardona stabs at the photograph and tells me, "This is a great image. The hands that can make this painting, those hands kill 200 people in this city every year."

AFTER SEVERAL MONTHS, things in Juárez begin to haunt me. I try to put my finger on what exactly is bothering me. I tell myself it is not simply the poverty—I remember being in delta shacks in the segregated Mississippi of the 1960s and people living almost like animals deep within the bosom of my own country. When I lived with these people for weeks and weeks, I ate what they ate—wild greens picked by the road and fried in grease, bootleg liquor made in the thickets by the river. Also, I can remember working on the west side of Chicago in districts that had the look and feel of Berlin in, say, the summer of 1945. But Juárez is different in a way that tables of wages and economic studies cannot capture: in Juárez you cannot sustain hope.

In the shadow of a maquiladora sprawls a Community for Public Defense barrio, one of at least twenty-six in Juárez. The police are afraid to enter CPD settlements. The residents work in maquilas and sell drugs, guns, and cars stolen from the United States. They also make bricks. It is dusk, and they have fired up their kilns using tires for fuel. Black tongues of smoke lick the shacks. The main dirt lane of the colonia is blocked by a circle of people sitting on buckets. They are having a community meeting. This is the order in the new world.

There are other hints of the emerging order. Jaime Bailleres is in a nightclub and at his editor's insistence takes a picture of a beautiful woman for the newspaper's lifestyle section. A man at another table is accidentally included in the frame. Suddenly two bodyguards lay their hands on Bailleres.

They do not want this picture published, understand? He wonders: Is this man now stored somewhere in his camera Amado Carrillo? But this thought is dangerous. Later, when I mention the name out loud at a bar, he looks around quickly to see if anyone has overheard. His eyes for a few seconds show true panic. Jaime is hardly a coward, but he is certainly not a fool like me.

We all have a deep need to ignore Juárez. We write off what is going on by saying that it is something our grandparents or great-grandparents went through. We tell ourselves that there are gangs and murders in American cities. This is true, but it does not deal with the reality of Juárez. We are not talking about darkness on the edge of town or a bad neighborhood. We are talking about an entire city woven out of violence. We tell ourselves that jobs in the maquiladoras are better than nothing. But we ignore the low wages, high turnover, and shacks. Then there is the silent thought: after all, they are Mexicans, not U.S. citizens. This kind of shrug brings to mind René Descartes nailing his family dog to a board alive and cutting it up to determine if it had a soul.

I AM STANDING BY THE Carranza sisters' cardboard shack in a part of Juárez called Anapra. They moved to the shantytown about ten months ago, when three years of drought ended their lives in a village in Durango. A half-dozen murdered, mutilated, and raped girls have been found about a hundred yards from their shack, and this frightens the teenage girls. Each morning they rise at 3:30 A.M., cook over bits of wood, and have some coffee. After a cold tortilla, they walk out into the darkness with their few possessions (a pan, a plate, knife, fork, spoon, and cooking oil) and bury them secretly in a hole; otherwise they will be stolen while they are gone. They are the lucky ones: five of them work in American-owned maquiladoras. The fifteen-year-old girl is a welder at 160 pesos a week (about $21.62 at current exchange rates). Bus fare consumes about half her salary. Today, the Carranza kids are fixing to plant eight pine seedlings. Tomorrow, they begin their six-day weeks at American factories.

The United States begins fifty yards away, where the North Americans are constructing a steel wall to keep Mexico at bay. In fact, the First World is so near that every few days a band of Anapra residents gather around 8:00 P.M. and walk the short distance to the border, where an American railroad almost brushes against the fence. Then, as the bend in the tracks slows the train, they expertly crack open a dozen or more boxcars, toss goods out to waiting hands, and rush back into Mexico—all in less than the two minutes it takes for cops to arrive. U.S. newspapers periodically print stories about these train robberies (600 in the last three years) and call the Carranzas' neighbors the new Jesse Jameses.

Jaime Bailleres says, "Sometimes I feel like I am in Bosnia." He tells me a story to make sure my feeble gringo mind grasps what he means. The paper wanted a soft feature on the lives of the rich, so one Saturday a photographer and his editor strolled through an enclave of wealth looking for the right image. The photographer brought along his wife and two children. As a rabbit hopped across the lawn of a mansion, the camera came up. Suddenly two bodyguards appeared with AK-47s, and one said, "Give me that fucking camera and film." They forced the photographer facedown on the pavement with the automatic rifles at his head. Then, in front of his wife and children and editor, they beat him about his head, ribs, and genitals. Police stood nearby and watched. That is the end of the story.

None of this matters. It is all a detail or an exception or an illusion. The authorities announced back in November of 1995 that 520 people had disappeared in Juárez that year and "an important percentage of them are female adolescents." By last March, the mothers of the missing were demonstrating and demanding justice. Then in April, the police made a sweep of the red-light district, bagged 120 suspects, and announced that the slaughter was the work of eight apparently gregarious sociopaths who hung out in a bar called Joe's Place. The next day the mothers of the accused protested the police torture of their sons. And, of course, the killings and disappearances continue—though reports of them were censored for a while.

Then, in July, one of the Juárez dailies published a front-page list of missing girls found dead in the Lote Bravo over the last year. Adriana Avila Gress was not on the list. It doesn't matter that I read of her disappearance in the same newspaper or read the account of her body being found in the same newspaper or examined photographs of her corpse in the morgue of the same newspaper. I can't find her family, so I'm hard-pressed to prove that she ever existed.

That same day, an American drug conference takes place at Fort Bliss on the edge of El Paso. The attorney general, the drug czar, the head of the FBI, and the head of the INS will be there, and for days the newspapers have bubbled with stories that the next candidate to make the FBI's most-wanted list will be one Amado Carrillo Fuentes. The night before, I was taken by a Mexican reporter to a mansion in El Paso surrounded by high walls and featuring electronic gates and an array of security systems. I was told that the building belonged to a family with serious organized crime connections and that for the past week Carrillo had been staying there to get some peace. I can't prove that Carrillo is inside the mansion; I couldn't do that if I entered and shackled him. No one really knows what he looks like. Besides, I've gone native. Reality comes and goes for me.

I come and go into Juárez, and then return to a different world where things still seem to work, where payday comes now and then, and where over a good dinner what I know and have seen can be buried. Alive. After all, I would rather smile and feel the sun against my face than think about Juárez or all the places like Juárez that are growing quietly like mold on the skin of the planet. When I go to the United States, no one ever mentions this place. It simply ceases to exist, even if I only travel to El Paso. I used to wonder about this fact.

I GO BACK TO THE GLOWING SCREEN in the dark room. I must see that blackened face again. Soft music calms me, the blackness of the room caresses me, the roar of the fan on the projector is oddly comforting. The beam of the white light defines reality now and keeps it locked up within a rectangle. Jaime Bailleres installs a slide carousel, and then I hear a click and color explodes. The photographers do not know whether this is art. It is not for them to say. *Nada Que Ver.* I face again the open mouth and clean white teeth. "Why do you want this picture?" Jaime Bailleres asks me. "You know it will never be published. No one will print it."

I have never told him the truth. I have never told him that the first night I saw the girl's face I thought it was a carved wooden mask, something made by one of those quaint tribes far away in the Mexican south. Nor have I told him that I keep a copy of it in a folder right next to where I work and that from time to time I open the clean manila folder and look into her face. And then I close it like the lid of a coffin. She haunts me, and I deal with this fact by avoiding it. I have brought a pile of photography books to Jaime's house to add to the communal archive maintained by the street shooters of Juárez. They are all here at this moment, sitting in the room staring at the screen. We are amigos now. I have rustled up a curio—a bottle of wine called NAFTA, with the label Mexican, the wine U.S., and the bottle Canadian. Everyone smiles at this farcical vintage. The photographers tell me after we have been drinking for hours, "You give us hope." It must be the wine.

I look up at Jaime Bailleres. The girl's face is still floating on the screen. "Yes," I tell him. "You are right. No one will ever print this photograph. But I want them to see it whether they print it or not."

He sighs, the way an adult sighs over the actions of a child.

I look up at the girl on the screen. I tell myself that a photograph is worth a thousand words. I tell myself photographs lie. I tell myself there are lies, damned lies, and statistics. I tell myself I am still sleeping. But she stares at me. The skin is smooth, almost carved and sanded, but much too dark. And the screams are simply too deafening.

NOTES

1. Former president Carlos Salinas de Gortari figured Mexico's drug cartels net $30 billion a year, more than the U.S. bailout of Mexico. In 1995, Salinas fled the country under suspicion of ties to the drug cartels.

2. Figures on pay in these factories are almost universally exaggerated. In October of 1995, *Newsweek* pegged the average wage at $15 a day. When I showed this issue to Mexican reporters, they insisted it must be a typographical error. Wages vary from one border city to another, but a fair range is from $20 to $35 a week.

3. Last spring the boss of the big worker-dominated bus company in Mexico City was found dead. The government determined that he had committed suicide. He had shot himself in the heart. Twice.

4. Over 90 percent of Mexican families have a television. In the barrios, where the houses are cardboard and the electricity is pirated, you will consistently find televisions. This part of the fabled global village actually exists.

Don Francisco Must Be Stopped

From *USA Today*, September 12, 1985

TUCSON, ARIZ.—Here is what we are up against in the international trade wars: one old Mexican man.

He lives a few miles south of the Arizona line in a windowless, dirt-floored cardboard shack. He fattens on beans, tortillas, and coffee, cooks over a wood fire, lacks a well or a privy, and fights the night with a kerosene lamp.

When the desert sun torches the air at 120 degrees, he sits in the shade. When the winter winds blow cold, he shivers. He smiles often.

When congressmen thunder about fiendish foreigners taking U.S. jobs, pocketing U.S. dollars, underselling U.S. industry, Don Francisco comes to mind. He reaches into all the forbidden places, draining off work, destroying the balance of trade, crippling U.S. enterprises.

For a few pesos a month, he guards the road leading past his shack to a cinder mine, a peasant-powered outfit that undercuts U.S. suppliers by cheaply selling building materials here. The first offense.

His wife lives in Los Angeles doing God-knows-what and doubtless without the blessings of the U.S. Immigration Service. The second offense.

His son, another uninvited member of our labor force, works as a chauffer in San Francisco. The third offense.

Then there are the piñatas, paper creations stuffed with candy and swung at by blindfolded kids at parties. When shattered, the beauty vanishes in a shower of sweets.

His dark hut glows with dozens of paper roses, bears, sputniks (Don Francisco hungers for the high-tech market), swans, clowns, horses, cows. All day long, he snips colored paper designs and pastes.

Once a month or so, he hitches a ride into a nearby border town and sells his goods to a shop, which in turn resells them to U.S. tourists for those fabled U.S. dollars.

Then Don Francisco buys some beans, coffee, and flour, heads back to his hut, and continues undermining the mightiest industrial state in the history of the planet.

He does not speak of this matter. He talks of his small dog, one pitched by rich people from a car on the nearby highway. He calls the dog "Little Gift."

He keeps snipping colored paper, guarding the cinder mine road, thinking of his wife in Los Angeles, his son in San Francisco.

There is no doubt about it: He's got to be stopped.

A SHORT NOTE

The revolution of 1910–1920 is the religion of the Mexican state and forms its main claim to legitimacy. Even the toppling of the ruling party in the election of 2000 by a conservative pro-business party has hardly altered this homage. In the United States, the revolution is barely remembered and functions as a cartoon of violence, rape, and mayhem. But it was the moment when the Mexican people asked questions of themselves and of their government, questions that have never been answered nor gone out of date. The most forceful questions were asked by Doroteo Arango, better known as Francisco Villa, or Pancho Villa. He has been made into both a monster and a buffoon in the United States and all but erased from the revolution in Mexico. He is part and parcel of the Mexican migration because ultimately this flight from Mexico stems from the failure of the revolution.

Villa terrifies people who hold power. On November 17, 1910, Villa murders Claro Reza, a federal cop, at a meat stall in Ciudad Chihuahua and then rides into the Sierra Azul with fifteen men. Soon he leads an army, then is arrested and jailed, then escapes and flees Mexico for Texas. At ten o'clock at night on March 6, 1913, he recrosses the Rio Grande into Mexico with eight men. They carry nine rifles, 500 rounds, two pounds of coffee, two pounds of sugar, one pound of salt, and a couple of barbed wire cutters. They are almost immediately fired upon but they slip south. Villa sends a telegram to the anti-revolutionary governor of Chihuahua who has taken over since the murder a few weeks earlier of President Francisco Madero in Mexico City.

> KNOWING THAT THE GOVERNMENT YOU REPRESENT WAS PREPARING TO EXTRADITE ME I DECIDED TO COME HERE AND SAVE YOU THE TROUBLE. HERE I AM IN MEXICO RESOLVED TO MAKE WAR ON THE TYRANNY WHICH YOU DEFEND. FRANCISCO VILLA.

In a year or so, the General has forty thousand men.

He is still out there, embodied in this new strange revolution called illegal immigration, an act by which poor Mexicans go from doom to a future, a movement which has enhanced the lives of poor people more than any policy attempted by either the U.S. government or the Mexican government.

People ask, why do they come here? People say Mexico has such low unemployment, so what is the problem? Consider this: you get up at 5 A.M. You live in a one-room shack and pay $59 a month in rent. Your address is on the outskirts of the world's second largest megapolis, Mexico City. You share this shack with your woman, a niece, and your child. At 5:30 A.M. you're on the bus, a ninety-minute ride for $2.45 a day roundtrip. You work in a tortilla shop for $1.64 an hour, eleven hours a day, six days a week. A gallon of milk at the store, the electricity that lights your shack, the fuel running the bus, all these things cost more than in the United States. Basically, everything costs more than in the United States—except labor. And there are other expenses. The water in the tap, should you even have running water, is not safe so you must buy other water or drink soda. You never save a cent, and when someone in your family becomes ill, you cannot afford medicine. You have essentially no education because after junior high you must pay for books and schooling and so, depending upon your circumstances, you quit school sometime between age twelve and fifteen. You will earn in a year less than six grand and almost everyone in your country lives the same way—or not as well. You will never take a vacation. Or see any future that is different from all the days you have known. But someone, a brother, a cousin, a friend will go to the United States and you will hear of life there.

Mexican civilization existed before the American people were even a thought. Americans have come to the game very recently, and like so many new arrivals believe they possess all the answers. At the moment, human beings are moving all over the planet to save their hides. Things have been upended, the moon rises at a strange hour, it is blood red, and dripping with hunger.

YELLOW DOGS LAZE IN THE afternoon of the plaza. Altar, sixty miles of dirt road south of Sásabe, is home to eighteen thousand people, and a way station for five hundred thousand, six hundred thousand, eight hundred thousand souls a year who pass through on their way to *El Norte*. No one knows for certain the actual number and hardly anyone really wants to know. But you can go to the bank with one fact: more Mexicans move through Altar and into the United States each year than the U.S. government admits enter across the entire 1,951-mile border. Altar is the beginning of the lie and the beginning of the pain.

At the moment, Holy Week in April, a holiday during which Mexicans make a desperate effort to be home with their families, at least two thousand people are passing through to the border each day. This is like Americans deciding to go to the office on Christmas Day. A month ago, an undercover Border Patrol agent surveyed the traffic and pegged it at five thousand a day. A visiting novelist, Phil Caputo, noticed the twenty-odd stalls selling black daypacks, black t-shirts and clothing and figured it for a migrant Wal-Mart. Two things happen to visitors in Altar: first stunned silence and then a search for some metaphor to wrap around the dusty town sixty miles of dirt road south of the American line. On the east edge of the community is one such effort, a boarding house for migrants (three bucks a day for enough space for one sleeping body) named *Éxodo,* Exodus. There are dozens of such flops in town.

Here is the basic script: you get off a bus you have ridden for days from the Mexican interior, increasingly from the largely Indian states far to the south. This is the end of your security. On the bus, you had a seat, your own space. Now you enter a feral zone. With money, you can buy space in a flop for $3 a night, get a meal of chicken, rice, beans, and tortillas for about $2.50. You stare out at an empty desert unlike any ground you have ever seen. Men with quick eyes look you over, the employees of *coyotes,* people smugglers. On the bus, you were a man or a woman or a child. Now you are a *pollo,* a chicken, and you need a *pollero,* a chicken herder. The price to get from this point to distant spots in the United States—North Carolina, Los Angeles, Chicago, and so forth—is at the moment $1700 and rising. Within three months it will pass $2000 and continue to rise. American Homeland Security is good for people smugglers. And this cost does not cover getting to the border or crossing the border or food or a place to stay. It only covers getting from a stash house in Tucson or Phoenix to some destination in *Los Estados Unidos*. You pay to learn how to be a chicken.

You will never be safe, but for the next week or so, you will be in real peril. If you sleep in the plaza to save money, thugs will rob you in the night, or if you are a woman, have their way with you. If you cut a deal with a coyote's representative (and 80 to 90 percent do), you still must buy all that black clothing and gear, house and feed yourself, and then one day when you are told to move, you get in a van with twenty to forty other pollos and ride sixty miles of bumps and dust to *la línea*. Each passenger pays ten to twenty dollars for the van ride—the price varies but keeps edging upward. The vans do not move with less than seventeen, prefer at least twenty, and do, at a minimum, three trips a day.

Fifteen miles below the border, you will face a checkpoint set up by *Grupo Beta*, the Mexican force supposed to help pollos. Here are signs warning of venomous creatures and high desert temperatures. And the officials are under an orange ramada, one with a crudely painted single word, *gallo*, rooster. The vans stop, the bodies are beat up, but the tires, always, are excellent. You will be sitting inside, possibly on an iron bar so that dozens of pollos can be packed in. The men of Grupo Beta will count you—everyone gets a cut in this business. The head of the state police in Sásabe, Sonora, the town just ahead on the line, takes in $30,000 a week. You are worth a little money now, though you are penniless, unemployed, and frightened. Two years ago, a friend of mine did the ride and counted 58 vans in one hour. Early this year, a group of American reporters stood at the checkpoint and counted 1,296 people in one hundred and eighty minutes.

You have entered a middle passage and it ends at the stash house. In between that bus from the interior you disembarked from in Altar and the stash house in Tucson or Phoenix, almost anyone could rob you or kill you or rape you. And many will try. At the moment, you are worth a few hundred dollars, almost like an oil future. But you must get to the stash house before you are worth real money and worth protecting. And you must do it by force of will. In this sector of the line, the three-hundred-mile-wide Tucson sector, four or five hundred of you will die, most in summer. Others will die and rot in the desert and go uncounted. A year ago, a woman from Zacatecas went down and died in late June. Her father came up and searched for weeks to find her body in the desert, a valley of several hundred square miles. In his quest, he stumbled on two other corpses before finding the remains of his own child.

At dusk on the line, you will go through the wire with twenty, thirty, or more Mexicans. There will be a guide. You will carry a gallon of water and that black daypack. The temperature in summer could be a hundred ten or fifteen degrees during the day. You will walk anywhere from ten to sixty miles depending on the route and what you have agreed to pay. There will be rattlesnakes, cacti, trees. And almost no signs of people or their homes. Everything will have thorns and rake your skin as you stumble through the darkness. You will keep up or be left behind. If you are a woman, you have a fair chance of being raped. And you will most likely never speak of these nights again so long as you live. You will have children and grandchildren and teach them many things. But if you are like the others who have passed this way, these nights will remain your secret.

A major strand of the largest known human migration on earth is passing through this section of the Arizona desert day and night in silence. No one is really counting the people, no one is really recording their journeys. They are items on back pages of border newspapers. Their Ellis Island is not marked on the map. Somewhere between Altar, Sonora, and Tucson and Phoenix, new Americans are being made and their souls are being forged in a burning desert. Soon, they and their descendants will number thirty million. And this vast silence is likely to be the savage part of their repressed history.

On the plaza at Altar, pollos sit in rows. They wear dark clothing, have daypacks and gallons of water by their side. They are waiting for their van rides. A mile to the west, two new motels have risen, one mainly for pollos, the chickens, the other for polleros, the chicken herders. A tourist would have a hard time finding lodging in Altar.

Everywhere around Altar, new houses are coming out of the ground. The nicest run two to five thousand square feet, have fine windows and doors, good walls surrounding the lot and flowering trees and shrubs. These belong to drug traffickers, sharks that swim in the same sea as the migrants and find that thousands of pollos mask their own hikes with backpacks full of dope. They tend to carry AK-47s as well as water bottles. The going rate for moving marijuana across the fence is ten dollars a pound—which means one night hauling a hundred pound pack can mean a thousand dollars.

There is a fantasy that drugs and migrants are separate matters. Both are often moved by the same organizations and both come north to satisfy American hungers. Sometimes, the two commodities flow together, and sometimes they are kept separate on the ground lest a group of poor people draws too much attention to a route and jeopardizes a shipment of high-grade heroin. But the networks are generally the same people because both commodities are about the same thing: billions of dollars of profit. And both mock the pretenses of Homeland Security. And both are relentless flows. They satisfy elements in each political party, those seeking people who will work for low wages and those seeking highs.

He's wearing a black Thunder Road chopper cap, is thirty-six, from Veracruz, and claims he and his mother and sister are on the way to Tijuana. He's almost certainly lying. No one sits on the plaza here dressed in black save pollos. Or the guides that haul them. But almost no migrant admits to being a pollo or a pollero. In part this is fear. Once I walked two blocks, sat on a curb, and watched eight people in a line at a pay phone (pollos try to report in to relatives despite Mexico's phone rates, among the highest in the world). Outside a flop, another half dozen pollos sat on a bench. I took my notebook from my pocket, flipped it open, and started writing. Every one of them fled.

Besides this fear of poor people far from home and suddenly facing a new and dangerous world, there is another reason for this deception. Shame. No one likes to admit their own nation has no place for them and that the nation they seek to enter holds them illegal and will try to hunt them down like animals. So the man from Veracruz says, "The United States? I have no papers for crossing."

Nearby are two guys from Guerrero in the regulation pollo black. They are Indians and plan to go to Taylor, Texas. They say they have friends there—pollos always say they go to friends, not family, another act of caution.

One guy is nineteen and he gives the basic biography of a pollo: "I have friends there. I have never been in the U.S. before. I plan to spend two years, a couple of years, and then go back to Mexico. There are no jobs in Guerrero. Why even go to school? When you graduate there are no jobs. Last week, in the state capital I saw three hundred young school teachers demonstrate because they could find no jobs. I work in the fields. I can grow beans, corn, and squash."

His eyes are anxious and he cannot seem to smile. He has heard there is work in the United States. He has heard Americans think people such as him steal jobs from them. But he does not believe this because "people who have been in the United States tell me Americans don't work in the fields."

He says he has two worries—dying in the desert, and not finding a job. He's heard of the recent big marches and thinks people have a right to march.

"Why," he asks, "won't the U.S. let us work and then go home? We don't want to do anything bad to America. In my village, 20 percent of the people have gone to the U.S. and in the state about 50 percent have gone. I've been in Altar two days waiting to cross."

He and his friend have no money and so they will cross without the help of coyotes.

He says he does not want to fail.

This story plays out of mouth after mouth in the plaza. There is no work in Mexico. Do you know where Oregon is? Do you know where Tennessee is?

Juan Hernández, a dark Mixtec Indian who has already been caught once by the Border Patrol, explains, "There is no work, no rain, nothing to do in the fields. We are very poor there. I don't know what the U.S. is like. I am about to give up. But a part of me wants to try again."

Already twenty to thirty people from his village have gone to the United States.

In the stalls, black T-shirts say: Retired Army, or U.S. Navy. They sport huge American flags, or soaring bald eagles. Racks hold medallions of Jesus Christ and Jesús Malverde. One was said to be a carpenter, the other a bandit hung in Culiacan, Sinaloa, in 1909 and now a favored *santo* of *narcotraficantes*. Amid the stalls, a line snakes out of the telegraph office where people wait to get money orders for the next leg of their journey. Against the side of the church is a sign: God Is Love.

There are two sounds: pigeons, and the low rumble of vans as they load pollos. The humans of the plaza are all but silent as they brace themselves for their new lives. Or deaths. Inside the church, pollos often light one-dollar votive candles before heading into their desert passage.

Francisco García is around forty, has smooth skin, black hair and moustache, and the slack gut of a man who does not work in the fields. Until recently, he was the *presidente* (the boss) of this *municipio* (think something the size of a U.S. county). Now he works for the Catholic church running an aide center for migrants six blocks off the plaza. Those defeated by the desert and the Border Patrol come here for food and shelter. And then they head north again—García knows one migrant that tried twenty-five times before he got through. He thinks at least 90 percent of the migrants get through.

He explains that the traditional economy of Altar was cattle and farming. Now it is pollos and drugs. Almost all the people in the pollo industry—the people running phone services and boarding houses, the coyotes—come from outside Altar. This is a common thing in the people-smuggling business all along the border.

"Altar," he offers, "is not only a path for migrants but a path for drugs. The migrants are like a curtain that hides the money of the drug business."

He dreads that the illegal migration might end, or move elsewhere. He dreams that migrant workers are made legal and that Altar becomes a kind of hiring hall and hub for American businesses. Regardless, he does not think the United States can successfully close the border.

He describes the people-smuggling business as like a string of beads on a rosary with each bead a self-contained cell. In the Mexican south, there are men recruiting pollos, then there are other men rounding them up and shipping them on buses to, say, Altar. Here another cell plants them in flop-houses and arranges van rides. Sixty miles north, another cell moves them through the wire. At the end of their desert trek, they brush against the next cell, one that loads them in vans and takes them to stash houses. Here a key representative of the coyote arrives, copies down names and phone numbers and destinations, makes the calls, and tells of the charge. Sometimes these people double the price from what had been earlier agreed. After forking over half the fee, the pollos are loaded in vans according to their destinations in American cities and towns. On arrival, another key figure appears, some blood kin of the coyote who pockets the rest of the money. The coyote remains in the shadows, he says, an intelligent, cunning, and mysterious figure.

This year García thinks 800,000 Mexicans will pass through Altar on their way to El Norte. The sign behind his desk advises that Jesus, Mary, and Joseph were migrants and were looking for a better life.

Down at the plaza, people line up at the public restroom (three pesos a visit). A Red Cross clinic in the trailer of a semitruck treats a woman who is losing the nail on her toe. She claims she hurt it in her house. This seems unlikely. She is dark and from Acapulco. Her name is Alicia Soriano, 49, and her face is awash in pain as the doctor clips off her nail. She has no one with her. Most likely she was separated from her man and family in the desert and walked and destroyed her foot. She is alone now in a strange town with blood gushing from her toe.

Outside, buses keep arriving and unload people from the south with dark daypacks and dark clothing and anxious eyes. Two mannequins stare at the pollos. One is a woman wearing a white bonnet and the mask of a Zapatista. The other is a man wearing an Australian bush hat and a rosary. Two pollos stop at a stall just before climbing into a van and buy foot powder. Vans depart more and more frequently. They will haul Mexicans until at least 8 P.M., then shift to the three or four hundred Central Americans who are generally moved in the dark of the night. They will be moving through the wire, if everything goes according to schedule, on Good Friday.

Where the road leaves Altar and heads north into the dust of the desert stand three crosses. One says "Children," the next "Family," the third states that "2,800 have already died on this journey and how many more must die?" The town priest put them up. Each year he came out one Sunday and said mass. Then he was shipped to the Vatican so he'd stop making such a fuss over this matter.

THEY WORK CONSTRUCTION IN THE hardwood forest and build mansions for people who speak a different language. North Carolina is one of those places that never saw it coming and now it is studded with new colonias of migrant Mexicans. On the weekend, open air markets erupt and look like those in rural Mexico.

A man works on his car out on the streets. He came up from Honduras and paid $5,000 to get to North Carolina.

A couple lives in a house. The man came north through Sásabe. He stood under a tree there and tore off his Mexican clothing and then changed into the garments supplied by a coyote so he would look American. I've stood there while men and women morphed into their new costumes.

He works construction and has brought his woman north through Tijuana. He's been here a year, she has been here a few months. She cleans apartments, the work goes very fast because strong chemicals are used—she has had to sign a waiver that says she will not sue if the chemicals harm her. They rent a house, they work all the time.

Everyone has dreams and they think of their former homes. But they will not be going back, except in their dreams.

Outback Nightmares and Refugee Dreams

From
Mother Jones,
March/April 2003

When a few thousand men, women, and children sought asylum in Australia, the Welcoming Country responded with prison camps, tear gas, and forced relocation to distant island jails.

THE DINGO FENCE MARCHES TO THE NORTH, a wire barrier twice the length of the Great Wall of China. To the west and northwest are the vast forbidden zones, legacies of nuclear testing in the 1950s. It is 100 degrees in the shade as the guard, a hefty guy in his 30s, wheels up in a truck, takes my measure, and says it is all but over, that the last person will be gone in two months. He works for Wackenhut, the American corporation that operates Australia's refugee internment camps. Leaving is never easy. One man was sedated by an intramuscular injection, a ball was placed in his mouth lest he cry out, then he was taken to the plane, arms taped to the chair, and flown back home. He also most likely left with a bill since the Australians commonly charge those who fail to qualify for asylum $60 to $70 a day for their imprisonment, a charge that can run more than $100,000 per person. Sometimes the flights end badly with the person being murdered upon arrival back home. In the camp, there were the incidents where men and women protested the conditions by sewing their lips together, others where men dug shallow graves, lay down in them, and had all but their faces buried. Sometimes people cut themselves with knives, drank shampoo, or leapt from treetops to attempt suicide. There were also the cases of teenage girls who regressed into incontinence.

I am standing outside a prison in Woomera, Australia. The name means "spear-thrower" in an aboriginal language and signifies the town's original reason for being: From 1947 to 1982, it was a secret community hidden in the vast desert of South Australia, about 200 miles north of Adelaide, where American and British military men and scientists tested rockets with the cooperation of the Australian government. Now it is down from a peak of 5,000 souls to 250—not counting prisoners and guards—and is a gas station, a hotel with floors named after rockets, a lot of empty houses, a few shops, and a prison in the parched outback, the heart of the planet's driest continent. The prison itself is that commonplace of such sterile centers—huge fences topped with razor wire, the simple bleak little buildings, barren ground, and a complete inwardness so that an observer sees nothing but metal and glare. As with all prisons, people are kept out of view.

Outside the fence, kangaroos and emus wander the land; cockatoos sit in the trees. The vast emptiness and open road whisper freedom. I have come here to meet with WMA 564, formerly known as Sharam Doraji. In the system, everyone becomes a number and is never addressed by name once given a number. They tell me he has been moved to another prison. When I go to it, my paperwork is not quite in order. I have failed to file it 72 hours in advance, which is true since I first sought to visit WMA 564 in Woomera before he was secretly moved. When I finally get things in order, my time in Australia has run out. But then that was the point of my visit to WMA 564—his asylum applications had run out and he too was rejected. Only, unlike me, he could be sedated, taken to his plane, and flown away taped to his seat.

At first, no one paid much heed to what Australia did with its refugees. In February 2000, for example, the Australian government flew Dr. Mohammed Taha Alsalami, a medical scientist and a leader in Sydney's Muslim community, to Curtin, a prison north of the Great Sandy Desert. He found 1,147 caged people, mainly Iraqis and Afghans. And 20 of them had sewn their lips together in protest of the prison's harsh conditions. A leading Australian newspaper, Melbourne's *The Age*, gave Alsalami's report three brief mentions of 50 words. The national radio network called the lip stitching "bizarre" and the premier of Western Australia, where the incident took place, said the refugees "had a nerve to be complaining" and decried them for not showing some "gratitude." Then the story went away. At that time, Australia had 3,000 such people locked up in six different centers.

Australia has faced a tiny refugee migration; since 1997 perhaps 10,000 people have entered the country without permission. The refugee crisis here is aflutter from a larger disturbance, the flight of people from Africa, parts of Europe, the Middle East, Latin America, and Asia to safety and shelter because of war and because of sea changes created by the global economy. Australia, which likes to call itself the "Lucky Country" or the "Welcoming Country," is one of the most civilized and civil places on earth. I wandered downtown Melbourne for three days before I heard a car horn. Yet this trickle of people prompted barbarism from the Lucky Country.

AUSTRALIA BEGAN ITS EUROPEAN HISTORY as a dumping ground for convicts and excess citizens of the British Isles. At the time of federation, in 1901, it adopted a whites-only immigration policy. After World War II, the government, with only 7.5 million citizens, set a goal of 20 million Australians who could protect the huge island continent from imagined Asian hordes. The whites-only policy continued—at first even Japanese war brides were banned and thousands of Asians and Polynesians who had found shelter here during the war were deported. In 1947, a poll revealed that only 17 percent of the population would accept refugees from the Holocaust. In the postwar labor government, Arthur Calwell, the minister for immigration, made statements such as "We can have a white Australia, we can have a black Australia, but a mongrel Australia is impossible." Of the Chinese, he informed Parliament in 1954, "Two Wongs do not make a white." During this same era, mixed-race children were seized from Aborigines and placed in white foster homes, a policy commonly known as "fucking them white."

This official stance was repealed in the 1960s and had vanished from government policies by the late '70s when the government adopted a policy of multiculturalism. But like an underground coal fire, it blazed on out of sight. In 1975, when Australia considered taking in 15,000 refugees from Vietnam, Prime Minister Gough Whitlam said in a private meeting that he was "not having hundreds of fucking Vietnamese . . . coming into the country," and two years later, his Labor Party called for the country to stop accepting refugees who simply landed on its shores. In 1992, mandatory detention for uninvited asylum seekers became law after a small influx—less than 1,000—of Vietnamese and Cambodian boat people occurred during a period of high unemployment and high legal immigration. Under U.N. rules, such detentions are permitted only for a few days or weeks while a refugee's identity and health are checked and can never be used to deter future refugees. Australia, however, made detention open-ended—in short, made it imprisonment. Through these years, the policy of rigid control cracked at times—for example, after the butchery of Tiananmen Square, thousands of Chinese students were given asylum, but their arrival prompted the government to change the law so that asylum, formerly permanent, was now granted only on a temporary basis.

By the end of the 20th century, Australia, though still one of the least densely populated nations on earth, had about 19 million citizens. The government, finally facing up to the limited resources of the continent (poor soils, almost no water, paltry fisheries, limited forests, and little arable land), planned to stabilize the population at 23 million (though the growing Green Party would like half that). Then, in 1997, increasing numbers of boat people began arriving from Afghanistan, Iran, and Iraq, and in 2000, 3,800 arrived. In keeping with U.N. accords, Australia was already slated to take in up to 12,000 refugees a year, but this small number of additional and uninvited arrivals struck a nerve. The old fears returned in force despite or perhaps because of the fact that in the previous 30 years Australia had swallowed 320,000 people admitted as refugees or for humanitarian reasons and despite the fact that 1 in 4 Australians is foreign born. In the summer and early fall of 2001, two things radically altered this effort at being kindly: an election, and what came to be called the "Tampa incident."

ON AUGUST 26, 2001, Captain Arne Rinnan and the Norwegian cargo ship *Tampa* were plowing the sea from Perth to Singapore when a call came from the Australian Maritime Safety Centre in Canberra that a wooden ferry was in trouble. Four hours later, the *Tampa* pulled up to the Palapa 1 and rescued 433 souls—including 70 children and several pregnant women—a number that overwhelmed the capacity of the *Tampa* and its crew of 27, a multitude that had to be sheltered in empty containers stacked on the deck.

The ship was only 75 miles from Australia's Christmas Island—a tiny territory of 1,500 people, 1,200 miles northwest of the mainland—but still in Indonesian waters. The Australian government ordered Captain Rinnan to take the people, all asylum seekers fleeing the Middle East, to the Indonesian port of Merak, 250 miles away. When told this, the asylum seekers became aroused and threatened to jump into the sea. The captain steamed toward Christmas Island, pausing just outside the official 12-mile limit. But he had entered the stormy waters of an impending Australian election. Already that month, more than 1,000 asylum seekers had made landfall in Australia. Throughout the 1990s, support for an anti-immigrant party, One Nation, had grown and the coalition government headed by John Howard wished to placate these voters. Howard told the media that the *Tampa* "will not be given permission to land in Australia or any Australian territories," and, although some passengers were near death, he sent elite Special Air Service troops to prevent the ship from docking at Christmas Island. After eight days of international protest, Howard cut a deal with the tiny 10-square-mile island nation of Nauru to imprison the asylum seekers in exchange for $20 million in benefits, effectively boosting Nauru's GDP by 33 percent. Most of the refugees were transported to the interior of the island, a phosphate wasteland abandoned by miners and inhabited by feral dogs. This, along with a $10 million deal cut with Papua New Guinea and a hoosegow built on Christmas Island, came to be known as the Pacific Solution and was the act that finally aroused some Australians to protest their government's policies.

Among other things, the Pacific Solution created a new legal entity, a person under Australian control in an offshore prison who nevertheless is not fully protected by Australian courts or laws. Today, some 1,500 people exist in such limbo. In October 2001, a month after the new policy of intercepting refugees and sending them to offshore prisons became law, a ferry of refugees went down with more than 353 lost, many of them children. In the speeches Howard gave while running for reelection that fall, he claimed the asylum seekers had tossed their own children into the sea for some kind of sport. There is an ongoing parliamentary investigation as to whether Australian intelligence in Indonesia sought to sabotage the frail boats favored by the smugglers of human beings.

But two things resulted from Australia's draconian solution to asylum seekers, a solution backed up by a naval blockade: The world began to notice and the boats soon stopped coming. And, of course, the Howard government was reelected because of overwhelming support of the new policy, support that continues to this day.

THERE IS A WORLD THAT HAS things and there is a world that wants things, a world of flesh in motion, a wave of men, women, and children that no one wants. This story is about one grotesque collision between these worlds, one that took place in one of the most decent and civilized nations on this earth. In the summer of 2001, Australia abandoned civilized norms as expressed in U.N. conventions it had earlier signed. In part, Australia became a victim of its own history, but mainly it succumbed to pressures that will eventually face all developed nations.

There are at least 35 million displaced people worldwide and at least 10 million people trying to get into the industrial West each year. Those who officially earn the designation of refugee—meaning they are likely to be persecuted if they go home—are merely a tiny subculture within this vast diaspora. Last July, Malaysia booted out a half million illegal Indonesian workers. The United States will face about a half million illegal Mexican migrants each year for the next 30 years according to the most optimistic projections by the government of Mexico. In response to such migrations, the United States builds giant fences and Europe is slowly but surely raising its drawbridges—Greece and Italy, for example, are keenly interested in Australia's harsh medicine as they deal with Turks and Albanians. In the summer of 2002, a memo slipped out of the Blair government revealing its interest in Australia's naval blockade as a possible tactic for stopping boats of immigrants from crossing the Mediterranean.

When Australia's minister of immigration, Philip Ruddock, went on tour last summer, he also found attentive ears for his nation's refugee policy in Tanzania, Southern Africa, Yugoslavia, the Czech Republic, Slovakia, and Austria. Ruddock perhaps best personifies the contradictions people are now facing. He is a lifelong member of Amnesty International and wears the group's pin on his suit as he peddles his nation's prison system for refugees. This past summer his daughter fled Australia for the Third World to do good works in penance for her father's actions.

THE SHOWERS HAVE PAUSED and the sun brushes the patio as the steaks and sausages sizzle on the grill. The Fitzroy Learning Network near Melbourne University entered the refugee world when an Afghan walked in the door and asked to learn English. Now it is one of the hubs of concern that dot Australia's cities. Most Australians are ignorant of such advocacy groups and would be hostile to their very existence. The old building is in Melbourne's bohemian district about a block from the Labour In Vain saloon and Barfly's Cafe. Fifty or sixty refugees mill around, mainly Afghans and Iraqis.

The Pacific Solution—along with the government's strict control of press access—has kept refugees at bay and out of sight, and the mainland camps are quickly being emptied, the asylum seekers shunted off to distant Pacific islands. To learn what happened, one must talk to the lucky few who qualified for temporary visas and were released.

A., who like many refugees does not want his real name used, is 24 years old, an Iraqi from Karbala. His family was tossed out when the Iraq-Iran war began because they were Shiites and so came to live in Iran for two decades. He is just out of an Australian prison and holds a temporary visa until his final fate is decided. All refugees have the same story: fear, escape, the terror of reaching a new, safe society, and eventually a brutal rebirth on some distant shore.

A. grew up stateless, his family lacking any papers in Iran and unable to return to Iraq. "They said," he notes of the Iranians, "'You are Iraqi; you must go back.' Finally, I didn't have any choice—if I go to Iraq, they would reject me. I couldn't find any place or anywhere to settle. They passed me back and forth like a basketball."

He tries to get recognition as a refugee from the U.N. office but fails to get any answer. He decides Europe and the United States are too hard to enter but "I hear Australia is a free country." The flight to Malaysia costs $500, and then the next leg to Indonesia is $100. He looks up a smuggler, and that is another $1,500. Two themes emerge in most refugee tales: first, a sense of general danger rather than a specific death threat. And second, expense. The dirt poor of the nations of the earth cannot buy their way out on airlines. A. is a slight man, maybe 120 pounds, of medium stature, the face fine-boned, the eyes careful and darting. He frightens easily. When he left Iran, he had to sign a paper stating he would not come back. This sense of statelessness terrified him and he dreaded what might happen if the Indonesian or Malaysian police nabbed him. He explains, "I have nowhere."

A.'s journey by sea began from the Indonesian island of Lombok, a Muslim island across a strait from Bali. There were 30 men, women, and children. They were terrified of the open water and yet strangely happy, he recalls, because "if they got to Australia, they would have freedom." They were three days and four nights upon the water and made landfall on an uninhabited Australian island on June 6, 2001. An Australian naval ship picked them up and took them to Darwin, and then they were flown to Woomera, the prison in the outback. There the food was bad, the facilities overtaxed. Fifteen hundred people were jammed behind razor wire. Everyone was given a number and no one had any sense of how their cases were progressing. The Wackenhut guards were often teens fresh off the dole, who were provided a couple days of training. They used riot equipment, tear gas, handcuffs, water cannons, and psychological torture. A federal judge would later compare their "thuggery" to that of S.S. guards. But at the time, the Australian press was barred, the refugees' plight unnoticed. Some people in Woomera broke and attempted suicide. A. saw people slash themselves with razors or go on hunger strikes.

"Now Australia," he says softly, "is like Iraq or Iran for me—they don't want me. That was horrible and painful for me. There is no place in the world for me to be settled. Why is there no place for people like me?"

All refugees enter a fog bank of international agreements and the various immigration rules of nations. They grow practiced at tailoring their stories to meet these requirements. But in the end, the stories touch the chords offered up by A.: the desire to be safe, to be free, to be settled, to be someone. And after a while, all the regulations and international accords begin to look like pious barriers erected by successful states to bar the losers of the world from entry.

And in Australia they enter a peculiar wound that warps all perceptions of them. The land here was seen as empty and so the Aboriginal population was pushed off or slaughtered without even the American fig leaf of treaties. Although for generations the white population was either brought in shackles or enticed with free passages, a national dread developed that others craved Australia, that yellow Asian hordes were poised to overwhelm this thinly populated European outpost. Even the displaced peoples brought from a ravaged Europe after World War II were segregated in isolated work camps until they had been properly Aussiefied lest they upset the resident population. The various plagues of the land, whether native dingoes or emus or introduced rabbits, were always seen as things that could be fenced out and controlled. This state of denial permeates the society and is the official face each refugee meets.

THE NIGHT BEFORE I MET A., a benefit—the Cha-Cha-Change A Refugee's World Ball—was held for the Fitzroy Learning Network. Two or three hundred guests gave around $10,000. I sat at a table with a half dozen refugees and one of their principal Australian defenders, Julián Burnside, a barrister of national reputation. Burnside has a big law office in downtown Melbourne, and if he walks into a courtroom, he earns around $8,000 a day. He is a graying man of around 50 and before the refugee matter came up was studiously apolitical, a man more interested in modern art (he is a sculptor and has written a successful children's book) than in refugees.

Recently, Burnside gave an address that tore to shreds the current policy of incarcerating refugees on the grounds that it violated both U.N. treaties and a core Australian value, that of a "fair go." He and his wife, Kate Durham, have held fundraisers for refugees, helped finance legal relief groups, and Durham even snuck into Nauru with a journalist to film a documentary about the Pacific Solution. But in the end, his position is simple. He doesn't care if the government policy is "bloody legal"—it is morally wrong. He explains this to me as we dine on Vietnamese chili chicken, cucumber salad, and pepper-crusted porterhouse steaks, all washed down with endless bottles of Australian shiraz. But when I ask him, "What if there were 40,000 refugees or 400,000?" he pauses and says, "Well, that would be a different matter."

Mohammed is 33 years old and comes from Ghazni, a Hazara community.

Western Afghanistan is largely Hazara and until about three centuries ago was part of Persia. The Hazara are descendants of the army of Genghis Khan and hated by the dominant Pashtuns and reviled by the Taliban. Mohammed fled Afghanistan in 1999 because his friends were disappearing. He borrowed $7,500 from family members to get to Australia and left behind his wife and children. He departed Indonesia with 38 people on a crowded boat for a four-day voyage that took ten days. They ran out of fuel and were down to bare rations of water when they hit an uninhabited Australian island on January 26, 2000. Next he was in Woomera, where he spent seven and a half months with 1,700 other people. They had one kitchen, one dining hall, no television, radio, or telephone. In the early days of Woomera, there were but two toilets for 700 inmates, and tampons were rationed to the women.

After five months, the protests began. And then one day, the inmates toppled the fence and hundreds of them walked into Woomera and simply stood around the public park, a peculiar place studded with missiles from the secret town's Cold War glory days.

Mohammed was eventually released with a temporary worker's permit in August 2000. He cannot go back to visit his family—any refugee who leaves Australia for any reason is denied reentry. So he works six days a week setting tile.

"No one," he teaches me, "wants to be a refugee. For me, there is nothing to dream. My children are there. My daughter has died from disease. My son and wife and my mother are alive. My future is dark. Everything is bad, bad, bad. I lost once. Maybe I will lose again. I am a loser."

I ask him if he finally feels safe.

He says, "Exactly."

He pauses and says with almost admiration, "People in Australia don't know reality. I escaped from something and I don't want to see it again."

I never meet a refugee who was not horrified by his time in Australian prisons, nor do I ever meet one who has had a single bad experience with Australians after getting out. Australia and the United States have different histories. Americans are hostile to illegal immigrants but programmed to believe in Ellis Island and the Statue of Liberty. Australians are trained to dread invasion and yet cannot stomach being unkind to any stranger. When I talk to Australians in bars and coffee shops, they tell me the refugees are lying, tearing up their documents, damaging the prisons—basically a bad lot of blokes, "whingers." But when I talk to the refugees they are all but in love with the Australians and their kindness.

THE LIGHT STREAMS INTO THE ALMOST bare room of the sixth-floor apartment. Shoes are lined up at the door of this small subsidized unit of the public-housing project in Melbourne. The three brothers serve coffee. Mohammed, 38, has been out for a spell. Hussan, 32, and Kamal, 40, just finished a year of detention on Nauru. Back in Baghdad the family was well-off with a chain of clothing stores. But then the trouble came.

Mohammed, trained as a physical therapist, began his journey 12 years ago when he got into trouble with the regime. He is vague on this point, but six months after Desert Storm swept through his world, he moved to Jordan with a six-month visa. Then he tried Turkey for three months and filed a refugee application with the U.N. High Commissioner for Refugees. The Turks arrested him and he spent two months in jail, a stint that prevented him from keeping his precious appointment with the United Nations. He was deported to northern Iraq, the Kurdish area, where he was safe from Saddam. He began his true statelessness. After a seven-hour walk through the mountains he landed in Iran, where he lived illegally from 1993 to 1999 and earned little beyond room and board. In those six years he was deported to northern Iraq six times. During one border crossing in 1997, a land mine went off, killing his three companions and injuring Mohammed. Then in 1999, Iran gave him two months to clear out. He landed in Australia in February 2000, was tossed into prison at Woomera, and spent half a year there.

Now he works in a nursing home and acts as a guide to this new land for his brothers. Mohammed thinks that if the borders were open every single person in Iraq would come to Australia. The brothers ask me if I know about the story of 4,000 Israelis being warned not to go to work at the World Trade Center on September 11. I tell them the story is a lie. The oldest brother, Kamal, then asks me if I am a Jew.

"What are your dreams?" I ask.

Kamal says, "If you offered me the entire United States, I'd rather have Saddam killed."

Mohammed says, "You think in our situation we have a right to dream? We have nothing."

Hussan says, "Find a safe place to live."

When Mohammed learns I am a U.S. citizen, he asks if he might see my passport. I hand it over.

He sits there on the sofa, slowly turning the pages, fondling each and every one. He says nothing but I can guess what he is thinking: If he possessed one of these documents, no one could touch him. No one.

IN 1999, WHILE MICHAEL OSAMA was visiting a city in his native Syria with a cousin, an attempted revolt took place. As they were leaving the city to return home from this holiday, their identity cards were noted. The next day, his cousin was taken away from his job and has not been seen since. For three weeks, Osama hid with friends; then he vanished into southern Syria for three months. He gave a smuggler $2,000 and was promised passage to South Africa. Eventually, he wound up on Lombok and boarded a boat. For three days he did not eat or sleep, simply smoked cigarettes and feared drowning in the ocean. He arrived in Woomera at 1 A.M. He thought this was okay, that in a day or two they would check him out and release him into the community.

The months roll by. Afghans start digging graves, climb in, and are buried save their faces. Osama joins a hunger strike. Then the fence goes down and he joins the march into Woomera. The inmates shout, "We Want Freedom!" During these few hours of liberty, Osama talks to the Australian press. He is a natural leader.

When Osama speaks, he looks off at a 45-degree angle. He can make out forms—that is all. He had to quit the university in Syria because of a progressive eye disease and gave up his schooling at about the same point he gave up his belief in God.

Now he works in a factory and gets around by bus or cab.

"No refugee can be illegal," he asserts. "I want to save my life. When someone, a gunman, wants to kill you, you should not have to write a letter and wait for an answer. There is no light at the end of my tunnel. And when there is no light, you cannot see. I have nothing. Nothing."

He taps out a number on a cell phone, and then a cab comes for him.

He says, "I am on a holiday from misery."

I ask him if the Australians have abused him since he left Woomera and he looks at me with shock.

"No," he almost snaps. "They have treated me wonderfully."

His temporary Australian visa runs out in the summer of 2003.

UNDER AUSTRALIAN LAW, you cannot be a legal immigrant unless you first file the paperwork in your country of origin. The Iraqis are terrified of going near foreign embassies. The Afghans lack documented identity—decades of war have destroyed doodads such as birth certificates. And so all such refugees, due to their clerical negligence, have failed in this preliminary filing and thus are banned from being legal immigrants. Also, under Australian law, in order to be a refugee a person must file for asylum within seven days of reaching a secondary country, meaning that an Afghan who manages to get to Pakistan has one week to file with the Australian Embassy. Failure to do so makes one ineligible for permanent asylum upon reaching Australia. The lucky few who manage to reach Australia are imprisoned and checked out. The government has spent at least $1.6 million running each refugee's speech pattern through a Swedish software program that can allegedly, for example, ferret out Afghans from Pakistanis and others pretending to come from harsh places. The software is keen on slang and other peculiar uses. It is fashioned by immigrants who have not been home for years and years and is thus out of date. These are just a few of the series of little hurdles facing refugees or those claiming to be refugees.

Against this apparatus, small legal organizations such as the Refugee Advocacy Service of South Australia (RASSA) in Adelaide wage legal appeals. Aleecia Murray, 23, will be admitted to the bar later this year, but for now she works 60- to 80-hour weeks helping refugees. So far, out of 170 cases, RASSA has won 8, and victory simply means that the refugee gets the chance to seek a temporary visa yet again. (By the end of 2002, refugees held on Nauru and denied visas had little choice but to accept Australia's offer of $2,000 and a plane ticket home. Meanwhile, riots erupted in Woomera, Christmas Island, and throughout the rest of Australia's gulag archipelago.) Until harsher laws were passed in the wake of the Tampa incident, the lawyers who formed RASSA won about 60 percent of such cases.

Murray says, "I think if someone has left a life and taken a risk and gotten here and then is subjected to detention, all you want to do is get them out. The biggest issue that concerns me with the refugees is that people don't care that we lock them up."

On her office wall is a quote from the Australian national anthem: "We've boundless plains to share. With courage, let us all combine . . ."

One of RASSA's clients, Huassan Varasi, a 27-year-old Hazara, knows the new reality in his bones. He paid $4,500 to get to Australia and spent 28 days on a tiny Indonesian boat with 73 others. He became one of the revolt leaders in Woomera after the Afghans asked him, "How long can we stay in this death house of liberty?" He led a hunger strike in which 80 Afghans sewed their lips together.

After 16 days the strike ended. Now he works in an auto factory and has a temporary visa.

Varasi first decided to leave Afghanistan when he was 18. And not because of the Taliban—persecution of the Hazari predated their reign. True, he was beaten in the streets, and also whipped. But he left because he has "a problem with fanaticism." He wanted to be free and live in a democracy. He has just bought a computer and is about to write a book about his ideas on the need for individual freedom.

Now he dreams of Canada because he thinks, just maybe, it might be "a rational country."

EVERYONE IS WAVING THEIR ARMS and talking at once. I am on Lombok, the Indonesian island from which so many refugees boarded the rickety ships of smugglers and sailed off into their Australian dreams. But since October of 2001, the ships have stopped coming. The Australian navy has put up a blockade, and the Pacific Solution, with its eerie echo of the American tactic of locking up Afghans in Guantanamo Bay, has apparently worked. And so for a year or more, close to a hundred Iraqis have been marooned in the town of Mataram on Lombok. They are mainly Shia, and the island is Sunni. They are not loved here and a local fatwa has allegedly been pronounced. Some of the women have been attacked in the street. And now the Iraqis have seized the ground around the office of the International Organization for Migration, an entity that works closely with the United Nations, camped out under the trees, and demanded that something be done about their fate. One man pulls off his shirt and shows me the scars from being tortured with electricity in Saddam's prisons. There is the man with scars from the fan treatment—tie the wrists to a ceiling fan, turn it on, then add weights to the body. One man has four children but one hand, a result of the war with Iran. A few days earlier, I am told, two teenage girls decided to make a point. They poured fuel on their bodies and struck a match. I am shown photos of them in their hospital beds. The IOM office is locked and no one within will deal with this throng. Basically, these people are doomed. To go back is death. Australia is off the table. And the local people have come at them with machetes.

And of course, as my local Muslim guide points out with contempt, the Iraqis are rich. He bases this on the fact that some have cell phones. He himself earns $45 a month because he knows English. And perhaps the Iraqis are moneyed. But their wealth avails them not at all this time.

We are supposed to do something—after all, there are tens of millions of refugees wandering the earth. We have U.N. accords to deal with this; we have our criteria. The small children press in on me as I take notes. Back in Iraq, one favored technique for prompting answers during interrogation is to torture your children in front of you. Or rape your women. Sometimes nails are driven into a person's skull to initiate a conversation. We can be appalled by the Australian response, one that at least in its naval blockade and indifference to death at sea seems taken straight out of our own playbook in dealing with Haitians. We can cringe at the thought of men and women stitching their lips together. We can recoil in horror at drugged inmates being taped onto airplane seats for their voyage back to their native hell, a bill tucked carefully into their pockets. We can even, perhaps, file appeals of individual cases in courts here and there.

But can we truly look into the regions of the uprooted and face all these helpless people? I am being overwhelmed by only a hundred men, women, and children, and I am both incompetent and incapable of sorting out who earns the lottery ticket as a genuine refugee. And I know they are simply a beginning of wave after wave that will inevitably splash against all our worlds.

Later, I go with my Muslim guide to a seaside restaurant. His life is in economic ruin due to the recent bombing on nearby Bali. No one comes to Lombok now. He tells me he has to feed his family. He may have to leave. He asks, What can I do? Earlier, he had taken me to the public market, where I bought Osama bin Laden T-shirts. He said many of his friends admire bin Laden and have doubts about America.

I ask why.

He says, "Because Americans always make war, war, war. No one can beat Americans."

And then we have beer and fish and other items on me, a tally that runs to about a third of his monthly wage. He has never been to the neighboring island of Bali. He cannot afford such a visit.

Back at the IOM office, the Iraqis have draped signs over the fence. The office is on a quiet side street and the signs are likely to be read by no one save uncaring Indonesian eyes. They read: HELP ME!!! HELP ME!!! WE DON'T WANT DIE HERE. HELP ALL CHILDREN FOR THE FUTURE. ALL CHILDREN WILL LOSE THE FUTURE.

Part IV

I don't trust the answers or the people who give me the answers. I believe in dirt and bone and flowers and fresh pasta and salsa cruda and red wine. I do not believe in white wine; I insist on color.

FROM "THE BONE GARDEN OF DESIRE"

Excerpt

From *Shadow in the City*

[Editor's Note: Joey O'Shay is an undercover narcotics agent who is deep into a transaction involving more than $50 million of high-grade Colombian heroin. Joey O'Shay is not his real name—everything else is real.]

The skin on his face is smooth, the skin of a child, skin without guile or worry, the skin that is supposed to come from some inner serenity. The skin is the ultimate camouflage of Joey O'Shay. When women see this face, they wince and they open up, they see hurt in the face, they see caring of some sort in this face, they sense vulnerability. Women fall in love with this face.

Men do not. They see the dead eyes, the relaxed skin, the lack of tension. Men see death in this face and they move on and do not want to discover what is behind this face because they already know and fear what they see.

When the face speaks, and it does this no more than is absolutely necessary, the words are flat, almost soft, and measured, the words never stumble or rush and there are no extra words. The words never pause, they simply march out of his mouth. They do not coax. They state. The face says always the same thing: Take it or leave it. But do not try to change it.

FOR SIX WEEKS, O'SHAY PUSHES the connection out of his thoughts. Cosima talks to Alvarez occasionally but the conversations are short. And coded. Talk about boxes, shipments. Business.

Alvarez comes back and they go to the apartment, a dull cell in a huge complex. O'Shay likes nondescript venues for his business. Alvarez has brought a sample half kilo, a testament to what commerce they could do in the future. O'Shay listens, one gunman hanging back in the room, Cosima fluttering about like a maid. No one talks but Alvarez and O'Shay.

The pornography business matters to Alvarez. He sees online porn services as an ideal way to launder money, a kind of ultimate restaurant where receipts can be dummied forever to explain income and where the details of cooks and food and storefronts can be avoided. O'Shay explains various options. Alvarez is keen for a webcam where someone can call in and direct the woman to do certain things on camera. He asks if O'Shay would like to invest.

"I don't need heat like that," O'Shay tells him. "It may be all perfectly legal but I have my businesses already. I have the trucks and the planes and I don't need the fucking feds coming around because I've got some bitches fucking on camera."

The talk goes back to heroin, to shipments, prices, purity. Transport. O'Shay is meticulous on such points. He hates sloppy work, he worships punctuality. He insists on sound habits from anyone he deals with. So he drones on about the details, about how the heroin will be packaged.

O'Shay says, "I know how you bring it in, stuffed in someone's gut and blasted out their fucking ass. But I do not ever want to touch this stuff until you've cleaned it up. Understand?"

"No, no, no," Alvarez interrupts. "You will never ever have that problem with me. It will be clean, my workers will clean it up. And you will not pay for the wrappings, they will be peeled. It will only be the sticks of heroin and they will be immaculately clean."

Suddenly O'Shay shifts back to the pornography business, starts talking about other possibilities there. Alvarez listens attentively. That is the moment O'Shay's aide leaves the room.

When he returns, the aide shoves a machine gun in Alvarez's face.

He is ordered down on the floor like a dog and he obeys.

He is forced to lie flat and spread his legs, put his hands behind his head. The cold barrel caresses his skull.

Alvarez is experienced in handling many things at the same time. As he sprawls on the floor and smells ruin and death nearby, he must consider other matters. He is involved in a scheme to murder a federal judge, and this cannot be escaped. The judge's fate is merely a chip in a larger game. A large Colombian player is in prison and wishes a way out. His people will arrange for a rival organization to murder the judge, he is told. Alvarez is to be with them, to help them set up the hit, to find them a place to stay. And then vanish and call his Colombian colleagues. They will sell the killers to the FBI, help prevent the murder of a federal judge. All this for a sentence consideration for their boss in prison. It will be a clean thing, and a thing Alvarez with his lost loads cannot possibly refuse. He smells the carpet that scrapes his face, feels the gun at his head, and also thinks he may fail in his assignment concerning the judge. He remains calm.

O'Shay does not rise from his chair but he watches attentively. He notes that Alvarez is horrified, his face ever so briefly awash with a wave of emotion. But still he remains calm. He does not whine or beg or weep. Some of them do. But he remains cool as the gun pushes against his head.

This is one thing O'Shay likes about his business. It trains people to a sound work ethic, it culls out those who are lazy or stupid. Or too greedy. The world, he thinks, has grown careless and fat. The wages are often too high and the work too easy. The price of failure is often no price at all. He sees it all the time in the police, their sloppy work, crude techniques, nine-to-five schedules. He despises a lot of police not because they arrest people and destroy people but because they almost always fail to appreciate excellence. They lack drive. They tolerate stupidity and do not weed out the stupid. As his industry grows, the authorities keep hiring more agents, keep raising their pay. And they keep failing. And this failure simply breeds the demand for yet more people and more offices. Waste. He cannot abide waste.

In his business, performance is everything. Just look at Alvarez on the carpet, a man behind in his payments, a man who has lost loads, and yet a man who comes to this city to do a deal, a man who expects no way out except one created by his own work and ingenuity. It is a wonder that such men ever go down to the police. But that is the cruelty of the business.

The police can fail and fail and fail and still their checks come, their jobs remain. Their work ethic has been steadily eroded by this pampering. Many of them retreat to offices and files and paperwork. They have lost the edge of violence, an essential for any success in the business. O'Shay has been in too many firefights. Sometimes he thinks the only really incompetent people he deals with in his business are the minions of the government.

O'Shay thinks that this will work, that this man can help him in his business.

They shackle Alvarez and take him to O'Shay's office. He hardly speaks, his black skin remains cool, his face concerned but still under control.

He says nothing about the voodoo altar. He seems relaxed by the turn of events.

O'Shay asks him if he needs to use the restroom because he knows that often men in such an instance desperately need a toilet. But Alvarez is fine, and says so.

O'Shay offers, "I want you to know this is not personal. It is simply business."

And then he gets down to business. Alvarez has two choices. One is self-evident. The other is to become part of O'Shay's organization and to work on its goals and not his own goals or his colleagues' goals.

Alvarez has a family, he has restaurants in New York, he has his life. He has many things he can lose. Or keep. He details all these things to O'Shay, it is hardly the time to withhold information. He explains that he comes from a large family, that most of his brothers and sisters are professionals. He explains that one sister is like him and that they both work hard in the business. Alvarez talks calmly of this, and that is his offer: he and his sister can deliver whatever is desired. And, of course, in return, keep what they already have.

"I can give you hundreds of kilos of heroin," Alvarez offers. "I can give you Southeast Asian heroin. My entire life has been as a liaison between the Colombians and the Dominicans and the Puerto Ricans and the blacks. I know Italians."

This is the moment O'Shay always enjoys, the moment when all those hours walking his dark house and thinking and plotting suddenly bear fruit. He observes such moments with full attention, waiting for a surprise that never comes.

Alvarez is like all drug dealers, on top of the world one moment, O'Shay thinks, and facing death and ruin in the next second. O'Shay prides himself on not being surprised. And yet, he knows that this lack of surprise is slowly killing him, extinguishing the fires inside him that keep him alive.

He sits there by his altar facing Alvarez and on the surface he is completely alert, but inwardly he feels like a robot executing programmed commands. And he does not care, that is always the sensation, this not caring. His big fists rest on his lap, his voice is soft and yet crisp in those few moments when he speaks. His eyes do not flicker, his face never reveals the slightest desire. A robot. The light in the office is sterile, a neutral light that makes everything pale and empty and tasteless. This light slowly saps the will from anyone O'Shay brings here.

They reach an agreement, just as O'Shay knew they would. But more than an agreement, they cross some dark waters and reach firm land on the other side. Because O'Shay knows he is going to release Alvarez back into his world, let him go to the airport and return to his safe places. And he knows that when Alvarez reaches his home, and his previous life is back, he will still obey. Alvarez will be sitting in one of his cafés in New York, slowly sipping a cup of rich coffee, softly giving commands to his staff, and he will feel O'Shay's breath at his neck.

Cosima likes to watch others dangle. She savors Alvarez's life: he is thirty-eight, he has children, he has a black Colombian girlfriend, he has businesses in New York and down there in the islands and now he is a man who was talking calmly an hour ago when suddenly a gun filled his eyes, a man who felt death near, then sensed a reprieve, then considered a deal.

She later tells O'Shay, "I don't think we should do this. We got a good thing here without him and his heroin. I don't think we should bring him in."

But O'Shay knows what Alvarez will do, that he will all but claw his way into the deal.

O'Shay plans, he thinks things through, he knows. He moves in a world where everything is covered by a fine dust and cobwebs, a kind of archive where even the future feels like the past. He suffocates as he plays Alvarez on a string.

Alvarez says one more thing: "You were really, really good."

O'Shay hands him a phone and Alvarez calls a man named García in Colombia.

"Hey, how's it going? I've got a real good connection here now. I need stuff. I'm going to give you my sister to handle it because I'm buried in other business."

García says that will be fine.

O'Shay senses he is in, has crossed some invisible line that separates people like himself from the rarefied air of international heroin merchants. He can almost smell the air at the other end of the line, the green tropical leaves, cool tile floors, leather furniture, small cups of intensely rich coffee, picture this stranger named García in some villa with a view of the hills, the Andes rising like gods behind him as he answers the phone, makes a few brief comments, and hangs up, staring out into the clear mountain air, and in O'Shay's mind it has to be clear, just as there can be no sound around the villa except for tropical birds raucous in the trees, it has to be this way, almost like a dream because in an offhand way, it has been a dream for him, to see if he can play with the big merchants and not simply hold his own, or cut a good deal, but absorb them, take them into his world and dominate them.

For O'Shay, it must be a pure thing, with a mountain villa, a phone on a fine wooden table, the cool red tile floors, the roof also red tiles with the daily showers splashing off it, and no whine of motor scooters, no barking dogs, no bad music blaring from cheap radios, no, a clean thing, this serene place where the game is simple, straight, and lethal.

Alvarez is almost relaxed now. The altar with burning candles by his side, O'Shay feels . . . closer but not close enough. He is in play, now he must not care, let it float, see what comes. But he cannot stop the feeling of desire, of breaking out of his routine into the mountain air where everything is washed by rain and green and clean. And clear.

It all seems too easy, too fast. But O'Shay knows that is the rhythm of the business. Endless delays, days waiting in motel rooms, quick phone calls followed by lonely hours. And then it all begins to move and happens very quickly.

THE WATER FEELS EARLY-MORNING, the glass that happens before the earth shakes off the night and begins to stir. Color touches this water but does not own it. There is a wash of blue, a faded blue, splotches of darkness that whisper the depths waiting below the surface. A bank of trees swirls in the background, shades of green, hints of rose, a turbulence of energy with barely the suggestion of form. To the right, an actual limb, branches, the dense mat of leaves reaching into the scene. It is summer, when time is rich and full. The sun will be hot, and beat down on the water. The boy is in the jon boat, each hand on an oar. He wears a green long-sleeved jersey, tan pants, and a large hat to fight off the rays that soon will come. His face turns out and stares, the mouth flat and expressionless, the eyes almost hooded and peering but giving away nothing except the knowledge that someone is watching.

The boy in the boat is alone. He has no doubt gotten up early, hoisted the jon boat on his back, walked a dirt track through the country woods to the lake in gray light, and launched in this elbow of quiet water. He is living alone, been left at this place for a spell. The painting says this. His face seems reluctant to speak, almost the face of a mute. His body is ready to row and yet relaxed, the limbs suggest not a particle of tension. He is facing the shore, his back to the big water beyond. Soon the oars will dip, bite the surface, and move out into more open waters. A line will be tossed, the little boat will float, and the sky will stream overhead as he leans back and waits for a tug on the baited hook.

Joey O'Shay stands back, looks, and listens to the jazz softly walking through his house. He picks up the brush, makes two yellow daubs on the surface, leaves, yes, leaves to show that time is frozen in the peace of the elbow of the big lake. He stares down at himself as a child, free and easy in the full stillness of the earth.

Or it is a different day for the child. He is down at the creek and there is honeysuckle blanketing the bank. The boy feels eyes burning into him and turns and sees a man hiding in the vines. And then he smells the Evil Creature, that odor, that dark, dank odor. And with that the man turns and walks away.

He knows the man meant him harm.

THERE HAVE BEEN A SERIES OF killings that have muddled O'Shay's affairs. As the Colombian heroin deal lumbers along, the murders provide a list of tasks he tends to.

He finds Johnny Boy. He is small, twitching, the eyes dart constantly, the habit runs $400 a day. O'Shay knows he will not talk, not now, that he is too armored by defiance. O'Shay simply wants a sense of him. In his mind, he knows he wants to choke him to death. But that can wait.

He tells Johnny Boy that his best friend, Big Dude, has been murdered. This causes a faint ripple of emotion to pass through Johnny Boy, then he is contained again. Johnny Boy and Big Dude botched a deal, so their colleagues hunted down Big Dude and killed him. It is a small matter, a business detail. Johnny Boy is thirty going on fifty, has been part of the organization since he was eighteen, when he got out of prison.

O'Shay can sense Johnny Boy was a bitch in prison, he can see this fact almost in neon across his face. He weighed maybe 120, and he was fresh meat. He was raped and stabbed eleven times and hid in solitary. When he was returned to the prison population, he fashioned a plan. He would be mean and crazy and safe. Upon release, he got into speed and killing. He was useful to the organization because of his appetite for death. But gradually he lost touch with his talent, his hits became sloppy. And now they have become pathological, serial slaughter.

. . . I would drown him and hope if there is a god, he would take this mutilated boy and rock him gently. Because he is forever lost . . . there is no hope . . . no fair shake . . . he is the creation of our need to erase what we do to each other. . . . I will see Johnny Boy again soon. . . . I will tell him I'm sorry for what I am about to do to him and I will describe the phases of his demise to him and I will apologize to him for what this world has done to him. I doubt he will do anything but curse me. But I would rather be around him and learn of the horror. He is reality.

But of course, O'Shay will destroy him.

He tracks down Johnny Boy's colleague, a twenty-year-old seeking to rise on the flow of Johnny Boy's violence. He can smell the weakness. O'Shay feels sure, certain of his powers. He looks into the kid's eyes and signals him that his life is over, that there is only one path left, confession, and by that act, redemption. In such a moment, and it is a feeling flowing through the room, a thing concrete and yet invisible, in such a moment, they always talk because they know finally and for probably the last time someone will listen.

O'Shay and the suspects soar like birds in this moment, rise up high in the sky and careen, wheel on the currents, dive and rise again, feel powerful and free. They can drop the disguise and finally be, and that sensation of being is such a relief they will endure any consequence once they have tasted it, go gaily to their deaths, happy to be unburdened. And O'Shay knows they will talk to him not because he can kill them with his bare hands, not because he is cold, intensely cold inside. They will talk because they know he is bad and so they will not be talking to a stranger.

O'Shay is always alone at such moments, quiet and barely leaning forward, his eyes focused and yet expectant of nothing but truth. He is empty of questions, prods, yes, now and then a prod to show he is present, but no questions, no loud voices, no tricks. Tricks would be an insult. They must know their life is over and then they can finally talk. And they do.

The boy looks up and squirms, then comes to rest. He opens his mouth and a poem falls out . . .

O'Shay listens, the pieces, the little details falling into place.

Johnny Boy and the boy will go down, be quickly forgotten. O'Shay will sit on his black couch near those French doors, sit there drinking past midnight, his head full of details of his big deal, his new connections, he will sit there going over every possible alternative, making sure he has missed nothing. He has a thread of good heroin now.

But briefly, as he raises the glass to his lips, perhaps for a second, just a second, Johnny Boy and his sidekick will flutter across his mind. And then leave and go for good into the darkness just outside the door.

IT IS THREE-THIRTY A.M. O'Shay sleeps flat on the bed, his face to the tin ceiling he has installed, when strange cries snap him awake. Off sounds always catch his attention, sometimes simply leaves fluttering in the pecan trees. But this is no movement of leaves in the night. He hears Awrr, Awrr, and he cannot identify the sound. He gets his gun and goes out.

He stares into the beam of his flashlight and sees a cat trying to kill a crow. The cat is hesitant as the crow uses his beak like a pile driver. One wing hangs, torn. O'Shay kicks the cat like a football.

He turns his attention to the crow.

O'Shay gets behind the bird, gets a stick and starts tapping and the crow stands, wobbly at first, and then tries to strut. Slowly, he herds it to the open door of his weight room.

The crow seems alert but calm.

O'Shay goes into the house, gets water and some bread. The crow spends the night.

O'Shay builds the bird a perch where it can look out at his garden. The crow starts to heal. When it sees him, it makes sounds that O'Shay realizes mean it desires food. And when he brings food, the bird hops up to him and will take it from his hand.

He puts food out in the yard so the bird will get some air and when he does, other crows come and the injured bird pretends to be perfectly fine while the other crows are around. If O'Shay comes out at such moments, the injured bird hops back into the weight room, almost as if it were ashamed of its companions.

He senses the free birds and the injured crow are all part of one flock, now separated by the violence of that night.

He builds perches at different heights in the yard.

Finally, he gets a cage to take the crow to the vet. O'Shay pays a hundred and fifty bucks to have its wing mended and to have it released in a wildlife refuge. On the papers, he fills out the bird's name as Joe the Crow.

He tells no one of Joe the Crow or spending money for his medical care.

The vet had told him that when the bird was finally healed and it was ready to fly again, it would most likely go back to its flock. O'Shay wondered how the bird could figure out such a trek and decided maybe it was the natural way that white trash gravitated to shithole bars.

He misses Joe the Crow, the way he would come up from the weight room and tap on the French doors and then O'Shay would fling food out at him. He almost seemed to dance at such times. He was a natural gangster.

He is in his back room, sitting on the couch, when he senses something is watching him and comes alert. He looks out and sees a crow looking at him. The bird takes off and flies away. A few moments later the bird is back and staring again.

He tosses some scraps out, and Joe flutters around and makes calls and does his dance.

After that, O'Shay feeds him every evening. Then Joe the Crow disappears and O'Shay figures he's out grifting somewhere, maybe looting trailer parks or doing some kind of deal. One day, he finds a crow dead in the alley and he's stricken. He gives it a burial under his Carolina jasmine.

And then one day he hears the tapping and it's Joe and O'Shay rustles around the kitchen, gets a pile of scraps, a box of cereal and tosses it out for him. He can see the rest of the flock waiting up in the trees. Joe does his dance and eats.

Then he goes away. But he comes back.

The Pariah

From *Esquire*, September 1998

Two years ago, Gary Webb wrote a series of articles that said some bad things about the CIA and drug traffickers. The CIA denied the charges, and every major newspaper in the country took the agency's word for it. Gary Webb was ruined. Which is a shame, because he was right.

HE TELLS ME I'VE GOT TO understand about when the Big Dog gets off the porch, and I'm getting confused here. He is talking to me from a fishing camp up near the Canadian border, and as he tries to tell me about the Big Dog, I can only imagine a wall of green and deep blue lakes with northern pike. But he is very patient with me. Mike Holm did his hard stints in the Middle East, the Miami station, and Los Angeles, all for the United States Drug Enforcement Agency, and he is determined that I face the reality he knows. So he starts again. He repeats, "When the Big Dog gets off the porch, watch out." And by the Big Dog, he means the full might of the United States government. At that moment, he continues, you play by Big Boy rules, and that means, he explains, that there are no rules but to complete the mission. We've gotten into all this schooling because I asked him about reports that he received when he was stationed in Miami that Southern Air Transport, a CIA-contracted airline, was landing planeloads of cocaine at Homestead Air Force Base nearby. Back in the eighties, Holm's informants kept telling him about these flights, and then he was told by his superiors to "stand down because of national security." And so he did. He is an honorable man who believes in his government, and he didn't ask why the flights were taking place; he simply obeyed. Because he has seen the Big Dog get off the porch, and he has tasted Big Boy rules. Besides, he tells me, these things are done right, and if you look into the matter, you'll find contract employees or guys associated with the CIA, but you won't find a CIA case officer on a loading dock tossing kilos of coke around. Any more than Mike Holm ever saw a plane loaded top to bottom with kilos of coke. He didn't have to. He believed his informants. And he believed in the skill and power of the CIA. And he believed in the sheer might and will of the Big Dog when he finally decides to get off the porch.

As his words hang in the air, I remember a convict who says he once worked with the United States government and who also tasted Big Boy rules. This man has not gone fishing.

This convict insisted that I hold the map up to the thick prison glass as he jabbed his finger into the mountains. There, he said, that's the place, and his eyes gleamed as his words accelerated. There, in the mountains, they have a colony of two thousand Colombians out of Medellín, guarded by the Mexican army. I craned my neck to see where his finger was rubbing against the map and made an x with my pen. That's when the guard burst into the convict's small cubicle and ordered him to sit down.

The convict is a man of little credibility in the greater world. He is a Mexican national, highly intelligent and exact in his speech. He is a man electric with the memory of his days working as a DEA informant in Mexico, huddling in his little apartment with his clandestine radio. He said I must check his DEA file; he gave the names of his case officers; he noted that he delivered to them the exact locations of thirteen airfields operated jointly by the drug cartels and the CIA. The man's eyes bugged out as his excitement shredded the tedium of doing time and he returned to his former life of secret transmissions, cutouts, drinks with pilots ferrying dope, bullshitting his way through army checkpoints.

He said, "I'll be out in six months or one year, depending on the hearing. We can go. I'll take you up there."

I have always steered clear of the secret world, because it is very hard to penetrate, and because if you discover anything about it, you are not believed. And because I remember what happened to one reporter who wrote about that world, about the Big Dog getting off the porch, about the Big Boy rules. So I thought about the convict's information and did nothing with it.

But this reporter who went ahead and wrote while I stopped, I kept thinking about him. When I mention him, and what happened to him, to Mike Holm, he says, "Ah, he must have drawn blood." Holm is very impressed with the CIA, and he wants me to slow down, think, and understand something: "The CIA's mission is to break laws and be ruthless. And they are dangerous."

I had been thinking about looking into the claim that during the civil war in Nicaragua in the eighties, the CIA helped move dope to the United States to buy guns for the contras, who were mounting an insurrection against the leftist Sandinistas. So I called up Hector Berrellez, a guy who worked under Mike Holm in Los Angeles, a guy known within the DEA as its Eliot Ness, and he said, "Look, the CIA is the best in the world. You're not going to beat them; you're never going to get a smoking gun. The best you're going to get is a little story from me."

What Berrellez meant by a smoking gun is this: proof that the United States government has, through the Central Intelligence Agency and its ties to criminals, facilitated the international traffic in narcotics.

That's the trail the reporter was on when his career in newspapers went to rack and ruin. So I decided to look him up.

His name is Gary Webb.

GARY WEBB LOVES THE STACKS OF THE state library across from the capitol in Sacramento, the old classical building framed with aromatic camphor trees. He enters the lobby and becomes part of a circling mural called *War Through the Ages,* an after-flash of World War I painted by Frank Van Sloun in 1929. The panels start with the ax and club, then wade through gore to doughboys marching off to the War to End All Wars. THIS HOUSE OF PEACE, the inscription on the west wall admonishes, SHALL STAND WHILE MEN FEAR NOT TO DIE IN ITS DEFENSE.

He was here in the summer of 1995 because of a call from a woman named Coral Marie Talavera Baca. She told him her drug-dealer boyfriend was in jail and one of the witnesses against him was "a guy who used to work with the CIA selling drugs. Tons of it." Webb was brought up short: In eighteen years of reporting, every person who'd ever called him about the CIA had turned out to be a flake. Webb started to back away on the phone, and the woman sensed it and exploded: "How dare you treat me like an idiot!" She said she had lots of documents and invited him to a court date that month. And so he went.

Coral's boyfriend turned out to be a big-time trafficker. She brought Webb a pile of DEA and FBI reports about, and federal grand-jury testimony by, a guy named Oscar Danilo Blandón. Webb was intrigued by government files that told of Nicaraguans selling dope in California and giving dope money to the contras. During a break in the hearing, he headed for the restroom and ran into the U.S. attorney, David Hall. Webb told him he was a reporter for the *San Jose Mercury News,* and Hall asked why he was at a piddling hearing.

"Actually, I've been reading," Webb answered, "and I was curious to know what you made of Blandón's testimony about selling drugs for the contras in L.A. Did you believe him?"

"Well, yeah," Hall answered, "but I don't know how you could absolutely confirm it. I mean, I don't know what to tell you. The CIA won't tell me anything."

Webb followed a trail of crumbs: some San Francisco newspaper clips, some court records in San Diego, where this strange figure, Blandón, had been indicted for selling coke in 1992 and, according to the documents, had been at it for years and sold tons. He and his wife had been held without bail because the federal prosecutor, L. J. O'Neale, said his minimum mandatory punishment would be life plus a $4 million fine. Blandón's defense attorney had argued that his client was being smeared because he'd been active in helping the contras in the early eighties. The file told Webb that Blandón wound up doing about two years, and that he was now out. The file recorded that at O'Neale's request, the government had twice quietly cut Blandón's sentence and that he was now working as a paid undercover informant for the DEA.

After about six weeks of this kind of foraging, Webb went to the state library. For six days in September, he sat at a microfiche machine with rolls of dimes and read an eleven-hundred-page report from 1989 compiled by a subcommittee of the Senate Foreign Relations Committee, a subcommittee chaired by Senator John Kerry of Massachusetts that dealt with the contras and cocaine.

Buried in the federal document was evidence of direct links between drug dealers and the contras; evidence, dated four years before the American invasion of Panama, that Manuel Noriega was in the dope business; drug dealers saying under oath that they gave money to the contras (and passing polygraphs); pilots talking of flying guns down and dope back and landing with their cargoes at Homestead Air Force Base in Florida.

Suddenly, Coral's phone call didn't seem so crazy.

Webb called up Jack Blum, the Washington, D.C., lawyer who had led the Kerry inquiry, and said, "Maybe I'm crazy, but this seems like a huge story to me."

"Well, it's nice to hear someone finally say that, even if it is ten years later," Blum allowed, and then he proceeded to tell Webb almost exactly what he told me recently when I made a similar innocent phone call to him: "What happened was, our credibility was questioned, and we were personally trashed. The [Reagan] administration and some people in Congress tried to make us look like crazies, and to some degree it worked. I remember having conversations with reporters in which they would say, 'Well, the administration says this is all wrong.' And I'd say, 'Look, why don't you cover the fucking hearing instead of coming to me with what the administration says?' And they'd say, 'Well, the witness is a drug dealer. Why should I do that?' And I used to say this regularly: 'Look, the minute I find a Lutheran minister or a priest who was on the scene when they were delivering six hundred kilos of cocaine at some air base in contra land, I'll put him on the stand, but until then, you take what you can get.' The big papers stayed as far away from this issue as they could. It was like they didn't want to know."

Webb was entering contra land, and when you enter that country, you run into the CIA, since the contras were functionally a CIA army. (The agency hired them, picked their leaders, plotted their strategy, and sometimes, because of contra incompetence, executed their raids for them.) This is hardly odd, since the agency was created in 1947 for precisely such toils and has over the decades sponsored armies around the world, whether to land at the Bay of Pigs or kick the Soviets out of Afghanistan. After a year of research, in August 1996, Webb published a three-day, fifteen-thousand-word series in the *Mercury News* called "Dark Alliance." It is a story almost impossible to recapitulate in detail but simple in outline: Drug dealers working with the contras brought tons of cocaine into California in the 1980s and sold a lot of it to one dealer, a legend called Freeway Ricky Ross, who had connections with the L.A. street gangs, and through this happenstance helped launch the national love of crack. That's it, a thesis that mixes the realpolitik of the-ends-justify-the-means with dollops of shit-happens.

The series set off a firestorm in black communities, where many suspected they had been deliberately targeted with the dope as an act of genocide (there is no evidence of that), and provoked repudiations of the story by the *Washington Post,* the *New York Times,* and the *Los Angeles Times.* The knockdowns of Webb's story questioned the importance of Nicaraguan dealers like Blandón, the significance of Ricky Ross, how much money, if any, reached the contras, and how crucial any of this was to the crack explosion in the eighties, and brushed aside any evidence of CIA involvement.

But while raising questions about Webb's work, none of these papers or any other paper in the country undertook a serious investigation of Webb's evidence. A *Los Angeles Times* staff member who was present at a meeting called to plan the *Times*'s response has told me that one motive for the paper's harsh appraisal was simply pride: The *Times* wasn't going to let an out-of-town paper win a Pulitzer in its backyard.

Later, when it was all over, Webb spelled out exactly what he meant and exactly what he thought of the CIA's skills: The series "focused on the relationship between the contras and the crack king. It mentioned the CIA's role in passing, noting that some of the money had gone to a CIA-run army and that there were federal law-enforcement reports suggesting the CIA knew about it. I never believed, and never wrote, that there was a grand CIA conspiracy behind the crack plague. Indeed, the more I learned about the agency, the more certain of that I became. The CIA couldn't even mine a harbor without getting its trench coat stuck in its fly."

After a while, the *San Jose Mercury News* series disappeared except on a few byways of the Internet, Gary Webb was ruined, and things went back to normal. Things like Oliver North's diary entry linking dope and guns for the contras, like Carlos Lehder, a big Colombian drug dealer, testifying as a prosecution witness in federal court during the Noriega trial about the Medellín cartel's $10 million donation to the contras, like the entire history of unseemly connections between the international drug world and the CIA—all this went away, as it has time and time again in the past. A kind of orthodoxy settled over the American press that assumed that Webb's work had been thoroughly refuted. He became the Discredited Gary Webb.

And so in June 1997, Webb wound up going to a motel room he hated. The *Mercury News*'s editors were supposed to fix him up with an apartment, but they never figured he'd show up for his dead-end transfer from investigative reporter to pretty much a nothing. So they made no arrangements, just shunted him to the paper's Cupertino bureau on the south end of Silicon Valley, his family 150 miles away in Sacramento. After a few days of the motel, he found himself in a tiny apartment. He was in his early forties, and his life and his life's work were over. He endlessly watched a tape of *Caddyshack* and tried to forget about missing his wife, Sue, his three kids, his dog, his work. He was an ordinary guy, by his lights, with the suburban home, an aquarium in the study, two games a week in an amateur hockey league. Now, during the day, he visited the bureau, and the guys there treated him okay, because they were all in the same boat, people who had pissed off their newspaper and been shipped to its internal Siberia, where they were paid to retool the press releases of the computer and software companies. Webb was fighting the paper through arbitration with the Newspaper Guild, and so while his case dragged on, he refused to let his byline run. But he did his assignments. After all, they were paying him a solid mid-five-figure wage; he was their star investigative reporter, the guy they had brought in from the *Cleveland Plain Dealer* in 1987 to do, in their words, "kick-ass journalism." Within two years, he'd helped bring home a Pulitzer with a team of *Mercury News* reporters who jumped on the San Francisco earthquake. Then he blew the lid off civil forfeiture in California law enforcement's practice of seizing property from alleged crooks and then forgetting to ever convict, try, or even charge them. That series got the law changed. He was hot. He was good. He kicked ass.

Now *Caddyshack* flickered against his eyes hour after hour. His thirteen-year-old son asked, "Why don't you get another job?" And Gary Webb told him, "That's what they think I'll do. But they're wrong. I'm gonna fight."

But fight how? He was one fucking disgrace. Oliver North described his work as "absolute garbage." Webb was stretched thin. The week the series ran, he and the wife closed on a new house and moved in. Payments. So each morning, he went to the Cupertino bureau, and there were assignments from the city desk. Seems a police horse died, and he was supposed to nail down this equine death.

So he did. He investigated the hell out of it and wrote it up, and, by God, the thing was good. Went on page one, of course, without his name on it.

The horse died from a medical problem, constipation. The horse was full of shit.

HECTOR BERRELLEZ STUMBLED ONTO Gary Webb's story years before Gary Webb knew a thing about it. His journey into that world happened this way: Hector was not fond of cops. He remembered them slapping him around when he was a kid. He was a barrio boy from South Tucson, a square mile of poverty embedded in the booming Sun Belt city. His father was a Mexican immigrant. After being drafted into the Army in the late sixties, Berrellez couldn't find a job in the copper mines, so he hooked up as a temporary with the small South Tucson police force to finance his way through college. And it was then that Hector Berrellez accidentally discovered his jones: He loved working the streets with a badge. The state police force hired him, and Hector, still green, managed to do a one-kilo heroin deal in the early seventies, a major score for the time. The DEA snapped him up, and suddenly the kid who had wanted to flee the barrio and become a lawyer was a federal narc. He loved the life.

In the DEA, there are the administrators, who usually have little street experience, the suits. And then there are the street guys like Hector, and they call themselves something else.

Gunslingers.

His hobbies were jogging, weight lifting, guitar playing. And firearms.

A Glock? Never. "Only girls carry Glocks," he snaps. "They're a sissy gun. Plastic. You can't hit anyone over the head with a Glock."

In September 1986, Sergeant Tom Gordon of the Los Angeles sheriff's narcotics strike force pieced together intelligence about a big-time drug ring in town run by Danilo Blandón. A month later, on October 23, Gordon went before a judge with a twenty-page detailed statement documenting that "monies gained from the sales of cocaine are transported to Florida and laundered. . . . The monies are filtered to the contra rebels to buy arms in the war in Nicaragua." He got a search warrant for the organization's stash houses. On Friday, October 24, there was a briefing of more than a hundred law-enforcement guys from the sheriff's office, the DEA, the FBI. That was the same day that President Ronald Reagan, after months of hassle, signed a $100 million aid bill that reactivated a licit cash flow to the beleaguered contras. And on Monday, October 27, at daybreak, the strike force simultaneously hit fourteen L.A.-area stash houses connected with Blandón.

That's where just another day in the life of Hector Berrellez got weird. Generally, at that early hour, good dopers are out cold; the work tends toward long nights and sleeping in. As Berrellez remembers, "We were expecting to end up with a lot of coke." Instead, they got coffee and sometimes doughnuts. The house he hit had the lights on, and everyone, two men and a woman, was up. The guy who answered the door said, "Good morning; we've been expecting you. Come on in." The house was tidy, the beds were already made, and the damn coffee was on. The three residents were polite, even congenial. "It was obvious," says Berrellez, "that they were told." The place was clean; all fourteen houses were clean. The only thing Berrellez and the other guys found in the house was a professional scale.

But there was a safe, and Berrellez got one of the residents to open it reluctantly. Inside, he found records of kilos matched with amounts of money, an obvious dope ledger, a photograph of a guy in flight dress in front of what looked to be a military jet, and photographs of some guys in combat. Hector asked the guy who the hell the people in the photographs were, and the guy said, "Oh, they are freedom fighters."

What the hell is this? Berrellez wondered. He left and went to a couple of the other houses that had been hit, and, Jesus, they were clean, the coffee was on, sometimes there were some doughnuts for the cops, and the same kind of documents showed up. But no dope, not a damn thing.

For a holy warrior, October 27, 1986, was a bad day. At the debriefing after the raid, Berrellez remembers one of the cops saying that the houses had been tipped to the raid by "elements of the CIA." And he thought, What? "I was shocked," he says now. "I was in a state of disbelief." He was supposed to believe that his own government was helping dopers? No way. "I didn't want to believe," he says.

And so he didn't. He was that rock-solid first-generation citizen, and he believed in America. He remembers having this ongoing argument with his dad about whether there was corruption in the United States like the old man had tasted in Mexico. His father would ask, Do you really think things are so clean here? And Hector would have none of it; damn right they're clean here. And he was clean, and he was in a good outfit (a position he is still passionate about—his absolute love for the troops he served with in the DEA), and he was in a holy war against a tide of poison.

In 1987, he was transferred to Mazatlán in Sinaloa, Mexico, to run the DEA station. Sinaloa was the drug center for Mexico; in the history of the Mexican drug cartels, all but one leader has been Sinaloan born and bred. He took the wife, got a beach house in the coastal city, and ran with the job. Two months into the assignment, *narcotraficantes* chased his wife and two-year-old daughter from the beach back to the house, and they had to be evacuated to the States.

In October 1988, Hector and some Mexican federal police hit a small hamlet that housed a ton of coke and twenty tons of marijuana. The firefight lasted three hours, with thousands of rounds exchanged. When three federales were mowed down on the field of fire, Hector managed to pull them to safety with another agent. He commandeered a cab to take the wounded to a hospital, then returned to the shoot-out. For this combat, Hector and two other agents at the scene were brought to the White House and given a medal by Attorney General Edwin Meese. He was on a roll that would eventually earn him twelve consecutive superior-performance awards.

In Mexico, Hector was running two hundred to three hundred informants, and he was bringing in a torrent of information on the drug world and its links to the Mexican government. But something else happened down there in Sinaloa that stuck in his mind. His army of informants was constantly reporting strange fortified bases scattered around Mexico, but they were not Mexican military bases. American military planes would land at these bases, and, his informants told him, the planes were shipping drugs. Camps in Durango, Sinaloa, Baja, Veracruz, all over Mexico. Hector wrote up these camps and the information he was getting on big drug shipments. And each month, he would go to Mexico City to meet with his DEA superiors and American-embassy staff, and he started mentioning these reports. He was told, Stay away from those bases; they're training camps, special operations. He thought, What the hell is this? I'm here to enforce the drug laws, and I'm being told to *do nothing*.

THE EMPTY ROOM SAGS WITH FATIGUE as the sports televisions quietly float in the corner. California's ban on smoking has emptied the watering holes. The hotel squats by a four-lane highway amid bland suburbs that blanket Sacramento's eastern flank against the Sierra Nevada. Everything is normal here; this is the visual bedrock of Ronald Reagan's America.

Gary Webb orders Maker's Mark on the rocks. He is a man of average height, with brown hair, a trim moustache, an easy smile, and laconic, laid-back speech, the basic language of Middle America. He moves easily, a kind of amble through life. His father was a marine, and his childhood meant moving a lot before finally coming to ground in Indiana, Kentucky, and Ohio. He's married to his high school sweetheart; they have three kids and live on a tree-lined cul-de-sac with a pool in back, a television in the family room, his Toyota with 150,000 miles in the drive, Sue's minivan, and on the cement the chalk outline of a hopscotch game. He looks white-collar, maybe sells insurance.

All he has ever wanted to be is a reporter. He started out as a kid, writing up sports results for a weekly at a nickel an inch. The Gary Webb who suddenly loomed up nationally with this bad talk about the CIA and drugs was a long time coming, and he came from the dull center of the country, and he came from an essay titled "What America Means to Me," for which he was runner-up in the fifth-grade essay contest, and he came from the smell of ink, the crackle of a little weekly where he nailed cold the week's tumult in the Little League.

Webb is not a drinker, probably because his marine father was, but now in the empty hotel bar, he is drinking. He is not used to talking about himself, because he is a reporter, and a reporter is not the story, but now he is talking about himself. When Gary Webb talks, he sometimes leans back, but often as not, he leans forward, and when he is really into what he is saying, he grabs his left wrist with his right hand as if he were taking his own pulse, and then his voice gets even flatter, and the words are very evenly spaced, and he never goes too fast, hardly any hint of rat-a-tat-tat—he is always measured and unexcited. But when he grabs that wrist, you can tell now that the words really matter. Because he believes. In facts. In publishing facts. In the fact that publishing facts makes a difference in how people look at things. Believes, without reason or question, believes absolutely. As for coincidence, it doesn't fit in with his mission. He also has no tolerance for conspiracy theories. By God, if he finds a conspiracy, it is not a theory, it is a fucking conspiracy, because it is grounded in facts.

When he was twenty-three, he was kind of drifting, living in the basement at Sue's house with her parents. He was writing rock 'n' roll stuff for a weekly, still grinding away at college, and about three units shy of a degree. His father walked out on the marriage, leaving his mother, a housewife, and his younger brother without a check. So Webb quit college to support them. A teacher in his journalism department told him that the strange guy who ran the *Post* in Lexington, Kentucky, set aside one day a week for walk-ins. Webb walked in and said, "I need a job."

The editor said, "Go do two pieces and bring them back in a week."

One was on the barmaids and strippers of Newport, Kentucky, the sin town across the river from Cincinnati. The editor tossed it aside and said, "Thrice-told tale." The other was on a guy who carved gravestones, that one the editor kind of liked. He said, "Bring me two more." Webb was shaken, went home and sat in the backyard, and then he thought, Fuck, I can do this.

This goes on for weeks. A kid calls the paper about the dog he's found run over in the street. He's taken it to the Humane Society; they want to put it to sleep, and the kid is very upset. Webb is sent out to see if he can do anything fit for a newspaper. He talks to the vet, who says it is hopeless, that the dog will never walk again, whether he operates or not. When Webb reports back to the editor, he says, "Get that guy on the phone," and after a few blunt words from the editor, by God, the vet is going to operate. And it works. The damn dog is leaping in the air. Finally, the dog goes home to the kid who found him, a kid in a wheelchair who seemed to identify with an injured mutt and was horrified at the idea that a cripple should be done away with. Story and photograph on the front page. Webb is hired. Years later, the old editor would tell him, "If that dog hadn't walked, you'd have never been hired."

There is a guy in the newsroom who is kind of burned out, a city editor. He watches the new hire for a few weeks. He tells him he will teach him the ropes, how to ferret out facts, how to find out damn near anything, how to be an investigative reporter. On one condition. He says Webb has to swear never to become a fucking editor. Webb agrees.

His first series was seventeen parts on organized crime in the coal industry. Then he moved up to a good job at the *Cleveland Plain Dealer* and was in heaven: Ohio was the mother lode of corruption in government. He got an offer from the *Mercury News* in 1987. After a brief bidding war, he moved the family west, great place to raise kids, and besides, during his father's wanderings as a marine, Webb happened to be born in California. Everything was fine. He was in the Sacramento bureau and so hardly ever in the newsroom, much less around editors. In a big story for the paper, he took on one of the area's major employers. After the first day of the story, the company bought a full-page ad refuting it. After the next installment, the company bought a two-page ad. Webb looked around and noticed that nothing happened to him. The paper backed him up.

GARY WEBB'S "DARK ALLIANCE" broke an old story. The history of the CIA's relationship with international drug dealers has been documented and published, yet it is almost completely unknown to most citizens and reporters. Webb himself had only a dim notion of this record. And so he reacted with horror when the implications of his research first began to become clear to him: that while much of the federal government fought narcotics as a plague, the CIA, in pursuing its foreign-policy goals, sometimes facilitated the work of drug traffickers. "Dark Alliance" is surrounded by a public record that bristles with similar instances of CIA connections with drug people:

- Alan Fiers, who headed the CIA Central American Task Force, testified during the Iran-contra hearings in August 1987, "With respect to [drug trafficking by] the resistance forces . . . it is not a couple of people. It is a lot of people."
- In 1983, fifty people, many of them Nicaraguans, were caught unloading a big coke shipment in San Francisco. A couple of them claimed an involvement with the CIA, and after a meeting between CIA officials and the U.S. attorney handling the case, $36,000 found in a bedside table was returned because it "belonged to the contras." This spring, when the CIA published its censored report on involvement of the agency with drug traffickers in the contra war (a report that exists solely because a firestorm erupted in Congress after Webb's series), this incident was explained thusly: "Based upon the information available to them at the time, CIA personnel reached the erroneous conclusion that one of the two individuals . . . was a former CIA asset." Logically, an admission that CIA "assets" can sometimes be drug dealers.
- n 1986, Wanda Palacio parted company with the Medellín cartel and started talking to Senator John Kerry's subcommittee, which was looking into the byways of the contra war and dope. Palacio said she'd witnessed two flights of coke out of Barranquilla, Colombia, on planes belonging to the CIA-contracted Southern Air Transport. She also had the dates and had seen the pilot. She also said Jorge Ochoa, another drug boss, said the flights were part of a "drugs for guns" deal. On September 26, 1986, Kerry took her eleven-page statement to William Weld, who was then the assistant attorney general in charge of the criminal division of the Justice Department. Weld

allowed that he was not surprised to find claims of "bum agents, former and current CIA agents" dabbling in dope deals with the Colombian cartels. On October 3, Weld's office rejected Palacio's statement and offer to be a witness because of what it saw as contradictions in her testimony. On October 5, 1986, the Sandinistas shot a CIA plane out of the sky and captured one of Oliver North's patriots, one Eugene Hasenfus. Palacio was sitting in Kerry's office when a photograph of Hasenfus's dead pilot flashed across the television screen. She whooped that the pilot was the same guy she'd seen in Colombia loading coke on the Southern Air Transport flight in early October 1985. An Associated Press reporter, Robert Parry, investigated the crash and obtained the pilot's logs, which showed that on October 2, 4, and 6, 1985, the pilot had taken a Southern Air Transport plane to Barranquilla, Colombia. Palacio took a polygraph on the matter and passed.

- Through much of the contra war, SETCO Air, an airline run by Juan Ramón Matta Ballesteros out of Honduras, was the principal airline used to transport supplies and personnel for the contras. Hector Berrellez later sent Ballesteros to Marion Federal Prison in Illinois to serve a couple of life sentences for dope peddling.

About the same time Gary Webb was making his bones at *The Cleveland Plain Dealer* and winning part of a Pulitzer at the *Mercury News*, Hector Berrellez was becoming a legend. After two years of living at ground zero in Sinaloa, he was brought home to Los Angeles in 1989 to take over the most significant investigation in DEA history: that of the murder of DEA agent Enrique "Kiki" Camarena. Camarena had been bagged in broad daylight from in front of the American consulate in Guadalajara in February 1986. His tortured body was found a month later. The investigation had stalled, so the DEA tossed it in Hector's lap. He ran with the new power, the raft of agents under his command, the huge budget for buying informants in Mexico. The case was a core matter for the DEA: The murder of Camarena was the event that gave the ragtag agency its martyr. The investigation was called Operation Leyenda, "Operation Legend."

During Operation Leyenda, a major drug guy in Sinaloa called Cochi Loco, "the Crazy Pig," put a contract on Hector's head. In the drug world, there are so many possible reasons for murder that a simple one is seldom clear. Whatever the immediate cause, in the early nineties a hit team was sent north to kill Hector.

One day in 1991, in the underground parking garage of the building in Los Angeles where the DEA and a bunch of federal agencies rented office space, someone walked up to a guy sitting in a car and clipped him in the head with a .22. The man died instantly and fell forward onto the steering wheel, and the sound of a car horn wailed through the garage. Hector remembers that they found him with the motor running, and neatly placed on the floorboard of the car was the gun, in a Mexican-tooled holster, and the two latex surgical gloves that had been worn by the hit man. Someone wanted a clear message delivered.

The dead man was a guy from the General Services Administration who happened to work in the same building as the DEA. He had been in some kind of a hurry and had pulled into a DEA parking space. The guy was a ringer for Hector's partner.

Three days after the hit, Hector picked up the phone in his office and heard the voice of Chichón Rico Urrea, a significant drug figure who was doing a stint in a prison in Guadalajara. Chichón told Hector, "You see what happened to your guy in the garage? That's going to happen to more of your guys."

Hector told the guy to go fuck himself, said he could kill all the fucking DEA guys he wanted.

But Hector was questioning his faith. The faith was the war on drugs. The faith was that he was a righteous soldier in this war. The faith was that he was risking his life for the forces of light against the forces of darkness. And he was Eliot Ness, goddammit; he was the most decorated guy anyone could remember in the DEA, the man running its key investigation, the guy who had killed people, the guy bloodied in the world of Mexican corruption. All of that Hector could handle—none of that could ever touch the faith.

But other things could. Things he saw and learned in Mexico. And things he saw in the United States. He began to doubt that there was a real commitment to win this war on drugs. He saw his government winking at too many narcotics connections. He took Kiki Camarena's murder personally, because as agents they were mirror images—gung-ho, committed drugbusters. And impediments to his investigation pissed Hector off. So in 1992, four years before Gary Webb sprang "Dark Alliance" on the world, Hector Berrellez sat down in his federal office in Los Angeles and picked up the phone and recommended action to the DEA. Things had come to his attention, and he thought, Somebody's gotta investigate this crap. In fact, he hoped to be that investigator.

Hector Berrellez wanted a criminal investigation of the Central Intelligence Agency. His $3 million snitch budget had brought in an unseemly harvest, report after report from informants that in the eighties CIA-leased aircraft were flying cocaine into places like the air force base in Homestead, Florida, and the airfield north of Tucson long believed to be a CIA base. And that these planes were flying guns south. One of his witnesses in the Camarena case told him about flying in a U.S. military plane loaded with drugs from Guadalajara to Homestead. Other informants told him that major drug figures, including Rafael Caro Quintero, the man finally imprisoned for the Camarena murder, were getting guns delivered through CIA connections. Everywhere he turned, he ran into dope guys who had CIA connections, and to a narc this didn't look right. "I can't believe," he told his superiors, "that the CIA is handling all this shit and doesn't know what these pilots are doing." His superiors asked if he had hard evidence of actual CIA case officers moving dope, and he said no, just lots of people they employed. All intelligence services use the fabled cutouts to separate themselves from their grubby work.

The DEA in Washington asked for a memo, so Hector fired off a summary of his telephone request. Agents were assigned, and Hector shipped every snippet of new information to this team. Nothing came of the investigation. The DEA team came out and debriefed him and some of his agents. And then, silence.

Hector's Camarena work had burrowed deep, very deep, inside the Mexican government and found endless rot. With the vote on NAFTA in the air in the fall of 1993, his investigation started to get pressure, then his budget was cut. By 1994, after Justice Department officials had been in Mexico City, he was told, "Don't report that crap anymore." It was clear to Hector that the Mexican government wanted this Camarena investigation reined in. In early 1995, he learned of his future in a curious way. One of Hector's informants in Mexico City called another one of his informants in Los Angeles and said, Hector's getting transferred to Washington. The guy in Los Angeles said, No, no, Hector's still here. Two months later, in April 1995, Berrellez was transferred to Washington, D.C. Over the years, Hector had become used to a certain amount of duplicity in the DEA. Some of his fellow agents, he had come to believe, were actually members of the CIA. The DEA had been penetrated.

At headquarters, Hector sat in an office with nothing to do. "There ain't no fucking drug war," he says now. "I was even called un-American. Nobody cares about this shit." He started going a little crazy. Each day, he checked in to a blank schedule. So he caught a lot of double features.

In September 1996, he retired. He had had enough. The most decorated soldier in the war on drugs kind of faded out at the movies.

IN THE NEWS BUSINESS, if you hang around long enough, you get a chance to find out who you are. Gary Webb was determined not to find out he was something ugly.

"I became convinced," he remembers, "that we're going to look back on the whole war on drugs fifty years from now like we look back on the McCarthy era and say, How did we ever let this stuff get so out of hand? How come nobody ever stood up and said, *This is bullshit?* I thought I had an obligation because I had the power at that point to tell people, Don't believe what you are being told about this war on drugs, because it is a lie. Very few people were in the position I was in, where I was able to write shit and get it in the newspapers. It was a very rare privilege. The editors at the *Mercury* gave me a lot of freedom because I produced. Then I got into this thing."

In December 1995, Webb wrote out his project memo, and suddenly, "I realized what we were saying here. I'm sitting at home, and this e-mail comes from a friend at the *Los Angeles Times*. And I had told him vaguely about this interesting story I was working on. I told him that he had no idea what his fucking government is capable of.

"And I was depressed because this was so horrible. It was like some guy told me that he had gone through the looking glass and was in this netherworld that 99 percent of the American public would never believe existed. That's where I felt I was. When I sat down and wrote the project memo and said, Here's what we're going to say, and we're going to be accusing the government of bringing drugs into the country, essentially; and we've spent billions of dollars and locked up Americans for selling shit that the government helps to come into the country—is just. . . . If you believe in democracy and you believe in justice, it's fucking awful."

For six weeks after his series came out, Webb waited in a kind of honeymoon. His e-mail was exploding, he recalls, "from ordinary people who said, 'This has restored my faith in newspapers.' It was from college students, housewives that heard me on the radio; it was really remarkable to think that journalism could have this kind of effect on people, that people were out marching in the streets because of something that you had written. There was a chance that this scab was going to come off, and we were going to see all the stuff that had been hidden from us all these years. The thing that surprised me was that there was no response from the press, from the government. It was total silence."

Finally, in early October, the *Washington Post* ran a story by Roberto Suro and Walter Pincus headlined, THE CIA AND CRACK: EVIDENCE IS LACKING OF ALLEGED PLOT. The story focused in part on the fact that Webb had given a defense attorney questions to ask Oscar Danilo Blandón about his CIA connections. It also quoted experts who denied that the crack epidemic originated in Los Angeles, disputed that Freeway Rick Ross and Blandón were significant national players in the cocaine trade of the eighties (pegging Blandón's coke business at five tons over the decade, whereas Webb had evidence that it was more like two to five tons per year). And, the article continued, there was no evidence that the black community had been deliberately targeted (the "plot" referred to in the headline and a claim never made by Webb), that the CIA knew about Blandón's drug deals (also a claim never made by Webb, who in the series merely connected Blandón to CIA agents), or that Blandón had ever kicked in more than $60,000 to the contra cause (the *Post* based this number on unnamed law-enforcement officials; Webb based his estimate of millions of dollars to the contras from dope sales on grand-jury testimony and court documents). Perhaps the best summary of the *Post*'s retort to Webb came from the paper's own ombudsman, Geneva Overholser, some weeks later: "The *Post* . . . showed more passion for sniffing out the flaws in San Jose's answer than for sniffing out a better answer themselves. They were stronger on how much less money was contributed to the contras by the *Mercury News*'s villains than their series claimed, how much less cocaine was introduced into L.A. than on how significant it is that any of these assertions are true."

In late October, the *Los Angeles Times* and the *New York Times* weighed in on consecutive days. The *Los Angeles Times* had two years before described Freeway Rick Ross vividly: "If there was an eye to the storm, if there was a criminal mastermind behind crack's decade-long reign, if there was one outlaw capitalist most responsible for flooding Los Angeles's streets with mass-marketed cocaine, his name was Freeway Rick. . . . Ross did more than anyone else to democratize it, boosting volume, slashing prices, and spreading disease on a scale never before conceived. . . . While most other dealers toiled at the bottom rungs of the market, his coast-to-coast conglomerate was selling more than five hundred thousand rocks a day, a staggering turnover that put the drug within reach of anyone with a few dollars." In the 1996 response to Webb's series, the *Los Angeles Times* described Ross as one of many "interchangeable characters" and stated, "How the crack epidemic reached that extreme, on some level, had nothing to do with Ross." Both stories were written by the same reporter, Jesse Katz, and the 1996 story failed to mention his earlier characterization. The long *New York Times* piece the following day quoted unnamed government officials, CIA personnel, drug agents, and contras, and noted that "officials said the CIA had no record of Mr. Blandón before he appeared as a central figure in the series in the *Mercury News*."

A common chord ran through the responses of all three papers: It never really happened, and if it did happen, it was on a small scale, and anyway it was old news, because both the Kerry report and a few wire stories in the eighties had touched on the contra-cocaine connection. What is missing from the press responses, despite their length, is a sense that anyone spent as much energy investigating Webb's case as attempting to refute it. The "Dark Alliance" series was passionate, not clinical. The headlines were tabloid, not restrained. But whatever sins were committed in the presentation of the series, they cannot honestly be used to dismiss its content. It is puzzling that the *New York Times* felt it could discredit the story by quoting anonymous intelligence officials (a tack it hardly followed in publishing the Pentagon Papers). In contrast, what is striking in Webb's series is the copious citation of documents. (In the *Mercury News*'s website version—cgi.sjmercury.com/drugs/postscriptfeatures.htm—are the hyperlinked facsimiles of documents that tug one into the dark world of drugs and agents.) But when Jerry Ceppos, the executive editor of the *Mercury News,* wrote a letter in response to the *Post*'s knockdown, the paper refused to print it because a defense of Webb's work would have resulted in spreading yet more "misinformation."

Despite Ceppos's initial defense of the series, the *Mercury News* seemed to choke on these attacks, and Webb could sense a sea change. But he kept on working, building a bigger base of facts, following its implications deeper into the government. When the *Mercury News* forced him to choose between a $600,000 movie offer and book deals and staying on the story, Webb picked the story. He kept discovering people who had flown suitcases full of money to Miami from dope sales for the contras. He documented Blandón's contra dope sales from '82 through '86. Gary Webb was on a tear; he was going to advance the story. Almost none of this was published by the *Mercury News;* the paper grudgingly ran (and buried) one last story on New Year's Eve 1996.

The paper had printed the story of the decade, the one with Pulitzer prize written all over it, and now was unmistakably backing off it. Webb entered a kind of Orwellian world where no one said anything, but there was this thing in the air. The *Mercury News* assigned one of its own reporters to review the series, using the stories of the *L.A. Times,* the *New York Times,* and the *Washington Post* as the benchmark for what was fact.

Webb wouldn't admit it to himself, but he had become a dead man walking.

WHEN HECTOR BERRELLEZ SPENT his year going to movies in Washington, he knew he was finished in the DEA. One day in October 1996, a month after he retired, Hector Berrellez picked up a newspaper and read this big story about a guy named Gary Webb. Hector had lived in shadows, and talking to reporters had not been his style. "As I read, I thought, This shit is true," he says now. He hadn't a doubt about what Webb was saying. He saw the reporter as doomed. Webb had hit a sensitive area, and for it he would be attacked and disbelieved. Hector knew all about the Big Dog and the Big Boy rules.

Hector's body aches from the weight of secrets. When we meet, he is in a white sport shirt, slacks, a blue blazer with brass buttons, and a shoulder-holstered 9mm with fifteen rounds in the clip and two more clips strapped under his right arm. He may be a little over-armed for his Los Angeles private-investigation agency (the Mayo Group, which handles the woes of figures in the entertainment industry—that pesky stalker, that missing money—for a fat fee up front and two hundred dollars an hour), but not for his history. For the rest of his life, Hector Berrellez will be sitting in nice hotels like this one with a cup of coffee in his hand, a 9mm under his jacket, and very quick eyes.

He saw a lot of things and remembers almost all of them. He wrote volumes of reports. In 1997, he was interviewed by Justice Department officials about those unseemly drug ledgers and contra materials he saw during the raid on the fourteen Blandón stash houses back in 1986. His interviewers wanted particularly to know whether anyone besides Hector had seen them. They then told Hector that they couldn't find the seized material anymore.

Before he retired, Hector was summoned to Washington to brief Attorney General Janet Reno on Mexican corruption. He talked to her at length about how the very officials she was dealing with in Mexico had direct links to drug cartels. He remembers that she asked very few questions.

Now he sits in the nice lounge of the nice hotel, and he believes the CIA is in the dope business; he believes the agency ran camps in Mexico for the contras, with big planes flying in and out full of dope. He now knows in his bones what the hell he really saw on October 27, 1986, when he hit the door of that house in the Los Angeles area and was greeted with politeness and fresh coffee.

But he doesn't carry a smoking gun around. The photos, the ledgers, all the stuff the cops found that morning as they hit fourteen sterile stash houses where all the occupants seemed to be expecting company, all that material went to Washington and seems to have vanished. All those reports he wrote for years while in Mexico and then later running the Camarena case, those detailed reports of how he kept stumbling into dope deals done by CIA assets, never produced any results or even a substantive response.

Hector Berrellez is kind of a freak. He is decorated; he is an official hero with a smiling Ed Meese standing next to him in an official White House photograph. He pulled twenty-four years and retired with honors. He is, at least for the moment, neither discredited nor smeared. Probably because until this moment, he's kept silent.

And Hector Berrellez thinks that if the blacks and the browns and the poor whites who are zombies on dope ever get a drift of what he found out, well, there is going to be blood in the streets, he figures—there is going to be hell to pay.

He tells me a story that kind of sums up the place he finally landed in, the place that Gary Webb finally landed in. The place where you wonder if you are kind of nuts, since no one else seems to think anything is wrong. An agent he knows was deep in therapy, kind of cracking up from the undercover life. And the agent's shrink decided the guy was delusional, was living in some nutcase world of weird fantasies. So the doctor talked to Hector about his patient, about whether all the bullshit this guy was claiming was true, about dead men and women and children, strange crap like that. And he made a list of his patient's delusions, and he ticked them off to Hector. And Hector listened to them one by one and said, "Oh, that one, that's true. This one, yeah, that happened also." It went on like that. And finally, Hector could tell the shrink wondered just who was nuts—Hector, his patient, or himself.

ON SUNDAY, MAY 11, 1997, Gary Webb was hanging wallpaper in his kitchen when the *San Jose Mercury News* published a column by executive editor Jerry Ceppos that was widely read as a repudiation of Webb's series. It was an odd composition that retracted nothing but apologized for everything. Ceppos wrote, "Although the members of the drug ring met with contra leaders paid by the CIA and Webb believes the relationship with the CIA was a tight one, I feel we did not have proof that top CIA officials knew of the relationship." Fair enough, except that Webb never wrote that top CIA officials knew of the contra-cocaine connection. The national press wrote front-page stories saying that the *San Jose Mercury News* was backing off its notorious series about crack. The world had been restored to its proper order. Webb fell silent. He had to deal with his own nature. He is not good at being politic. "I'm just fucking stubborn," he says, "and that's all there was to it, because I knew this was a good story, and I knew it wasn't over yet, and I really had no idea of what else to do. What else was I going to do?"

What he did was have the Newspaper Guild represent him in arbitration with the *Mercury News* over the decision to ship him to the wasteland of Cupertino. "I'm going to go through arbitration, and I'm going to win the arbitration, and I'm going to go to work," he says. "I was just going to fight it out. This was what I did, this was me, I was a reporter. This was a calling; it was not something you do eight to five. People were not exactly beating down my door, saying, Well, okay, come work for us. I was . . . unreliable."

So he went to Cupertino, and he wrote stories about constipated horses and refused to let his byline be printed. And then he went to his apartment and missed his wife and family and watched *Caddyshack* endlessly. He was a creature living a ghostly life.

The only thing he didn't figure on was himself. Webb slid into depression. Every week, the 150-mile drive between his family in Sacramento and his job in Cupertino became harder. Every day, it was harder to get out of bed and go to work.

And he was very angry most of the time.

He says, "I was going to live in my own house and see my own kids. At some point, I figured something was going to give." Finally, he couldn't make it to work and took vacation time. When that was used up in early August, he started calling in sick. After that, he went on medical leave. A doctor examined him and said, "You are under a great deal of stress," and diagnosed him as having severe depression. He couldn't sleep. He couldn't do much of anything. He decided to write a book about "Dark Alliance," but this time no one wanted it. His agent was turned down by twenty-five publishers before finding a small press, Seven Stories, that operates as a kind of New York court of last resort.

A job offer came from the California state legislature to conduct investigations for the government-oversight committee at about the same money he made for the *Mercury News*. His wife said, Take the job. Why hang around in this limbo? Webb thought about her words and told himself, What do I win even if I do win in arbitration? I get to go back to my office and get bullshitted the rest of my life. He watered his lawn, worked on the house, read more and more contra stuff. Drifted in a sea of depression.

"I didn't know what to do if I couldn't be a reporter," he says "So all of a sudden, I was standing there on the edge of the cliff, and I don't have what I was doing for the last twenty years—I don't have that to do anymore. I felt like I was neutered. I called up the Guild and said, 'Let's see if they want to settle this case.' They sent me a letter of resignation that I had to sign."

Webb carried the letter with him from November 19 until December 10 of last year. Every day, he got up to sign the letter and mail it. Every night, he went to bed with the letter unsigned. His wife would ask, Have you signed it? Somebody from the *Mercury* kept calling the Guild and asking, Has he signed it yet?

"I mean," he says softly, "writing my name on that thing meant the end of my career. I saw it as a sort of surrender. It was like signing," and here he hesitates for several seconds, "my death certificate."

But finally he signed, and now he is functionally banned from the business. He's the guy nobody wants, the one who fucked up, the one who said bad things. Officially, he is dead, the guy who wrote the discredited series, the one who questioned the moral authority of the United States government.

If Gary Webb could have talked to a Hector Berrellez in the fall of 1996, when his stories were being erased by the media, Hector would have been like a savior to him. "Because he would have shown what I was reporting was not an aberration," Webb says now, "that this was part of a pattern of CIA involvement with drugs. And he would have been believed." But Webb was not that lucky, and the Hectors of the world were not that ready to talk then. So Webb was left out there alone, one guy with a bunch of interviews and documents. One guy who answered a question no one wanted asked.

I CAN HEAR HECTOR BERRELLEZ telling me that I will never find a smoking gun. I can hear the critics of Gary Webb explaining that all he has is circumstantial evidence. And I remember that American prisons are full of people put there by circumstantial evidence. Like anyone who dips into the world of the CIA, I find myself questioning the plain facts I read and asking myself, Does this really mean what I think it means?

- In 1982, the head of the CIA got a special exemption from the federal requirement to report dealings with drug traffickers. Why did the CIA need such an exemption?
- Courthouse documents attest to the fact that the Blandón drug organization moved tons of dope for years with impunity, shipped millions to be laundered in Florida, and then bought arms for the contras. Why are Gary Webb's detractors not looking at these documents and others instead of bashing Webb over the head?
- The internal CIA report of contra cocaine activity has never been released. The Justice Department investigation of Webb's charges has never been released. The CIA has released a censored report on only one volume of Webb's charges. The contra war is over, yet this material is kept secret. Why aren't the major newspapers filing Freedom of Information requests for these studies?
- The fifty-year history of CIA involvement with heroin traffickers and other drug connections is restricted to academic studies and fringe publications. Those journalists who find themselves covering the war on drugs should read Alfred McCoy's massive study, *The Politics of Heroin: CIA Complicity in the Global Drug Trade,* or Peter Dale Scott and Jonathan Marshall's *Cocaine Politics: Drugs, Armies, and the CIA in Central America.*
- Following the release of "Dark Alliance," Senator John Kerry told the

Washington Post, "There is no question in my mind that people affiliated with, on the payroll of, and carrying the credentials of, the CIA were involved in drug trafficking while involved in support of the contras." Why has the massive Kerry report been ignored to this day?

- On March 16, 1998, the CIA inspector general, Frederick P. Hitz, testified before the House Intelligence Committee. "Let me be frank," he said. "There are instances where CIA did not, in an expeditious or consistent fashion, cut off relationships with individuals supporting the contra program who were alleged to have engaged in drug-trafficking activity, or take action to resolve the allegations."

  Representative Norman Dicks of Washington then asked, "Did any of these allegations involve trafficking in the United States?"

  "Yes," Hitz answered.

The question is why a mountain of evidence about the CIA and drugs is ignored and why the legitimate field of inquiry opened by Webb remains unpursued and has become journalistic taboo.

Maybe the CIA is great for America. But if it is, surely it can roll up its sleeves and show us its veins.

WEBB AND HIS WIFE, SUE, are standing in the driveway with me after a Thai dinner in Sacramento. The night is fresh; spring is in the air. A frog croaks from the backyard on the quiet and safe suburban street. Sue has just finished rattling off details from one facet of the contra war, the CIA drug-airline operation run out of Ilopango airfield in El Salvador. She seems to have absorbed a library of material over the last three years of her husband's obsession. Before, he always worked like hell, she knows, but on this one he brought it home. He could not keep it separated from his wife and family and his weekly hockey games. So Sue, with her winning smile and cheerful ways, has become an authority on America's dark pages. And we stand there in the fine evening air, the rush of spring surging through the trees and grass and shrubs, talking about the endless details of this buried episode in the secret history.

And I wonder how Webb deals with it, with all the hard work done, with all the facts and documents devoured, and with all this diligent toil resulting in his personal ruin, depriving him of the only kind of work he has ever wanted in his life.

And I remember what he said earlier that day while he sat in his study, leaning toward me, his right hand gripping his left wrist: "The trail is littered with bodies. You go down the last ten years, and there is a skeleton here and a skeleton there of somebody that found out about it and wrote about it. I thought that this is the truth, and what can they do to you if you tell the truth? What can they do to you if you write the truth?"

From the editors: In 2004, Gary Webb was found dead with two gunshot wounds to the head. His death was officially ruled a suicide.

Ike and Lyndon

Portrait of the Artist and the President

From *Harper's*, March 2000

HE KNOWS ALL THEIR FACES, Washington from memory, the other presidents from books, and he's been nailing them with pastels, tempera, pencil sketches, and oils since the late 1970s. Sometimes he identifies them—Jackson, Washington, Lincoln, and the like—sometimes not. But mostly, he just lays their faces out there for the world to see. After all, they're former presidents of the United States of America. His own name he always signs: Ike Edward Morgan.

Austin is his town; he was born in the area in 1958. He started painting here in the seventies, though at that time it was fire hydrants for the city. Since 1977 he's lived mostly in the state mental hospital, and he works all the time. He rises, gets his morning meds around 7:30 or 8:00, drops by social worker David Edington's office to say hello, and then is off to work. When the fever of creativity is really on him, he might knock out a dozen portraits a week. They're not always presidents, but the presidents are the ones that first catch a person's eye. His work is collected, hangs in New York and Europe. He belongs to that vast band of people who are self-taught, the kind of people who tend to come up the hard way yet have this feel for life. Critics now call the kind of thing Ike Morgan does Outsider Art.

He is a handsome man, with fine dark skin, a soft smile. He moves with grace and concentration as he bends over his favorite object, a blank piece of paper, canvas, or cardboard, and begins to draw. The movement of his hand is light but not tentative. Nor does he wonder about color. He knows, he just knows. He is said to get a special smile whenever he goes shopping for art supplies, and some think this smile comes from contemplating all the reams of paper and piles of colors waiting to be made into something with form and fire and feeling. He lives a life as dedicated as that of a Benedictine monk.

His images are on display at a gallery in Waxahachie, just south of Dallas. I stand there in a huge room with dozens of presidents staring down at me, and I mean staring, because if there is one thing Ike Morgan never misses it's the eyes, the burning eyes of human beings looking out with wonder or caution at the world. He lives in a world of color. I'm standing here with Bruce and Julie Webb, the gallery owners, Ike's friends, and passionate fans of Outsider Art. We're looking at Ike Morgan's $1 bill. It's about five feet by three feet and orange, and Washington's face is a rage of emotion, dotted with daubs of paint, and looks a lot like those stop signs deer hunters shoot up during the season. I kind of wish they'd use this design for the new model of the single they're planning, not because it would be hell on counterfeiters, though I'm sure it would, but because it captures the rage and energy that makes me love my country, the high-stepping, hog-calling, hip-hopping style that never rests, the blues bleeding out of Mississippi and the Sousa marches wailing so soulfully out of West Point and the constant flood of elevator music rising ominously above the levees, the lack of ease, the need for black coffee, hard liquor, support bras, and automatic weapons, the pedal to the metal, freeway love at 3:00 A.M., and hold the mayo. It is all there in Washington's face, raked with buckshots of paint, screaming off an orange background that is hot to the touch. I tell you this is blowtorch money, currency from hell, and it is hanging on a wall in a huge old gallery in Waxahachie about a half block from the courthouse square where a monument to the big war—the one that ripped this nation open and spilled its guts out; you know, Mr. Lincoln's war—stands tall and proud in the shape of a Confederate soldier at attention forever in the stone ranks of the lost cause. I need a wad of this orange money so it can sing to me in the morning and scream out Charlie Parker riffs at midnight.

I amble over to this big table and riffle through piles of Ike Morgan's paintings—down in Austin the state of Texas has had to rent space to store Ike's work, since he is a working fool and the state has been in charge of him since 1977—and there is Lyndon Baines Johnson. I'd already seen Ike's black Richard Nixon, with red lips, intense blue eyes, and a green background that looks electric. But Lyndon is special; he's part of what I've come for. I got up one day and had a notion: that in the state mental hospital in Austin, Texas, one Ike Edward Morgan, diagnosed psychotic, was capturing the color and fury and song—well, some of the song, since Ike is an eight-track man loyal to the musical technology loose in the republic at the time he was locked up—and love and history of my times as we grind and stagger into yet another millennium. And that a mile or two or three from Ike in a huge white building—a monstrous thing that looks, honest to God, like some white whale that beached itself deep in the heart of Texas, a presidential library that opened in the early seventies to the howls of 2,000 protesters and the only one of the eleven that has no admission charge—Lyndon is rising from his long black night, shaking his big-eared head, brushing those damned yellow rose petals off his britches, and coming awake after all those years of JFK worship, after the ringing in his ears from punks like me shouting, HEY HEY LBJ / HOW MANY KIDS DID YOU KILL TODAY! getting up as the American presidency toddles through the Clinton years after crawling through the Bush years and spending what out of kindness we might call the Dreamtime of the Reagan years. Lyndon's arising, clearing his throat, and letting loose with a yowl that cuts right through the cloud of Prozac hanging over the republic like the scream of a mountain lion coming off the peak in the night, and we snap alert and realize that after this cavalcade, one captured in paint by Ike Morgan—this cavalcade of Nixon, Ford, Carter, Reagan, Bush, Clinton—Lyndon Baines Johnson, the man who took us to Nam in a handbasket, the man described by George Reedy, his own presidential press secretary, in this way: "Were there nothing to look at save LBJ's personal relationships with other people, it would be merciful to forget him altogether. But there is much more to look at. He may have been a son of a bitch, but he was a colossal son of a bitch . . ." Well, this Johnson may have been the last president who knew how to run the government and the last one to really have any practical handle on this vision stuff.

I know, you think I'm into the paint thinner again, but listen up: Head Start, civil rights, education, endowments for the arts and humanities, Medicare, clean air and water, wilderness protection, urban housing—that terrible big government we denounce and then we hitch up our pants and belly up to was built by Johnson. John Kennedy went down in Dallas November 22, 1963, with a legislative program that had been largely frozen since he took office, and by June 1964 LBJ had begun to ram 400 bills through the U.S. Congress. The man was compulsive. When we put the boots to him, and he went back to his ranch on the Pedernales, he told his hands, "I want each of you to make a solemn pledge that you will not go to bed tonight until you are sure that every steer has everything he needs. We've got a chance of producing some of the finest beef in this country if we work at it, if we dedicate ourselves to the job. And if we treat those hens with loving care, we should be able to produce the finest eggs in the country. Really fresh. But it will mean working every minute of every day." Yesssssssssir.

So I snapped alert one day with this waking nightmare—that Lyndon Baines Johnson was back—and looked and listened hard to Johnson's first year in office, four cassettes called *Taking Charge: The Johnson White House Tapes, 1963–64*, and realized I hadn't heard such talk since I and millions just like me chased LBJ from public life and put him in this big damned tomb of a presidential library a few miles from where Ike Morgan captures American history in the state mental hospital. So once this notion came to me, there was really nothing I could do.

Except go.

And visit the two great artists of the End Time.

VIETNAM RAP ARTISTS

WEDNESDAY, MAY 27, 1964

LBJ: *Got lots of troubles.*

SENATOR RICHARD RUSSELL: *Well, we all have those.*

LBJ: *What do you think of this Vietnam thing? I'd like to hear you talk a little bit.*

HARDLY GOT JFK UNDERGROUND and the family moved in, and hell's a-popping all over the place. Because it always is that way around Lyndon Johnson. Most presidents leave office and disappear into the boredom served up by American historians, a native class of the enfeebled. But not our boy Lyndon. I'm up in the stacks, 36 million documents all snoring in red boxes on black shelves, the air holding steady at seventy degrees, the humidity an even 50 percent, so that the Vietnam War can endure and rage on here for centuries. All the voices still talk here, because Johnson, that tricky son of a bitch, taped everybody who talked to him. He just forgot to tell them about it. On one tape he wants to get out front on this Negro issue—especially being a southern man and all that—so he's going to appoint Carl Rowan, a newspaper guy, to replace Edward R. Murrow as the head of the United States Information Agency. But Johnson knows he's got to slide this appointment through John McClellan's Senate committee, and he knows that McClellan of Arkansas is a stone-cold segregationist. So he picks up the phone on January 16 and says, "John, I've got a little problem. I don't want to embarrass you in any way, and the best way to avoid it is talk to you beforehand so you know what the problem is. Mr. Ed Murrow is dying with cancer of the lung. . . . I've got a good solid man that's went around the world with me. . . . But he's a Negro . . ."

McClellan says evenly, "I doubt if I'm going against this. You do what you want to."

But Johnson is having none of this. "I know what your problems are," he offers. "I don't want you to cut his guts out because he's Negro. And I've seen you operate with a knife and I have seen a few people get de-nutted."

McClellan, well, hell, he's a United States senator, and this sounds like a bit much to him, so he says, "I wouldn't say that."

Johnson fires back, "I didn't want you to . . . send him home one day without his peter."

"I'm not going to do that."

"I've seen you operate, John."

HARRY MIDDLETON WORKED FOR Johnson as a speechwriter from 1966 to 1968, when everything was falling apart. Now he runs the LBJ presidential library. But what he has really done is make one key decision: to open up the tapes. There are 9,500 recordings, half opened already, the rest to be made public over the next few years. When Middleton first decided to open them, he didn't know what was in them—they were a "pig in a poke," he says.

But he wanted them opened on his watch.

Because he had to know that if anything was going to bring Lyndon Johnson back from the historical trash can, it had to be his voice operating, doing deals, and bullying a nation to his will.

LIVE OAK, THIN SOIL, AND BLUE SKY cover the land, and under the hill country, just below the skin, is the rock, and when ground is abused the soil flows away and rock slaps the world in the face. Fine limestone gates frame entryways to big ranches hidden in the trees, and then the fist of the hill country takes over, and lonely trailers or houses on piles pop up and goats chew the ground. The sign outside the smokehouse says YOUNG ROASTING PIGS. Down the road a taxidermist touts white-tail mounts with limited lifetime warranties. Just outside Johnson City, a dead raccoon lies by the road. LBJ's hometown is a hamlet of 1,100 souls selling pop and lunch to the straggling visitors to the dead god. The earth cries out for strong drink and gets Baptist churches. This is the place where white people learned to sink into the blues.

A sign at the LBJ National Historical Park gives a brief outline of the world he long ago found in these green soft hills of cactus, trees, and thin soil: NO PLUMBING. NO ELECTRICITY. . . . NO PLACE TO BUY A LOAF OF BREAD OR A POUND OF MEAT. Just down the street is Johnson's boyhood home, a white clapboard thing with a swing on the porch and not much else (it's bigger inside than it looks, a park guard advises).

Fifteen miles or so to the west, LBJ sleeps in his family's burying ground, and the hills roll on, and come spring and some rain the wildflowers bloom and his ranch, the one he bought in the fifties with the loot that befalls a senator, looks like the way life ought to be. You come from this kind of place, and you stay hungry. In the fifties, when LBJ was Senate majority leader, he prided himself on getting one of the early car phones, and then one day it rang while Johnson was out rolling around and it was Everett Dirksen, the Senate minority leader, calling up to tell Lyndon he'd just got a car phone. Johnson cut him off with an excuse me, I have to go, since my other car phone is ringing. Johnson could never get enough love, enough applause, enough of anything, and his hunger made millions dislike him. When his body lay in state in the white whale of a library in Austin he'd built to guard his reputation, Harry Middleton assigned a guy to count just how many people went by the coffin. When asked at the time why in the hell this mattered, he said, "Because I know that somewhere, sometime, President Johnson's going to ask me."

I stand there in the bright sun and let the clean air wash my soul and wonder when the war will end. Johnson City is the kind of crossroads where a lazy dog can cross the highway without a care. And Johnson lived and died a dumb shitkicker in the eyes of a lot of people. But then country boys for generations have been fleecing people who saw things that way. When Charles de Gaulle came to bury John Kennedy in November of 1963, he said: now this man Kennedy is the country's mask, but this man Johnson, he's the country's real face.

RUSSELL: *And I don't see how we're ever going to get out of it without fighting a major war with the Chinese and all of them down there in those rice paddies and jungles. . . . I just don't know what to do.*

LBJ: *That's the way I've been feeling for six months.*

HIS HANDSHAKE IS SOFT TO THE touch and so is his voice. He is not keen on eye contact but he recognizes the power of eyes, and they blaze right out of each of his portraits. It is about eighty degrees today but Ike Morgan likes the feel of a lot of loose clothing, and so he wears two pairs of pants, a bulky sweater, and a parka. It took the state of Texas hardly more than a month to decide he was not competent to stand trial back in the spring of 1977, and then after two years he got out of the state hospital for the criminally insane and wound up here at Austin State Hospital, in the heart of the city, with its generous smear of live oak trees. For a time he had spells when he still felt the anger, but then the drawing took hold, and also one of the hospital workers, Jim Pirtle, noticed his work and showed it to a Houston art dealer, and Ike Morgan was on his way from being state case number #086146 to being an artist. Ike still sometimes draws Jim Pirtle, even though he moved on years ago.

Since 1991, he's been on Clozaril, one of the newer drugs for psychotics, which David Edington, for years his social worker, believes has stilled Ike's anger and given him the feel for more speech. Now the state is easing Ike into a kind of halfway house, but he is not anxious to move. He likes the routine of the hospital, he tells me, and likes the room and time for work. "I don't got nothing against being here," he rolls on with that soft voice. "I forget what the days are. I work and accomplish things. People wonder why I want to stay at a dump like this, but it evens out."

"I started doing artwork," Ike explains, "about the same time I learned to tell time—when I went to school."

So he stays in and draws turtles, birds, bears, rock stars, apes, and presidents—especially presidents. He shows twenty-seven poster-size George Washingtons he recently whipped out (four or five hours a piece he figures). I particularly like the Washington with yellow hair, a purple-brown face, blue suit, and yellow ruffled shirt. Ike goes with whatever colors he finds in his box and has no prejudice in these matters—"I like orange, red, blue, and green and lots of other colors."

I tell Ike Morgan that I am very fond of the purple and brown Washington, and he says, "That is a very nice thing to say."

Across the lawn, just past Guadalupe Street, the straight and woolly world of Austin begins. I point to it and ask Ike, who comes and goes and now rides the bus into town for classes three days a week, what he thinks of all that out there. He looks where I point and says, "I've been out there. I've got friends out there. And sometimes you've got to draw the line."

WE TALK ABOUT HOT PEPPERS, decent French cookware, and why a career officer, a good Catholic boy from San Antonio, the father of six children, Major Ted Gittinger, walked out on the United States Army. Now he is part of the staff of the LBJ presidential library; in fact, a telegram he sent in 1956 to Senator Johnson seeking an appointment to West Point (he didn't get it) is part of the collection. But by 1970, after a tour in Vietnam as an artillery officer, he was teaching ROTC at Sam Houston State in east Texas and his graduates were coming home with tales of the collapse of military discipline. He'd already had a taste of that during his tour in Nam, with an army starting to be devoured by cheap dope and a racial Grand Canyon where there was no color line when the bullets flew at the front and there was hell to pay between whites and blacks when on leave at the rear.

"I resigned," he says flatly. "I was sick at heart at what I had seen in the army and the country. I was afraid my country was coming apart at the seams."

So he became a college teacher and wound up at the library doing oral history. In a real sense, he's spent a quarter century or so in Saigon.

Looking into this thing called Lyndon Johnson, Gittinger says, "I lost friends. He lost my war. But I'm not bitter. I just didn't have the heart to go on and do any job in the military. We weren't going to win, and I didn't want to be the last guy killed in Vietnam."

So he goes over and over this war, especially that tape with those Vietnam rap artists Ice LBJ and Senator Richard Snoopy Dogg Russell, and he's left with, well, they meant well, and yet everything got fucked up.

Downstairs a guard tells me that one thing he learned on this job is to never ask Vietnam veterans about Johnson.

I ask why.

"Because a lot of them don't like him."

Gittinger doesn't feel that way, but still he's not all that settled on the war yet. He thinks maybe forty years from now scholars will get a better bead on it, that things will sort of calm down once guys like him and me die. Because for a whole bunch of us, whether vets or goddamn protesters, it just doesn't seem to end. He eyes me and says, "You know how you can tell a bullet's close? You hear this whump, that's from air filling the hole as it goes by you."

So we talk inside Johnson's tomb about this monster named LBJ. Part of what neither of us ever saw coming was that this paranoid, overbearing, egotistical braggart would overwhelm our defenses by abandoning his own.

LBJ is the dead man talking.

Later, Gittinger walks me away from this cacophony of voices into the outside pavilion and points to the blooming mountain laurels.

"Smell it," he encourages me.

I do.

"What's it like?"

I say it reminds me of a whiff off a fine cheap whore.

He smiles and offers, "Grape Kool-Aid."

I hear Jimi Hendrix's "Purple Haze" ringing in my head, and, yes, we are trying to be one nation.

SOMETIMES, LATE AT NIGHT, or at least I want it to be late at night, Ike Morgan dips into the money he earns from selling his artwork and orders up a pizza or some burgers, or best of all, some chicken wings. And they deliver them to the Texas state mental hospital in Austin, and it all tastes so good. Afterward he'll have a Camel or, if he's trying to save up for his art supplies, he'll roll a little Bugler and have a smoke and relax. Because its damned hard to have over two centuries of presidents of the United States pouring through your hands. Not to mention various singers and movie stars and other children of the Lord.

He is the official historian of the United States, the man who left the busy streets in 1977, the eight-track man, the fellow who can hardly remember anything before 1977, or at least one day in April of 1977. And yet he does portraits of all those presidents, and some of them are so damn obscure probably not even their wives could bring to mind their scent or faces. That's the hell of it for the LBJs. You get to be king of the world, and then you die, and then it's another millennium and I'm in a fish joint in Austin just a bare mile or two or three from that huge LBJ presidential library, and I ask the twenty-three-year-old bartender what she thinks of LBJ, and she says, "I don't really know much about him, but I suspect he had some doing in the killing of Kennedy."

But Ike Morgan does. I've seen his portrait of LBJ, and the lips are very red, red like lipstick, and the eyes very blue. And the face is black.

I think of another Texan I went to school with back in the sixties at the University of Wisconsin in Madison. He'd been recruited in Texas by the CIA to fight the Commies and then served in Europe as a representative at various international student things and then one day, as the war in Vietnam got hotter and hotter and more and more body bags came home, he'd thought, what in the hell am I doing? And then he came home.

I met him afterward, when the news from Vietnam was especially black, and he was walking near the campus, and some guy was walking toward him and laughing and having a perfectly fine time, and he snapped alert and looked at the laughing guy and punched him in the mouth. And then walked on without saying a word.

I remember another time I was at a student-faculty type meeting and the war was raging and the South was still unsettled over civil rights and a professor made some statement that sounded to me like we all have our differences over the war but that doesn't mean we have to hate each other. When he finished, one of my fellow students stood up and said, "Look, as far as I am concerned, everything south of Canada is Mississippi."

And I didn't think that was true, but that wasn't what caught my notice. It was that every single person at that meeting knew exactly what he meant.

I was one of those wayward academic types who bumbled through the war on a student deferment, but I can still smell the sulfur in the air and feel the breath of the dragon on the back of my neck. The Beatles were losing ground, and the Stones were gaining, and no one who listened to *Let It Bleed* ever wondered why. I remember going to a drive-in movie in like '67 with a friend who had no time for college so he didn't go, and it is a James Bond movie, lots of action and women with large breasts, and in the morning he'll go for his physical, but no matter, he's been there before and his ticker is not so good. So we're drinking 40-ounce jugs of beer, because they're damn cheap, and pissing by the car, because this is not too fancy a drive-in, and no one is worried, because they always look into his heart and send him home. And he goes down the next day and that is the last I see of him for two years.

David Edington remembers sitting on the plane that was going to take him across the pond to Vietnam and somebody had a radio on and just as they began to take off the damn thing played "Leaving on a Jet Plane."

It got like that at times.

LBJ: *How important is it to us?*
RUSSELL: *It isn't important a damn bit, with all these new missile systems.*
LBJ: *Well, I guess it's important to us.*
RUSSELL: *From a psychological standpoint.*

I'M LISTENING TO THESE goddamn tapes, and it is a Thursday, June 11, 1964, and LBJ is again talking on the phone to Senator Richard Russell of Georgia, a man who loved the Constitution and fought against civil rights, and LBJ is whining about Vietnam, and this at a time when Kennedy is hardly cold in the ground and the rest of us can't find the place on the map, and LBJ wails, "I'm confronted. I don't believe the American people ever want me to run. If I lose it, I think they'll say I've lost it. . . . At the same time, I don't want to commit us to a war. And I'm in a hell of a shape."

Senator Russell offers, "We're just like a damn cow over a fence out there in Vietnam."

Ah, but Lyndon says, "I've got a study being made by the experts . . . whether Malaysia will necessarily go and India'll go and how much it'll hurt our prestige if we just got out . . ."

All this talk going on without me, going on before I knew where such countries were, going on even before I'd popped out of the car at the Bond movie and pissed into the desert night. And Ike was not even ten and hadn't entered into his genius with color and his toils in history.

WE LOVE PERIODS, ORDER, SEQUENCE. I'm standing in Waxahachie with Bruce and Julie Webb, going through piles of Ike Morgan's art. Waxahachie is an Assembly of God town—Jerry Lee Lewis once studied theology here before being seized by great balls of fire—and Bruce's grandparents settled here after missionary work in India. When they died, he and Julie came here to find space for their passions. They fit in fine—Bruce signed up with the Masons and Odd Fellows—and created this sanctuary for Outsider Art. Ike, as it happens, began with a Dumpster Period. This covered the years when he'd scrounge behind the hospital in the trash for something to draw on—pieces of cardboard boxes, covers torn off tablets, sheets of paper. A lot of the paintings have leaves stuck to them, a reality for the Outside Artist. There also is a period when he drew noses in a particular way, and then these series would come, sometimes explained by a book that came his way and sometimes not explained at all. Right now, for example, Ike is heavily into an homage to Dr. Seuss. And Sarah Bernhardt. Unlike many artists, Ike draws without a concern for the market, and, unlike just about any other dealers, Bruce and Julie never suggest he make something the market wants.

Ike's life has apparent order in two places: inside their gallery, with its carefully filed, loved, and preserved artworks; and inside that big blue book that David Edington sometimes consults, the one stuffed with twenty-odd years of reports and notes on the case of Ike Edward Morgan.

All of my life I've had trouble with order, knowing it was a way to make sense out of things and yet sensing it was a way to squeeze the life out of things. For decades Ike and Lyndon have been trapped in their madness, and we've said we couldn't make heads or tails of them. Ike stayed stashed in the state hospital, Lyndon buried in the tomb of a library he threw up in Austin. Inside, a huge glass wall opens up to the stacks of documents like a window into a brain, and I've stood there staring in at the millions of pieces of paper, all those voices, and I've leaned forward and could almost hear them shouting and screaming in their desperate effort to make themselves heard through the thick glass that keeps them in their place.

Douglass Cater, one of Johnson's presidential assistants, remembers how he had these newswire machines in the Oval Office—the kind with a roll of paper, keys flying like hell, and the whole thing inside a soundproof cabinet—and LBJ would get up during meetings and go over and stare through the glass and see what was going on in the world, and then, if it really caught his eye, he'd open up the cabinet and "disappear down into the bowels of the thing to read it as it was actually being typed out on the spindle. He wanted to get even farther ahead of the news before it could surface." I tell you, you can hear voices in this library. Sometimes I've thought that the place needs a dumpster artist, an Outsider Artist. And then, with the issue of the tapes from the first year of LBJ's reign, the voices came out of the dumpster and began to twist and shout, and there he is, hair down to his shoulders, face painted with peace symbols, and lipsticked across his forehead is the word LOVE, and he's crooning in that cool cat way of his:

When the truth is found to be lies
And all the joy within you dies
Don't you want somebody to love?
Don't you need somebody to love! . . .
You better find somebody to love.[1]

NONE OF THOSE PRESIDENTS Ike Morgan is making us face, not a one, ever got there by being shy and retiring. But still there is something about Johnson's ego that puts your basic power-junkie-self-centered-maniac-president in the shade. On January 8, 1964, LBJ had given his first State of the Union address, and that afternoon he called a big muckety-muck national columnist to get his reaction. His operators found the man traveling in North Dakota.

Johnson discovered the columnist had not even heard the speech, so he told him, "I got eighty-one applauses, in 2,900 words. It was a twenty-five-minute speech, and it took forty-one, because of the applauses . . ."

And the horse you rode in on, too.

LBJ: *I'm afraid that's right. I don't think the people of the country know much about Vietnam, and I think they care a hell of a lot less.*

RUSSELL: *Yeah, I know, but you got to send a whole lot of our boys out there—*

LBJ: *Yeah, that's right. That's exactly right. That's what I'm talking about. You get a few. We had thirty-five killed—and we got enough hell over thirty-five—this year.*

RUSSELL: *More than that . . . in Atlanta, Georgia, have been killed this year in automobile accidents.*

LBJ: *That's right, and eighty-three went down in one crash of a 707 in one day, but that doesn't make any difference . . .*

HE KNOWS THINGS A LOT OF US DON'T. On Saturday, April 9, 1977, Ike Morgan, age eighteen, was told to do some cleaning by his grandmother, Margarite, sixty-two. It was Saturday night, and she went into the bathroom wearing her nightgown to take a bath. The babysitter was over from next door to look after Ike's younger brothers and sisters. They heard some shouting. He slipped a nine-inch butcher knife into his grandmother's heart and stomach.

"I don't know," he almost whispers. "That's the hardest thing I could think of. I should have been in school instead of hanging out around the streets. I don't know how to explain that. I can't put all the blame on my grandmother. It was not a very right thing or good thing to do. I've tried to change what I can change. You can't be too hard on yourself. My grandmother loved me, but she didn't like some things. When she was bringing me up, she was nice and sweet. Some of the nicest days I ever had."

And then he goes off and then he comes back. The murder of his grandmother is hard ground for Ike Morgan to visit, and his memories over the years have been blurry, as if that day were hidden in the mists. "I came up in those neighborhoods," he continues on. "I couldn't just back off, you know." And then he is back at the hospital, where he found safety. "These people," he explains, "gave me more reason to be strong, and that's all a guy needs sometimes."

He is drawing Dr. Seuss characters on a poster. Two big birds, a couple of trees, a bear, a rabbit, a worm, some turtles. In the left-hand corner is a bush with huge berries—"Birds love to eat berries," Ike explains. He holds the pen like a brush between his thumb and forefinger and sketches out this peaceful kingdom. After decades he is the silent member of our community who now has the gift of speech, the one we ignored and then buried alive in our institutions, and now he has color and form and gives us our presidents.

The neighbors later told the reporter that Ike had been walking up and down the block acting kind of strange for days. When they got to his grandmother in the bathroom, blood was running out from under the door.

I FOUND HIM AT A TRUCK STOP during a Teamsters' strike and hopped in because he was heading west and going east was against the grain. There had been shootings, so he rode with a .44 magnum on his lap as he guided his Peterbilt toward L.A. It was the early 1980s, and Ike was deep into his art by then, going out back of the hospital to scavenge paper and cardboard from the dumpster for his art supplies. Lyndon was deep in his grave and pretty much forgotten except for biographers who periodically dug him up and flogged him with whips made in Saigon. Once in a while Republicans had at him and made the phrases Great Society and War on Poverty sound like something you did back of the barn with a sheep.

My truck driver was quiet at first, and then we fell into those black hours after midnight—carefully studying each freeway overpass for snipers—and he returned to Saigon. He'd gone during the white heat of the war, 1967, and the next thing he knew he was an Ohio farm boy looking out the back door of a chopper as a gunner. A fellow in black pajamas was under him looking up, the pilot was barking into his ears through headphones, and he hesitated on the trigger and then cut the guy in black pajamas in half. After that, he told me, it got kind of automatic, and then a year later the U.S. military dropped him back in Ohio as if it had never happened. He remembered walking around the yard at his folks' farm with his mother, and he was wearing a suit, and all of a sudden there was a loud sound, and he flung himself down in the mud. He never forgot the look in his mother's eyes when he got back up all wet and covered with mud.

He decided to go to college and enrolled in the National Guard to help pay for it. A few weeks later he was at Kent State and heard gunshots again. He decided, to hell with college, and became a trucker. He showed me a photo album of favorite cargoes, and he kept an apartment in Oklahoma City. He hardly ever got to visit the place, but he made damn sure he had a home and damn sure it was in the heart of the country.

And then there was the carpenter who finished off my office and introduced himself as a baby killer. He'd come up from Chihuahua as a field hand, enlisted to get a footing in the U.S. of A., and wound up with some weird secret team in Cambodia cutting throats in the midnight hour. When he got back to the world and walked off the plane in Oakland, a woman spat at him and he broke her arm. Told me it was a reflex. He said his wife would find him sometimes slumped in the corner of the bedroom weeping. He loved baseball.

And there were people talking guns and explosives over the beer and wine in the sixties. Finally, the heroin hit and then the coke, and the whole thing vanished, slipped away except for the wounds. And I'm left standing in Austin with a presidential library and a presidential artist.

RUSSELL: *It's a tragic situation. It's just one of those places where you can't win. Anything that you do is wrong. . . . I have thought about it. I have worried about it. I have prayed about it.*

LBJ: *I don't believe we can do anything—*

RUSSELL: *It frightens me 'cause it's my country involved over there, and if we get into there on any considerable scale there's no doubt in my mind but that the Chinese will be in there and we'd be fighting a danged conventional war . . .*

LBJ: *You don't have any doubt but what if we go in there and get 'em up against the wall, the Chinese Communists are gonna come in?*

RUSSELL: *No sir, no doubt about it.*

THERE IS SOMETHING ABOUT George Washington that touches Ike Morgan. "I like the first one more than the other ones—the vision of him.

He's too nice looking, the scenery of him." And so he does him over and over and sees him with a red face, a purple-brown face, an orange face, and a black face. We can't see Washington at all. He's not a man or a face or a form; he's a blur as we hand over the money, a cartoon on our currencies.

Ike has created his own iron constitution out of his own hard lessons from life. "If you don't try," Ike offers, "you'll never know what can happen anyway. Keep hanging in there. If there wasn't for people helping out, I don't know if I'd be here today. You just gotta be yourself. I can't do what everybody says to do—you gotta figure out what is right to do and make a decision and stick to it."

And then he turns back to his drawing and adds eyes to the rabbit.

"Go to a restaurant, get yourself a bite to eat. Get away. Do something special, you know. Early in the morning you can see wildlife pass through. Good to go bicycling. When the sunlight comes out, that is just enough. It keeps the body warm."

He sketches in a crescent moon in the upper left-hand corner.

"Sometimes people need moonlight."

EVERYTHING ABOUT THE WAR IS simpler now, and it seems like a detail that it devoured LBJ's presidency, his reputation, denied him a second term, and chased his ass back to Texas, where he built his library, grew out his hair, and went to his grave looking like some deranged street person. Now the ground is shuddering as he comes back up into a world that thinks a virtual war like Operation Desert Storm is the real thing.

Jesus, it is evening on April 30, 1964, and Johnson is on the horn with Robert McNamara, his brainy secretary of defense, and he's pissed about reports from this Vietnam.

"Let's get some more of something, my friend," he offers, "because I'm going to have a heart attack if you don't get me something. . . . We need somebody over there that can get us some better plans than we've got, because what we've got is what we've had since '54. We're not getting it done. We're losing."

McNamara almost intones his brief reply: "I know it."

Great, the fucking secretary of defense knows he is losing a war in a place only he and a handful of bureaucrats know exists.

"Tell those damn generals over there," Johnson orders, "to find one for you, or you're going to go out there yourself."

And McNamara picks right up on the boss's mood and says, "That's one reason why I want to go back. A kick in the tail a little bit will help."

That's the spirit, that's the can-do shit that LBJ wants to hear. But he makes sure McNamara understands when he says, "What I want is somebody that can lay up some plans to trap those guys and whup hell out of them and kill some of them."

Nail that damn coonskin to the wall, you hear?

And while he's straightening out this Vietnam mess, the damn generals bogged down like some old truck in the mud, while he's getting that all ironed out, he's fiddling with the biggest civil rights act in the history of these United States, and deep into the longest goddamn filibuster in the history of the U.S. Senate, a southern choke hold on the bill that will rattle on seventy-seven days before Lyndon Baines Johnson, that Southern Man, stops it dead in its tracks and signs the bill into law.

Besides that, he's got this War on Poverty he wants to win, and he's fired up to kick Barry Goldwater's ass in the fall election, and he's just gotten the country out of a winter of mourning for JFK, and he's trying to figure out a way to ship Bobby Kennedy to some outer darkness, and if all that ain't enough, he needs some britches.

So on August 9, 1964, at about 1:16 P.M. he gets Joseph Haggar Jr. of the Haggar Company on the phone and says, "You-all made me some real light slacks. . . . Now, I need about six pairs for summer wear."

And, by God, Mr. Haggar says, "Yes, sir."

But that's not enough, and LBJ rolls on. A man's got needs, and, yes, even the president of the United States must sometimes stand naked, but also he must wear britches that don't irritate him, and so listen up, "The crotch, down where your nuts hang, is always a little too tight. . . . Give me an inch that I can let out there, because they cut me. They're just like riding a wire fence."

And now you want to task me with this intern and a cigar story? Enough of that, I tell you he is rising, those yellow rose of Texas petals are a-fluttering off, and he's coming back, the president who said of JFK's womanizing, hell, that he had more by accident than Kennedy ever got on purpose, the man who laid secretaries on White House desks and what's this chickenshit you're saying about a cigar? The man who took us to Saigon and Mississippi and Bed-Stuy, the guy who got into all our business and finally ended this stuff about only white people voting. I tell you he's coming back, ready or not.

It's around 8:35 P.M. on Tuesday, August 4, 1964, and his wife, Lady Bird, calls this monster up, and he says, "Darling?"

And she says, "Yes, beloved."

And he says, "Did you want me?"

And she says, "I just wanted to see you whenever you're all alone, merely to tell you I loved you. That's all."

And Lyndon Baines Johnson says, "I'll be over there."

LBJ: *I've got a little old sergeant that works for me over at the house and he's got six children, and I just put him up as the United States Army, Air Force, and Navy every time I think about making this decision and think about sending that father of those six kids in there. And what in the hell are we going to get out of his doing it? And it just makes the chills run up my back.*

RUSSELL: *It does me. I just can't see it.*

I ONCE WAS WALKING A BEAT with a skid-row cop, and as we entered a dive a guy raced for the bathroom to dump his kit, and the cop, a huge guy, grabbed him by the throat and held him off the ground against a wall. The guy pleaded, "I'm clean, I'm clean." The cop said evenly and cold as ice, "You can't be clean here."

You can't be clean around Johnson. He got too much done.

He's talking, man's always talking, and it's June 23, 1964, second day into summer, and it's about four in the afternoon, and he's on the line to Senator James Eastland, the god of Sunflower County, Mississippi, and they're talking about a woman named Fannie Lou Hamer of Ruleville, and my ears get big because I knew Fannie Lou Hamer. She was a piece of work, a woman I've thought about most of my life because when I choke I think, well, hell, she did not choke, and sometimes when I think that I fire up enough nerve to push on. She and her husband lived in a shack, and when I sat there I could look at a wall and see daylight coming through the cracks. She was the granddaughter of a slave and just about drove Lyndon Johnson and James Eastland crazy. For a while she worked for SNCC (the Student Nonviolent Coordinating Committee) organizing and helping black people to register to vote, a project Senator Eastland never fit into his schedule. One day in June 1963, just about a year before Johnson and Eastland chatted on the phone, she walked into a whites-only restaurant in Columbus, Mississippi, and got jailed and the hell beat out of her. Folks would fire into her shack from time to time. But she never gave in and by June of 1964 had welded together something called the Mississippi Freedom Democratic Party and was fixing to show up at Lyndon Johnson's convention in Atlantic City and demand the seats of the traditionally lily-white delegation, the one Senator Eastland was so fond of. Also three civil rights workers had vanished in Mississippi two days earlier on a Sabbath.

So Johnson says, "Jim, we got three kids missing down there. What can I do about it?"

"I don't know," Eastland grumbles. "I don't believe there's three missing. I believe it's a publicity stunt."

And then he rolls on and my ears get big: "I happen to know that some of these bombings where nobody gets hurt are publicity stunts. This Negro woman in Ruleville [Fannie Lou Hamer] that's been to Washington and testified that she was shot at nineteen times is lying. Of course, anybody that gets shot at nineteen times is going to get hit."

But Johnson presses on. He's friendly, but he senses he's got a problem with these missing civil rights workers, though he doesn't know they've already been buried in a dam. He's in fine form, asking Eastland about the weather and commiserating with him about the lack of rain, and then Eastland offers the insight, "It'll take a crowd to make three men disappear."

And LBJ says, "That depends on the kind of men, Jim. . . . It might take a big crowd to take three like you! I imagine it wouldn't take many to capture me."

And they go on like that bantering back and forth—the boys, you know—and I remember being there four years later, sitting in Fannie Lou Hamer's shack, being there after the dead boys were dug up and the civil rights bill was made law, after the big changes, and still it was lively, hell, Martin Luther King had just been murdered up the road in Memphis. But what I notice is that call from Eastland ends and immediately Johnson is on the phone with J. Edgar Hoover, and Hoover says they found the car and it's burning so hot they can't peek in to see if there are bodies. And then—bam—Eastland is back on the line, and he says he talked with the governor of Mississippi and the governor "expects them to turn up with bruises and claiming that somebody's whipped 'em. He doesn't believe a word of it."

Johnson drops the big one by saying, "Now, here's the problem, Jim. Hoover just called me . . ."

Eastland bleats, "Well, I know nothing about that."

I really hated Johnson back then, and I'm not sure I've mellowed much as I listen in and hear Mrs. Hamer come up and remember those Mississippi days and nights. But I have to notice, as I listen to the tapes, that the filibuster is grinding out and the man is always on the goddamn phone and the government, that rude beast, is awakening.

And you can't be here and stay clean.

THIS AIN'T NO DISCO. This is work, and work is not necessarily what you have been told. It must be done, these things in the head must be born, be given color and form. Life has its drives. "Life is not building up too much stress," Ike advises. "Sometimes I wake up and I decide I'm gonna do something nice for someone. They say you don't want to do work, well, then why eat. All you do is art, they say. And it is good to eat." And then he pauses, he's still working on his Dr. Seuss drawing, then continues. "You know how some days are, all day out in the yard playing with water. Sometimes in life you just can't draw. And sometimes you can stay behind it."

When the weather is good, he likes to work outside, get away from the gray-feeling building with light green concrete walls, dull linoleum floors, and the weight of government, the dimly lit halls, and the doors that open freely to get inside but are locked when you try to go outside, to the pastoral grounds with big trees and grass imprisoned by the whir of traffic on each side.

So Ike Morgan takes his stuff out to the concrete picnic table, the one all splattered with paint from his work, and he'll be at it for hours. Sometimes David Edington will see him out there in the wind with four different paintings held down by garbage-can lids, and Ike'll be bent over working on a fifth.

LIKE THAT OTHER GREAT American president, Elvis Presley, LBJ went to flesh in the end. After he left office and moseyed back to the ranch, he kind of seemed to give up on things. His hair grew out, and the people around him didn't quite know what to make of him and his new do. A man with a bad ticker, he started smoking a couple of packs a day, boozing into the wee hours on that Cutty Sark and hitting the Night Hawk diner on South Congress in Austin, gobbling up burgers. One day in January 1973, he showed up at his presidential library to talk to an aide, Mildred Stegall. Johnson looked like hell, skin pink and gray, and he had the air of a dying man. He told her how to take care of the many tapes he made of phone calls and meetings when president—they should be sealed for fifty years, and some of them should never be opened. A week or so later he died at the ranch, and Stegall sealed the material, as instructed, until 2023. This decision was later overruled for various reasons, including fear of public lawsuits, and because it was pretty clear Johnson really did want everyone to finally listen in on him. Just after the library opened, Harry Middleton tried to censor some stuff, and Johnson roared, "Good men have been trying to save my reputation for forty years and not a damn one's succeeded."

But what strikes me is Johnson's attitude that January day as he gave his weary orders with his long white hair curling down to his shoulders. He had the air of a dead man walking, a man who didn't care. Whereas the Kennedy library close by Harvard gives us history as a veneer and never mind the garter belts, Johnson's joint is serving up history with the bark on. Just before his big library had opened, he'd noticed that the museum section didn't have any hate mail, and, by God, he was a world-record beater in the hate-mail department. So Lyndon Johnson, disappointed by examples dug up by his staff archivists, waded into the millions of pieces of correspondence himself looking for the meanest letter "I ever got." He finally settled on a postcard from Linden, California, that read: "I demand that you, as a gutless sonofabitch, resign as President of the United States." So it went on display.

Vietnam could do that to you. David Edington remembers finally finishing his tour in Nam and riding home with a planeload of other guys. Just before they made it to Seattle, the pilot came on the intercom and told them to get all sharp objects out of their pockets and to tuck their heads down because the landing gear refused to come down.

What Edington remembers of the planeload of guys finally coming home is that they all figured they'd die in the attempted landing and no one gave a damn. Not one guy. The plane was perfectly quiet and serene as they glided toward oblivion.

LISTEN UP NOW. This is simple. First, horror movies are okay, just as long as you remember they're not true. That's what Ike Morgan advised me, and he's seen true horror and come back from it. And second, we gotta stop dismissing people, because the hour is getting late, we've blown out all the candles on the last thousand years, and Saigon won't go away and neither will Lyndon. He's pulled the hat trick. No, not the War on Poverty; they said that didn't work even though it did. No, not the Civil Rights Act; that worked so damn well everybody forgot what a bitch life was before it got passed. And forget the Great Society; everyone else has. What is bringing Johnson back is the past served up raw and bloody. John Kennedy, he's got his Harvard center tending to the holy remains and ducking every time an old squeeze shows up, but Johnson, he figured out something better than all the spin masters, all the pet house historians, all the loyal lying retainers a man could muster. He stockpiled the greatest show on earth, brutal and bawdy power lashing against our hides like a whip.

And he's coming back from his tomb. He's pulled that wooden stake from his heart just about the time we've wearied of focus groups, false piety, and clambering about looking under the bed. We've lost our appetite for Rhodes scholars and are a little more open to Outsider Artists, to the self-taught, to the guys who have been there.

Ike and Lyndon are back with their reports. And it's not the way we think it should be, and it is not polite, and it is not always pretty. So come down the lane of pain and take a look. Good morning, millennium. Time to chew some bones. The weather forecast today is purple haze.

Ready or not.

RUSSELL: *It's one of these things where "heads I win, tails you lose."*

LBJ: *Well, think about it, and I'll talk to you again. I hate to bother you, but I just—*

RUSSELL: *I wish I could help you. God knows I do, 'cause it's a terrific quandary that we're in over there. We're just in the quicksands up to our very necks. And I just don't know what the hell is the best way to [go] about it.*

LBJ: *I love you and I'll be calling you.*

NOTE

1. Jefferson Airplane, "Somebody to Love." When you tour the library and hit the part called Images of the Sixties you can hear this song, plus "Hair," "Riders on the Storm," "Twist and Shout," "Hello, Dolly!" "Puff the Magic Dragon," and "This Land Is Your Land." Oh, yeah, and of course "She Loves You, Yeah, Yeah, Yeah."

Extra-ordinary Rendition

The following piece is an early draft of an article that eventually appeared in the November 2007 issue of *GQ*, about the artist Fernando Botero. When Botero read the Seymour Hersh article in the *New Yorker*, an article that was the first in a series of articles that brought to light the torture by American soldiers at Abu Ghraib, Botero responded with art depicting the torture. His Abu Ghraib paintings appeared in New York in October and November of 2006 and then Berkeley in January 2007. They caused a stir. Critics called the pieces anti-American propaganda. Subsequently, the Abu Ghraib pieces were dropped from his North American tour. No institute would touch them. When this article was published in November 2007, the Abu Ghraib pieces were on display at the American University in Washington, D.C., making their second debut in the United States.

HE BELIEVES IN AMERICA. The terrace spreads before the house built around 1780 on the Tuscan hillside. His wife Sophia serves olives from their own trees and pours glasses of white wine as the sun sinks over the Mediterranean. On a clear day, Corsica looms into view. The house itself was a ruin when he found it twenty-five years ago. He'd come here to do sculpture and the medieval village with its ancient walls has been a center for marble and metal workers for centuries. Pietrasanta means Holy Rock and the Popes sent their emissaries here for the stone that became St. Peter's.

The house itself once housed peasants—the family living upstairs, the animals on the first floor. He paid $25,000 and now three bedrooms line the top, and the barn part has become a bedroom, with two big statues at the foot of the bed, a living room and a kitchen. He spends two or three months a year here supervising the casting of his bronze statues, and then dealers buy them for a million dollars or more. He has done 150 major sculptures, maybe three thousand paintings. He is probably the most recognizable living artist on earth with his inflated human bodies all sharing blank faces and brilliant colors. They have become part of the visual vocabulary of our time. He is despised in the art world.

As he sips his wine on the terrace, he says simply, "They hate me. In Milan, one of my statues was sprayed with graffiti and the papers said, 'Who could blame the vandals?'"

There have been thirty books written about him but he says with some pain, "When the critics write about me, it is to kill me. They hate me because I was not made by them."

He rises early, showers out in the garden, then he has coffee on the terrace and reads the newspapers. At ten, he walks down the hill to his studio, stands before a canvas and paints for eight hours with only a slight pause for lunch. He is seventy-five years old and he follows this routine seven days a week, fifty-two weeks a year—sometimes in Mexico, sometimes New York, then Paris and finally back to Pietrasanta.

His work is widely pirated for posters and as a veneer on furniture. He does nothing about this theft because legal action would eat into the time for work. Since 1991, the paintings go for about a million and now nouveau riche Chinese in Shanghai are plopping the huge bronzes in their gardens. He has more money than he will ever need—a few years back he donated his $200 million art collection of masters to Colombia so that young artists could see the real thing.

But now he is in the center of a controversy that he did not see coming.

Fernando Botero says, "I was very shocked and mad because the U.S. were torturing in the same prison used by Saddam Hussein. The United States violated its ideals of freedom and human rights."

The light is failing, the gardens glow on the hillside, the world looks safe and wholesome and eternal but Botero cannot stop speaking of his hurt.

"The American press," he continues, "was courageous because they did this revelation. If this had happened in other countries, it would not be published. This thing was too much because the policy of the U.S. government allowed this to happen. They keep doing definitions of torture so that you can keep torturing. You see torture in Africa or Latin America and you expect the worst. But you do not expect this from the United States; the most powerful country in the world doing this is a scandal."

In 2004, when the story of Abu Ghraib broke in the *New Yorker,* Botero was on an airplane reading Seymour Hersh's exposé. He set down the magazine and began sketching. He did nothing but Abu Ghraib and a year later had produced one hundred paintings and drawings.

At the time, nine U.S. museums had accepted a touring Botero show. And then, they saw that part of the show were the Abu Ghraib works. They all canceled. Finally, some of the work was hung briefly in the library at the University of California, Berkeley. And in November 2006, Botero's gallery in New York, the Marlborough, displayed the work. Armed guards were hired, and visitors wrote hate notes in the gallery's comment book.

Botero was stunned. He has not lived in Colombia since 1956; he has spent more than a decade in the United States and it is in many ways his second home.

Now his Abu Ghraib works will finally see the light of day in November 2007 in Washington. It responds to a fragment of the new America, a single prison in Baghdad that is part of a new constellation of black sites and other locations where people vanish and are asked questions under various methods.

He refuses to sell the work because he does not want money from torture. Here is what he wants from the United States: he will give the Abu Ghraib works to any American art museum for nothing if it will put it on permanent display because he never wants this to be forgotten. Or repeated.

THE MAN SUDDENLY LIFTS HIS ARMS but the pigeon dodges and gets through the trap. The birds are everywhere and sweep past strollers like guided missiles. Afternoon seeps across the Piazza della Scala where a statue of Leonardo da Vinci stares down at the people flowing past the opera house. No one pays much attention to the wizard of the Renaissance except for the pigeons that shit on his head.

Off in the corner of the piazza, a new woman is gathering a crowd. She's huge and her naked bronze body seems to parody the notion of voluptuousness. She is called "Standing Woman" and people serially pose with her. The women stand before her waiting for the photograph to be over. The men like to pose beneath her giant ass and many stroke a buttock for their keepsake shot. A few rub her crotch. The children in the piazza scamper about and ignore the statue. There is something about the work—tall, fat, and bronze—that turns children into adults and adults into children.

The statue by Fernando Botero has been placed to lure visitors to the nearby museum where a retrospective of his work is on display. Botero may be the most recognized and popular artist in the world. His fame is on display out on the street where people take gag shots by his giant bronze creations—a reclining naked woman, a giant version of a cat. For forty years, Botero has been a brand famous for fat men and women, or so they look to most people. To Botero, they are simply inflated torsos, shapes made huge and bulbous in order to devour space and create calm. He's insistent on this point and denies his creations are fat people. No matter. They are the benign visual background of the last decades and everyone knows their look even if they do not know the name of the artist.

And now they are being tortured every minute of the day and night inside the museum in Milan. But their real origin is within the government of the United States and that fact is why they hang in Italy and not in the homeland.

Behind the cathedral, a giant reclining naked woman gathers her own crowd and people reach up to hold her hand while a photo is snapped. Just down the street is another Botero, a giant bronze horse. Children flock to this statue and their parents lift them up so they can pose on the pedestal inside the four giant legs.

I sit on the pavement and watch the two statues for an hour more. The longest gap in people posing is a single twenty-second void. And when the people pose—men, women, and children—they always smile.

A blind man sprawls on the sidewalk cradling a saxophone as I watch the statues in the midday glow of light. Suddenly, he begins improvising on George Gershwin's "Summertime." The man's face is old and grizzled, and he is mainly bald. The music rolls out like a carpet on the piazza and after ten minutes I walk over and drop about $10 in the hat that every busker has. He nods and "Summertime" plays against the old stone walls as people smile and pose against giant bronze casting that comes from the mind of some Colombian they probably do not know.

I walk over to the museum, enter, and after about six rooms I hit it.

A European couple stares at a small drawing in the corner. A man writhes, his hands and feet bound, his eyes blindfolded and the only real note of color is a yellow arc raining down on him as one of my fellow citizens pisses.

I am standing in Milan looking at images my country prefers not to see.

HE IS BORN POOR IN MEDELLÍN and then gets poorer. His father is a traveling salesman—there is a photograph of him astride a mule in the Andes peddling his wares. He dies when Botero is two. His mother is a seamstress trying to feed three sons. Uncles help out and the family struggles. Botero studies to be a bullfighter but leaves the school the first day the training entails facing a real bull. His uncles get him into a Jesuit high school and he is doing okay until he publishes an essay at age sixteen on Picasso as a hero of art and freedom. The dean of the school calls a meeting of the students out on the patio, denounces Botero, and expels him in 1948.

This is the very beginning of La Violencia, the ten-year civil war that slaughters at least 200,000 people in Colombia. Botero decides to be an artist, he goes to Bogotá and tries to teach himself art. When he is eighteen, a friend tells him to go to Tolu on the coast, a village of black fishermen where a man can live on almost nothing.

He finds a thatched hut with a dirt floor and shares the place with a fisherman and a schoolteacher. His tiny room runs him five bucks a month. He lights a candle and hears the rustle of wings. The ceiling is covered with vampire bats. In two or three months, he does maybe twenty paintings.

In the village, there is a small inn and he paints the walls with images of princesses and trades this work for food.

One day, he is bathing in the sea and he looks up at the beach.

"I saw," he remembers, "two policemen with a pole on their shoulders and a bound man is hanging from the pole who is screaming."

La Violencia has paid him a visit. He goes back to his hut and paints the scene. In 1952, he enters the painting and wins a national prize in Colombia, one worth $7000. He is twenty. For the next three years, he haunts Europe. He lives in rooms with no heat—in the winter he goes to bed with his gloves and overcoat on. He spends maybe a dollar a day on food. He is in Madrid, Paris, then Italy, and he spends his days copying the old masters in museums so that he can teach himself their tricks. The paintings he peddles to tourists for a pittance, anything so that he can buy a meal.

Botero has never had a single job except his art. He decides a painter is a person who paints and sometimes he goes hungry and sometimes he can afford food. But he never betrays his chosen vocation.

In 1956, he is living in Mexico City painting a mandolin and one day he makes the soundhole in the instrument tiny and then, he realizes the volume of the instrument has been expanded to a giant size. He feels a change and years later he says that when he painted that tiny hole it was like a door he walked through and then suddenly he was on the other side. And on that side is the world now called Botero, where people are gigantic and fill the frame of a painting, and the flowers are huge and beautiful and the countryside beckoning and safe. It is the Colombia he has never known because it is the Colombia that has never existed. Like his contemporary, Gabriel García Márquez, he enters a fantasy world so that life becomes bearable.

He paints priests, he has a cardinal in a bathtub, he has huge men and women dancing, there are circuses and valleys lush with green, and still lifes of huge fruits and flowers. He goes to New York and struggles in Greenwich Village, selling his art for food and rent. He is the man out of step with his times. The art world is deep into abstract painting, he is playing with giant people populating a lush countryside. He does not fit. William de Kooning, a giant of abstract painting, has a Colombian girlfriend and so they hang out together and Botero learns a vital trick—always clean your brushes with Mr. Clean—something he has done ever since.

One day in 1958, there is a knock at the door and it is Dorothy Miller of the Museum of Modern Art. She was visiting someone else in his building and the guy told her she should take a look at the stuff done by this strange Colombian. He has a painting on the easel he'd done in Colombia of a young girl with the trademark giant head. When he'd first painted her, a cleaning lady was in his room and she said it looked like Mona Lisa. So Botero reworked the smile and entitled it "Mona Lisa, Age 12." The next day, MoMA sends someone to box it and then, it is hung in the museum.

For Botero, it was that close. He thinks, what if I had been out at the store when Dorothy Miller knocked? What if I had a different painting than the Mona Lisa on the easel? He pauses as he remembers that moment and sighs because no matter how hard you work at art, you must also face the terror of being lucky or unlucky.

He now sees light at the end of the tunnel, though the bad times do not end instantly. One day in 1961, he realizes he has three things—a wife he has left, three children he supports, and twenty-seven dollars on earth. But that night someone buys a painting and he is never that close to failure again. By 1964 or '65, he is box office, and after that he never worries about money. He meets Che Guevara, he is hosted by Latin American presidents. He buys a tiny house on Long Island and spends four months a year there painting without distractions. He simply lives as he has always lived: painting eight hours a day, seven days a week. In the early seventies, he teaches himself sculpture. By the early nineties, he is everywhere, instantly recognizable, and maintains homes on three continents.

But Colombia moves beyond his reach. Eleven years ago, eight men came to his house to kidnap him. He happened to be out. They shot his two dogs, stole 22 paintings and two sculptures, and ended forever any hope of being safe where he was born.

He is very rich, he is beloved.

And one night, as we finish a three-hour dinner in Pietrasanta with a small army of empty wine bottles glowing in the candlelight, he looks up and says, "The critics hate me, hate me."

And he is right.

Which is why his Abu Ghraib work has caused a stir.

The critics hate him but they need the paintings he has done on torture because the art world has fallen deaf and dumb in the face of Abu Ghraib. Suddenly, this guy they have despised shows up with 100 paintings and drawings that scream out that something shameful and terrible has happened and it has been done by the people and the nation he admires.

He explains that he may be anti-social (he hates parties or anything that takes up time when he could be painting or thinking of painting) but he is not anti-American.

Botero muses that he is also an anti-modern modern.

"What I have done," he says quietly, "nobody did before. It is new but it does not follow the fashion of the day. I have all my life been swimming against the river and it was always very hard to swim against the river all of the time."

And now, the critics are swimming alongside him because in the moment of Abu Ghraib, he is one of the few that dove into the angry and bloody water.

HE IS A CULTURED, CALM MAN. He wears the round black glasses that are almost a uniform among European intellectuals, he reads widely and he is immersed in the history of western art and almost swoons when he thinks of the Quattrocento, or of Velásquez or Goya. He is the man everyone wants to meet after work for that quiet drink at the café while the sun sets and the turmoil of life can be briefly set aside for the joys of music and painting and literature. But his work, those thousands of paintings, those huge statues, are messages from a soft and kindly world, the place we dismiss with one word—sentimental.

The show in Milan opens on grace notes—a giant cat, a man and woman dancing, the big bronze people outside the museum. The early rooms are explosions of color. Clerics, lovers, circus people, giant flowers and fruits beckon and you think this is the way a child sees the world and suddenly, you want to be that child. Colors smear the eye—blue, green, pink, red, yellow, brown, black—streams of color and the room feels warm and the shapes soft, the priests, the whores, the man out on the town, lovers, naked women, old women, seamstresses, even a suicide floating down through the air with that huge Botero body, a trim moustache, and a blank face. A watermelon the size of a truck stares out from the wall with cool pink flesh, a monstrous mandolin with that tiny hole—one of many copies Botero has made since he sold the original to eat and now he cannot find where it has gone. Clowns prance, a sword swallower glides the blade down his throat, a big woman parades in brilliant tights on a unicycle, another Botero Amazon reclines on a tiger, there are homages to his heroes and Van Gogh's passionate flowers now have swelled and blaze out of the frame, a sixteenth-century Van Eyck classic has been made a Botero as the couple looks out from huge bodies.

The walls are white, the paintings presented like jewels, and then you go through a door and walls go gray and a naked man with a brown beard and black hood sits on the floor, his arms chained to the wall, or three men are bound and blindfolded and blood flows from two while the third vomits, a fierce dog snarls near another blindfolded man's face.

Botero's drawings and paintings do not spring from the photographs that exploded across the world in March 2004. There is no Lyndie England holding the leash of a collared man on the ground. He read the published U.S. reports and then imagined not how such things look but how such things feel. And how they feel not simply to the flesh but how they feel to that place all interrogators seek, the mind. In almost none of the images are U.S. personnel present since for Botero it is the torture that matters, not the face of the man doing the torture. And of course, the American government strongly agrees since it has chosen in many instances since 9/11 to employ anonymous CIA contract employees to supervise the destruction of the will in other human beings. Once in a while, there is an admitted error—David Passaro, one such contract employee in Afghanistan, was convicted and sent to prison when his zeal in asking questions killed the person. But in the main, no one really learns who is doing the work, just as until the photographs accidentally surfaced, no one was really willing to admit the work was being done. So Botero imagines a world that officially never existed, and in this world people who never officially exist torture other human beings who never really mattered.

And his famous figures change in the Abu Ghraib paintings and drawings. The human beings are still huge, but now they are taut and muscular, as if in order to express his anger and despair at the United States sanctioning torture, he had to pluck the example of Michelangelo's giant people on the ceiling of the Sistine Chapel in the Vatican.

THE LIFE IS VERY NICE AND VERY SIMPLE, the hours regular, and of course, the money helps. But there is something clean about seeing a man of seventy-five who sells bronze statues to rich men in China for their gardens at a million a pop roll into the piazza on a motor scooter, and then walk over to a small café and sit at an outside table and have his evening Campari with orange juice. He is the congenial man in Pietrasanta, where everyone seems to know who he is—one of his huge statues dominates a piazza a few blocks away—but no one pays any particular attention to him.

He says, "All of my life I have thought about dictators and military juntas. Torture is something refined and cruel and done in cold blood. It is worse than violence."

And he knows violence, having come up during the bloodbath of La Violencia in Colombia and having kidnap attempts on him there—he now visits his family members secretly for very short periods of time with bodyguards hired out of New York. Once he was in a private plane on the runway with his bodyguards for a lightning visit to Medellín when the president of Colombia called and warned he must abandon the trip because of danger.

Botero is the man who lives part of the year in New York City because of the rush he feels from the energy of the place. He cannot live in Colombia because he will be either murdered or kidnapped and he cannot give up his Colombian passport because he feels that his fellow countrymen would then, rightly, see him as a traitor. One of his sons became Secretary of Defense in Colombia in the early '90s. He was in line to be the next president when he was sent to prison for two years for collecting drug money for the then current president. Botero called him once in prison and then did not speak to him for three years because he was enraged that after an education at Harvard and the Sorbonne, that when he could have a fantastic life, he ruined it. In part his rage is a father's rage but in the main it is the rage of a poor boy who sees someone squander an opportunity he never had. And then when the cartel leader Pablo Escobar was finally murdered, Botero learned he had been collecting his paintings and this disgusted him. He did a hundred works on the violence in Colombia, including one of the killing of Pablo.

The bright colors and almost happy paintings of Botero come from a dark place he is determined to escape.

TORTURE IS THE MOTHER'S MILK of Western art, and Italy is studded with torture art. A block or so from the main piazza in Pietrasanta there is a small church and Botero did two frescos there—one of paradise and one of hell. In hell, Hitler's head bobs in the burning lake. But all over Italy there are these buildings where saints are shot full of arrows, where men writhe in agony on crosses. Almost every women wears a cross dangling from her neck. It is difficult to escape visual references to the violation of the flesh. The nation houses over ten centuries of art focusing on butchery and blood and gore.

So the debate over torture art seems quaint, a debate that asks if it is proper to display such things, a debate that asks if it denigrates pain to show it. There is a legitimate debate over torture itself, one that asks if it is moral to deliberately put another human being in pain and destroy the mind in pursuit of information and if torture actually produces accurate information. There was a time when such practices were widely cited as one of the reasons that Saddam Hussein must be overthrown. In those olden times, I sat with Iraqi refugees in Indonesia and listened to them tell of their time in Hussein's prisons. Some of the tales then were about nails being driven into a man's head. None of the men could proceed very far into their stories before they began to shudder and then had to fall silent for long moments. Because in the end, torture is always about breaking a person, about destroying the mind and will, about stealing the soul. I have sat in John McCain's senate office as he walked me through his five and half years in the Hanoi Hilton and the beatings and the screams. I have sat in the office of a comandante in a Mexican police station while next door a man screamed at the top of his lungs and the comandante spoke calmly as if nothing were happening and I spoke calmly as if nothing were happening.

And in a way, that is how torture happens. We go on with our lives as if torture were not happening.

THE BISTRO TABLE AT THE Café Teatro is very small. Rain sprinkles just before Botero arrives from his day of painting and the air in the piazza is clean and fresh. He is buoyant from his eight hours of thinking of nothing but color and composition and harmony. Since he finished his Abu Ghraib stint, he has gone to the circus in his mind and now there are forty canvases of midgets, clowns, and trapeze artists, of the gaiety that comes to town when the big top is raised.

But mention of Abu Ghraib makes him suddenly somber and he says things like "Art is a permanent accusation."

He asks out loud if anyone would remember the bombing of civilians at Guernica in the Spanish Civil War if Picasso had not made his famous painting.

He says, "You do things like Abu Ghraib as a testimony. You don't think you will change things. You want it to stay in the mind as something very wrong. There are things that have to be seen."

When he says the words "very wrong" his hands stop moving and his voice has that pain of a small child who is shocked and hurt. Then, he returns to being Botero, the person he invented at age eighteen when he decided he would do no work but art and live in a peaceful world of bright colors.

His life has a simple geography. He escapes poverty and violence in Colombia by painting a man being tortured. He then struggles and creates the world we now know as Botero where all the people seem plump and all the life seems good and fine. Even when he had to confront the guerrilla war in Colombia in the nineties, his canvases retained the familiar colors and shapes of his happy paintings. And then, three years ago, he was exiled for a year from his happy kingdom and did a hundred drawings and paintings in earth tones of men being urinated on, of men having broom handles shoved up their asses, of men beaten, of men chained to walls, of men in agony.

No one in my country wished to display such things. Botero offered the whole set of work permanently to any institution that would keep it up on the walls. The phone did not ring.

This November they make a visit to the capital city of the United States.

I am sure some of my fellow citizens will denounce them as anti-American or as lies or as things that should never be on exhibit. I have read art criticisms of the Abu Ghraib paintings that suggest they exploit suffering. As for me, I hear the man screaming in the room next to the comandante's office while he and I speak calmly as if nothing is happening.

I look across the table at Botero and now he is lost in his love of Velásquez and Goya and Picasso and Van Gogh, and his face is smooth and ageless as he revels in this long line of artists he wishes to join where humans paint and create beauty and joy.

I am the man who loves his country and must face the brutal truths of that love.

He is the man who believes in America.

Epilogue on Edward Abbey

Intro draft for Bowden's review 5/24/91

This is a copy of the original typed letter sent to James Bishop Jr. for the epilogue to the book *Epitaph for a Desert Anarchist: The Life and Legacy of Edward Abbey* (1994). Bowden wrote this in Alamos, Sonora, where he lived for a year and a half in the early '90s.

AS I WRITE THIS, Ed's been technically dead about two years, and I've had a hard time with what's happened to his career since he died. The guy I knew has become an object, a category, a legend of sorts, and something that almost seems to be spelled in capital letters: EDWARD ABBEY.

I have never really recovered from his death. The day he died was the first time in years I raised my hand in anger at another person. For days, I felt violent, and I was appalled at myself, but it felt good. Why did this happen? I think because of a kind of selfishness and a kind of fear.

I knew I would no longer have anyone to talk to about the words as music. Not that we ever said a hell of a lot. But that's the point. We didn't have to say much because we both felt the same way. I think of him a lot. Not in any concrete way, remembering a moment or some stunning pronouncement, but in a vague way, like he's a friendly ghost watching over me.

And judging me! I can give you a dime store version of what he gave me: don't write just for money; don't write anything you don't believe; don't listen to others; don't quit, don't ever quit. And don't believe the good things they say about you. You see? It's all rather obvious. But I still think of him, because even though these thoughts, these admonitions, are common, to live them and practice them is very uncommon.

I have a hunch Abbey is delighted at this new change in his status. As they said of Elvis' death, "good career move." But this new guy, he's not the one I knew or would ever want to know.

The Abbey I knew, an anarchist, a quiet loner addicted to classical music, bouts of solitude, and strict work habits, hardly knew the creature he had created and admitted as much in his essay "Confessions of a Literary Hobo." But then there were a lot of Abbeys, and different people knew different men parading about under that name.

I still remember that hotel squatted by the Los Angeles airport, the corridors clogged with magazine people in full rut at an industry convention. I was an editor at that time, and my major investor was sweating blood as he stood before me. He told me he had just talked to his office and discovered that it was going to be picketed by Mexican-Americans, that there might be violence, that some fabled end was near. There had been angry phone calls, he sputtered. All because of Abbey, because of what Abbey wrote—an attack on Hispanic culture as anti-nature, anti-democratic, as patrón-ridden—and what I had decided to print . . . ah, the power of words.

Then I fielded a call from a Mexican-American leader in the community who wanted to talk to Abbey, wanted to correct in an honest discussion the errors of his way. I said I'd call Ed (the phone number by that time in his life was a minor secret, unlisted and known to only a few thousand people here and there) and have him call back. So I did.

It was early in the morning and overcast, the kind of half-rainy day where cars sing on the asphalt as they roll past, and Abbey's voice was slow, soft, and with wide spaces between his words.

That was normal. He often was not much of a talker. I told him of the tempest he'd created and of the man who wanted to talk to him. I said the man deserved to be answered. So he said he'd give him a call. Then he paused and sighed, and continued that he wished he'd never written that piece, that it had hurt too many people and raised too much bad feeling for whatever value the ideas in it might have. Words can do that too.

Words, that is really a lot of whatever friendship existed between Ed Abbey and me, words, the mystery of words. Abbey could be wrong-headed, angry, vicious at times, but not careless when it came to words. He delighted in their exact value, the same way a gunfighter was into the ballistics of various cartridges . . . at times he seemed to favor magnum loads.

I'll tell you about the Abbey I knew. He'd promised to write about a kind of stand-off with a local developer–car dealer for a newspaper where I worked in Tucson. And when it was due, I called him and he'd forgotten all about it. So I drove out to his house to get it, while he typed out a piece in a semi-panic.

When I got there it was finished, the pages were full of pen marks moving sentences, scratching out words, adding new thoughts. The damn thing looked like a snake pit packed with writhing serpents and he was still at it with his pen as I pried it out of his hands.

Or, there was the Abbey I was having lunch with once when I happened to mention a passage in John Steinbeck's *The Log of the Sea of Cortez,* a few paragraphs describing Bahía Concepcíon. He'd read the book years before and started quoting the description from memory.

This is the man who was my friend and whom I remember. A guy who sweat blood over words and never by his own standards got it right. The man who never rested on his laurels, who constantly read other writers, who every single time I met him was shoving books into my hands and insisting that I read them, telling me in that flat, soft voice that I had to read this or that.

Basically, a hillbilly from Appalachia who mainlined the English language and never recovered from his love for it. That feeling is very rare, at least it has been in my life. I have by accidents of employment been around a lot of people who write down words, and sell them, but Abbey was about the only person I ever knew who shared my own passions for the language.

We were both essentially children, semi-dolts, in awe of the sound of words. I must emphasize the sounds because Abbey was a product of spoken language, of the music of words. I think of this sense of language as music, as rhythm, resulting from his early rearing in the hills.

In my case, I remember a childhood of people talking in the kitchen, of men sitting there with quarts of beer and talking, telling tales, commanding attention through their sense of editing of quirky words, of comedy mixed with pain; of women at the sink or bustling about the stove and counters and telling tales of their life with men; of vocabulary being a chest of tools for constructing narratives of life as a song, the words as notes, the people or characters being melodies. For me, and I suspect for Ed, reading books came later, and by that time we could not alter this sense of language as music.

Basically, he thought writing was a moral task dedicated to moral issues and if it were not, then it was a bunch of bullshit. Hence, his endless rage against the Henry Jameses and John Updikes of the world. He also believed that writing was to be read.

The students he taught could not get an A unless their work in class was accepted by some publication—I know because they would show up at my editorial office door with his recommendation for immortality.

I happened to agree with him on these matters, and so, while our conversations tended to be about writing, we didn't say a lot because we agreed. We carried on more of a wink-and-nod sentence fragment kind of conversation.

Anyone who wonders how he felt about words should simply read a couple of pages of him. Then pick a paragraph and try to remove a sentence. Then take a sentence and try to scratch out a word. Or change a word. It's not easy to do.

Abbey wrote in the vernacular style, the words sounding as if they were coming out of his mouth as he sat on the bar stool next to you. And this makes his writing look off-handed. But it is tight, very tight.

I can't recall asking him a direct question about what someone should do and say and write. I'm not sure I cared. People ask me things now as if I had been keeping detailed notes, making tape recordings of penetrating talks with the Master. Well, I didn't. I'm not that kind of person.

I know people who dream about him. Some of them never met him, but they still dream about him. I don't, but I believe they do. I'm now living in Mexico, that place and culture that Abbey skewered so harshly and yet efficiently in an essay that temporarily ignited the magazine I once worked for.

I never agreed with the essay or Ed about Mexico or Mexicans. But I loved the way he constructed a demolition job on the culture and I don't doubt he believed every word of it. So I live in Mexico, and that's just one more thing Ed Abbey technically disagreed about.

From time to time in the press now, I read attacks on Abbey as being racist, sexist, rednecked, and having other failings. I never feel any need to respond to these attacks. I don't think they are entirely fair, but I don't care. Any writer who is dead and still raises hackles must have done his work properly.

In a way, I hope I never have to write about him again. I'm a little ill at ease with the Abbey industry that has flowered since he died—and I'm not thinking of this book when I say this. I mean the people I know that didn't give a damn about him, who envied him and cut him up behind his back, and who now base part of their public identity on some kind of intimacy with the late, great Edward Abbey.

Oh. Well, the hell with it. Abbey can take care of himself. He always has. And now I've got to walk down to the weekly market in the arroyo. Let me know, Jim, if this is what you had in mind.

Chuck Bowden
Alamos, Sonora
Mexico

The Bone Garden of Desire

From *Esquire*, August 2000

Rossini, the great opera composer, could recall only two moments of real grief in his life. One, when his mother died. And the second time was out on a boat when a chicken stuffed with truffles fell into the water and was lost.

SOMETIMES, WHEN HE WAS NEARING DEATH, I'd go over to help Art cook. I'm down on my knees on the patio, and Art is sitting in a chair with a beer. He has grilled steaks to a cinder and caught the juice. And now I pound the meat with a claw hammer until it's infused with cloves of garlic and peppercorns. Then I shred it with my fingers, put it all in a bowl with the saved juice and herbs, and then simmer. This is *machaca* according to his late wife's recipe and it takes hours, and this is life, or the best part, he believes as he sits in the chair while I bend and pound to spare his battered old joints. It is a deep taste of something within his bones.

We are outside in the old downtown barrio while I pound in the desert sun, and nearby are the *justicia* flaming-orange flowers and the *chuparosa* with the buzz of hummingbirds and the *nicotiana* reaching up twelve, fourteen feet, the pale green leaves, the spikes of yellow flowers, the costa hummingbirds with purple gorgets that seem to favor it, and Art beams and says, "My birds, my plants."

He takes another swig of beer, and beads of cold moisture fleck the can. Maybe it is the mouth, I think, as I sit down in the garden, swirling red wine in my mouth, dry wine, the kind that reaches back toward the throat and lasts for maybe half a minute on the tongue.

Anyway, when we made the machaca, Art was alive then, and being alive is gardening and cooking and birds and green and blue, at the very least. He was relaxed. I pounded the garlic and pepper, and grilled flesh hung in the air. He told me that during the Korean War, his navy ship made a run from Philadelphia to Europe, and during the Atlantic crossing five officers went over the side and nobody ever writes about stuff like that. But he knows, he was there and all fell overboard at night. They were all assholes, he said.

The beef was tender, the chiles hot, but not too hot, just enough to excite the tongue, and the seasonings bit, the garlic licked the taste buds, and I began to float on the sensations as Art drank his beer and the plants grew and stirred, the hummingbirds whizzed overhead and then hovered before my face, my tongue rubbed against the roof of my mouth, and it is all a swirl of sensation as I remember that summer day cooking.

I also remember Art (died February 11) sitting down in my garden in a chair on a Sunday in January, the last day he left home under his own power. He could barely walk then, his chunky body dwindling as the cancer snacked on various organs, and his skin was yellow from the jaundice. He held on to my arm as we crept through the garden, down from the upper bench, past the bed of *trichocereus,* under the thin arms of the *selenicereus* snaking through the tree overhead. He looked over by the *notocactus,* with their dark green columns, their tawny rows of bristles and small bubbles of white down on their crowns where the yellow flowers would finally emerge; he looked over there where I'd scattered Dick's bone and ash and he said brightly, Hi, Dick (died August 23).

We sat in plastic chairs surrounded by garden walls that were purple, yellow, and pink, colors to fight back all the nights. He knew he'd be dead in two or three weeks, and he was. He knew he'd never see this spring, just as Dick had never made it to the previous fall. And five months before Dick had been Paul (died March 9). And five months after Art would come Chris (died August 6).

THE COOKING HAD BEGUN EARLIER, like the gardening, but both took hold of me around the time my friends started dying. I remember walking to the market, coming home and flipping through books for recipes, and then cooking. While the sauce simmered, I would open a bottle of red wine and begin drinking. There was never enough red wine, never. I was always cooking from Italian recipes because they were simple and bold and I loved the colors, the red of the tomatoes, the green skin of the zucchini, and because I liked peeling garlic and chopping onions and tearing basil. The oil mattered also, the thought of olives, and I preferred the stronger, cheaper oils with their strong tastes. I used iron pans coated with green enamel on the outside. There would be scent in the air.

The garden also went out of control. I put in five or six tons of rock. Truckloads of soil. I built low terraces and planted cactus and a few herbs. I had no plan and the thing grew from someplace in my mind.

I must tell you about this flower, *Selenicereus plerantus*. It opens only in the dark; it begins to unfold around 9 P.M. and it closes before dawn, slams shut at the very earliest probes of gray light. When it blooms, no one can be alone at night, it is not possible, nor can anyone fear the night, not in the slightest. This flower touches your face, it kisses your ear, its tongue slides across your crotch. The flower is shameless, absolutely shameless. When it opens its white jaws, the petals span a foot and lust pours out into the night, a lust as heavy as syrup, and everything is coated by the carnality of this plant. It opens only on the hottest nights of the year, black evenings when the air is warmer than your body and you cannot tell where your flesh ends and the world begins.

A month, maybe a month and a half, before Chris died, he came over in the evening. He could not control his hiccuping then—the radiation, you know. And he found it better to stand in his weakness than to sit. He wore a hat; his hair was falling out. So we were out in the darkness, him hiccuping and not drinking—he just did not want that beer anymore—and the flower opened and flooded the yard with that lust, the petals gaping shamelessly, and we watched it unfold and felt the lust caress us and he hiccuped and took it all in.

He understood that flower, I'm sure of it.

BLIND OLD HOMER WROTE THAT no part of us is more like a dog than the "brazen belly, crying to be remembered." By the twentieth century, there were fifty or sixty thousand codified recipes in Italian cooking alone. By the mid-twentieth century, Italians were eating seven hundred different pasta shapes, and one sauce, Bolognese, had hundreds of variations.

What can death mean in the face of this drive? What can death say at this table? I tell you: Art called up when things had gotten pretty bad and said he had this craving for strawberry Jell-O.

There must be something about the mouth, about the sucking and the licking and the chewing and the sweet and the sour. The pepper also, and the saline. An English cookbook of 1660 suggests a cake recipe that consumes a half bushel of flour, three pounds of butter, fourteen pounds of currants, two pounds of sugar, and three quarts of cream. There is a leg of mutton smeared with almond paste and a pound of sugar and then garnished with chickens, pigeons, capons, cinnamon, and, naturally, more sugar.

The dark green flesh of the cactus glows with life from the ash and ground human bone. I've come to depend on the garden, and so I stare at the Madagascar palms, their thorny trunks bristling under the canopy of the mesquite tree. Red wine swirls against my tongue because this bone gardening, this wall of green flesh, has all become hopelessly oral with me. I eat, therefore I am. I appreciate nothing, devour everything.

ART FOUND OUT ABOUT THE CANCER after Thanksgiving. He couldn't really eat. It wasn't the chemotherapy, since he'd passed on that after having a first bout with the colon cancer, and to be honest, the doctors didn't recommend chemo or any other therapy. They gave him prescriptions for opiates and advised him to take lots of them and not to worry. But he didn't like them, didn't like having his mind turn to mush, and besides, he was an old narc, and I think pill popping didn't quite sit right with him. But he couldn't eat, just had no appetite, and when he ate, he felt kind of sick. The cancer was everywhere, of course, with the liver just being the signature location.

So I took him over some marijuana brownies and that evening he took two and then spent half the night in the kitchen—frying steaks and potatoes, whipping up this and that, and gorging. And after that, he refused ever to take another brownie.

Art said they upset his stomach.

But, Lord, that one night, he came alive and tasted deeply.

SHE HAS THE GIFT OF WRITING exactly the way she speaks and speaking exactly the way she thinks. For years I have gotten letters from Barbara, and they are always fresh and clear and without any of the filters we generally use to guard our hearts. When she writes of her son's death, her words remain the same. Paul was not a surprise to her. She is an artist, her father was an artist, his father was an artist. And it has never been easy—art is not made by the easy, but it has been in the house for generations and felt like a part of life. She told me that's what she put on his tombstone: ARTIST.

At first she was very angry. Not at Paul, at least not in a way she was ready to say, but at the people around him who introduced him to heroin and then did nothing as the drug took over his soul. Shouldn't they have done something? Didn't they realize what they had unleashed? Aren't they responsible? And, of course, the questions were sound and the answers were deserved and Paul was still dead.

She works, she organizes his papers, letters, his art work. She revisits the studio, the pipe, the rope, a boy hanging there. She writes me, "Found out Paul hung for over 8–9 hours. That would not have happened had I been there. 8–9 hours after he was found. Fuck the criminal codes. My baby hung by his neck for as long as 14 hours. I didn't think there could be more pain."

THEY TAKE AWAY THE MINTS because the case is metal. They scrutinize the carton of cigarettes also and then I'm allowed on the ward. Dick is puzzled by the shower, why the head is buried up some kind of funnel in the ceiling. It takes him weeks to figure out they are trying to prevent him from hanging himself. Of course, he cannot think clearly, what with the steady dose of electroshock treatments. He'd checked himself in after the suicide attempt failed. He had saved up his Valiums, taken what he figured to be a massive dose, and then, goddammit, still woke up Monday morning when by any decent standards he ought to have been dead. It was the depression, he told me, the endless blackness. He could handle the booze, and when he was rolling, that was a quart or two of vodka a night, plus coke, of course, to stay alert for the vodka. There was that time he'd checked into detox with blood oozing from his eyes and ears and ass. But he could handle that. He was working on the smoking, didn't light up in the house, you know.

But he couldn't take the depression, never tasted blackness like that. I'd go out in the evening to the ward and we'd sit outside in the walled yard, kind of like a prison, and for two days I tried to get him to pitch horseshoes. Finally, on the third night, he tried but couldn't make the distance between the two pits. The shoes, of course, were plastic, lest the patients hurt one another. But we worked on it, and he got to tossing okay.

We'd been friends for a good long time, business partners once, and we'd survived being in business together, so we must've really been friends, and he'd always been like me, riding a little roughshod over the way life was supposed to be lived, but he'd kept his spirits up. Not now.

When he got out, I'd go over and take him to the store. He could not move. I'd walk him from the car into the market and then walk with him up and down the aisles. He could not connect with food. I'd buy him bananas because his potassium was low, and lots of green vegetables. He couldn't abide this; he told me he'd never eaten anything green since he was five. Then I'd take him through the checkout and home. The place was a wreck. One day I showed him how to clean off one square foot of the kitchen counter. He watched me do it. I said, Look, you do a foot a day and if you don't do a damn thing else, you'll feel like you did something. His face remained passive.

I'd bring him over and cook dinner and make him eat it. Then we'd sit in the yard, he'd stare out at the cactus and trees, and his eyes would glaze at the twisting paths and clouds of birds. He could hardly speak. The blackness, he'd say by way of explaining.

My huge Argentine mesquite arced over the yard. Nobody believed I'd planted it myself, dug the hole and everything, and that when I put it in the ground, it did not come up to my knee. I remember when I planted it, a woman was over and I told her what this little sapling would become and she said, Nope, it ain't gonna happen. But it did.

I kept trying to get Dick to plant trees. But it was like the horseshoes. It came hard.

IN 1696, MME. DE MAINTENON, Louis XIV's longtime mistress, writes, "Impatience to eat [peas], the pleasure of having eaten them, and the anticipation of eating them again are the three subjects I have heard very thoroughly dealt with. . . . Some women, having supped, and supped well, at the king's table, have peas waiting for them in their rooms before going to bed."

Peas are new to the French court and all those lascivious mouths and expert tongues are anxious for this new sensation. I applaud this pea frenzy. Who would want a stoic as a cook?

Mme. de Maintenon, sixty-one years old, now secretly wed to the king, stalwart of court etiquette, she likes her pea pods dipped in a sauce, and then she licks them. Yes, she does.

GOING UP THE STAIRS, I instantly miss the sunlight. Outside, Brooklyn in January is brilliant and the sea is in the air. The stairs feel narrow and dim and cold and dank, and it is like leaving childhood behind for the grave. In my memory, Paul is a child, permanently around the age of, say, ten. I've seen his later photographs on driver's licenses, and the face seems gaunt, the eyes hollow. I'm afraid of finding the room those eyes came from, finding it upstairs at the end of these seemingly endless flights of stairs, with almost no light, a chill in the air, and that dampness that says no one cooks in the kitchen and the woman is never in the bed.

But the machinery standing in the gray light of the big room comforts me. I have stumbled into a surviving pocket of the nineteenth century, that time when people still believed that they could throw themselves at problems and wrestle with materials and fabricate solutions. The morning bleeds through the large windows and glows against the shrink-wrap machine. He had a thing about shrink-wrap—the more you stressed it, the stronger it became. I soak up the room and feel at peace. This is a proper shop for a craftsman and his craft. His craft was pretty simple: he was going to be the best fucking artist in the world and show that all the other stuff was shit. He was going to cut through the fakery and the fashion and get to the ground floor, the killing floor, the factory floor. He was not about tricks or frills or style. He was brutally simple and industrial-strength. I can feel him here, his mouth a firm line, his hair carelessly framing his totally absorbed face, his body bent over slightly as he tinkers with some project, oblivious to everything, including himself, pushing on relentlessly toward mastering a riddle that only he sees or feels or can solve. He's forgotten to eat for a day, his dog watches him silently from a corner of the big room, a stillness hangs over everything and is only slightly broken by the careful movements he makes.

Over in a corner of the shop is the apartment he carved out of the vast cavern of the old factory, and sketched on his door is an arrow pointing down to the floor and a message to slide the mail under here. It has the look of something a twelve-year-old would do. And enjoy doing. I half expect Orville and Wilbur Wright to tap me on the shoulder, or to hear old Henry Ford laconically announcing idiot-savant theses about the coming industrial age. I'm in the past, a place Paul picked to find the future. There is a feeling of grime everywhere, an oil-based grime that has come off machines as they inhaled and exhaled in the clangor of their work. I stand over a worktable and open a cigar box of crayons and carefully pluck two for myself, a blue and a red. I ask a friend of Paul's a question, and he visibly tightens and says suddenly that he can't stay in here anymore. He says he is still upset. So I go alone and look down the narrow hallway to the door to this loft/studio/factory floor and glance up at the stout pipe; it looks to be six or eight inches in diameter. Then I come back to the factory room and see a piece of a black doormat that Paul had nailed to the wall. It says quietly, GET HOME.

I think, Well, shit, so this is where he hung himself.

KING SOLOMON'S PALACE WAS PROBABLY one warm home. He lived with seven hundred wives and three hundred girlfriends and somehow everybody tore through ten oxen a day, plus chunks of gazelles and hartebeests. The Bible said the wise old king had twelve thousand horsemen charging around the countryside scaring up chow for the meals back home.

Money does not replace the lust for food. Or the flesh. Nothing replaces it, nothing. Sometimes it dies, this appetite, sometimes it just vanishes in people. But it is never replaced. By 1803, one restaurant in Paris had kept its stockpot bubbling twenty-four hours a day for eighty-five years. Three hundred thousand capons had gone into the pot over the decades. This is what we like to call a meaningless statistic. Until we open our mouths. Or catch the scent of a woman. Or lean over into a bloom raging in the night.

I'D COME OUT TO THE RANCH, a two-hundred-acre remaining fragment of the fifty to eighty square miles that once wore his family's brand, and we'd sit on the porch and have a beer. Chris worked as a carpenter and enjoyed life. He knew every plant and rock for miles around. He didn't seem to give a damn about being born into money and now living without it. I never heard him say a word about it. He cared about when one of his cows was going to calf. And he liked not owning a horse—he prided himself on getting along without one and in wearing sensible boots instead of narrow, high-heeled cowboy boots like every other person in a western city.

He'd show me things. The foundations of a settler's cabin down the hill. The little collapsed house he and his first wife lived in along the arroyo. An old Indian village.

I remember the village clearly. We walked for an hour or two or more and then hit a steep incline under the palisades. Chris paused and pointed out the hawk and falcon nesting sites. Then his legs went uphill at a steady pace, like pistons. At the top, we slid through a narrow chute and were upon a small village on a mesa. At the entrance was a low wall and piles of rocks for throwing at invaders. This was clearly a fort people fled to in some time of trouble five hundred years or more ago.

Chris had been coming here since he was a boy. The place, like almost everything else in the area, was his secret. We sat up there in the sunshine, swallowing a couple hundred square miles of scenery and saying little. He was like that. I hardly ever heard him complain. Things just are. And if you look around, they're pretty good. Have a cold beer, a warm meal. And take in the countryside.

IN THE FIRST CENTURY, Apicius put together a manuscript that lets us visit the lust of the Roman palate. The empire made all things possible—Apicius once outfitted a ship because he'd heard some good-sized shrimp were being caught off North Africa. The emperor Vitellius, said to be somewhat of a pig at table, favored a dish of pike liver, pheasant brains, peacock brains, flamingo tongues, and lamprey roe. Apicius is supposed to have killed himself when he was down to his last couple of million bucks because he could not bear to lower his standard of living. Before there was a language of words on paper, there must have been a language of food. Speech begins with the fire and the kettle. I am sure of this.

WHEN I WAS DRINKING AT THE GRAVE, I didn't feel quite right. I'd been uneasy about leaving Dick, worried about two days away. I'd gone down and gotten him bailed out a few days before, done the shopping trips, talked to him about the importance of cleaning a counter. All of that. We had sat in the yard and watched the woodpecker eat insects in the throb of the August air. His speech was very slow and nothing seemed to ever lift, nothing. He'd been fired, the drinking had come back, the electroshock didn't seem to do much good, and the gambling dug in deep until he had about a hundred thousand on the credit cards. So we'd sit in the yard and I'd explain that you can't beat a slot machine, that you can't win. He'd say, That's it, that's it, you can't win.

So when I left for a memorial mass in a distant city for a murder victim named Bruno Jordan who'd crossed my path, I felt ill at ease. Out at the cemetery after the mass, we stood around the grave drinking beer and talking, and then we went back to the house in the barrio for dinner, one cousin looking down at the grave and saying, Hey, Bruno, see you back at the house.

The next day, when I came through the door, the phone was ringing. They'd found the body. Dick had been dead two days. He'd died clean, nothing in his body. He'd accidentally tripped on the rug, hit his head on the dining room table, that was it. He'd been working on a book about the drinking life.

Dick had always had one terror: that he would die drunk. So God smiled on him.

I FEEL SURPRISINGLY AT PEACE. Walking the few blocks from the subway, I take in the Brooklyn street, warming to its resemblance to the endless warrens of houses and factories I knew in Chicago. It looks just like the places Paul lived as a boy, and I think, You cagey guy, you found the Midwest in New York. Behind the factory-now-loft stands a Russian church, thrown up in the 1920s by those determined to keep the lamp of faith lit on a distant shore. Across from that is a small park with beaten grass, the kind of sliver of light our urban planners have always tossed to the inmates of our great cities. It all feels very comfortable to me. When Paul was a small boy, I can remember walking across the tundra of Chicago to visit his parents' apartment and passing scenes just like these in this pocket of Brooklyn. And the workspace itself, with its patina of grime from machines, its workman's bench, its monastic sense of craft, hard work, and diligence, recalls the various places Paul toiled as a boy—his room, the cellar, the corner grabbed in some cottage in the country. That's part of the sense of peace I feel pervading me. I think to myself, Paul, you kept the faith.

I've gotten up before dawn and gone over his letters, which I've brought with me, and the bank statements, all the while sipping coffee in a mid-Manhattan hotel. The numbers on the statements blurred as I sat amid businessmen who were studying CNN on the lounge television, and then I'd look back down at the bank statements and feel as though I were watching the spinning dials of a slot machine, only this machine always comes up with the same result: a hundred dollars a day. December, January, February, the steady withdrawals are punctual and exact. I thought to myself, Paul, you create order even in your disorder. So later when I stand in the big room where he tore at the limits of what he called art and plunged into some place he hoped was behind that name, when I touch his row of tools on the workbench and admire his shrink-wrap machine in one corner, whirring in my head is this blur of numbers as he swallowed his earnings in a grim, orderly fashion. I look over at the wall, the one punctured by the hallway leading to the doorway and the stout pipe against the ceiling, and read once more the doormat still whispering, GET HOME. I reach up and rip the black message from the wall. This one I am taking home.

Paul was up to something here. I know this in my bones.

HE KIND OF SCOWLS AND comes limping across the kitchen at me, saying, No, no. He takes the knife and says, Here, see, you gotta do this rocking motion, and with that he chops the hell out of the cilantro. Art will be dead in three weeks, and this is his last hurrah, teaching me how to make salsa cruda. He's real yellow now, wheezing all the time, and beneath the yellow is the color of ash.

He's got these papers to straighten out, and we go over them. He's going to do a bit of writing, and so I bring the office chair and computer. But then he can't sit up anymore, and we try to jury-rig something in the easy chair. And then that's too much and the damn fluid is building in his body, he's all bloated and distended, and, by God, he tells the nurse who comes to the house each day, he's gotta get the swelling drained at the hospital. And she says, That won't do any good, you're not sick, you're dying. He listens without so much as a blink, I'm sitting right there, and then he pads down the hall to his bedroom, lies down, and sleeps. In twenty-four hours, he goes into a coma. The next day, he's dead after a night of family praying and shouting over him—ancient aunts hollering messages in his ear for other family members that have gone to the boneyard ahead of him. His cousin, the monsignor, says the funeral mass.

I can still taste the salsa and smell the cilantro and feel that rocking motion as he tries to show me the right way to wield the knife. And to make salsa, his salsa, as he learned it from his wife, Josie, who learned from her parents, and back into the brown web of time. Like everything that matters to the tongue, it is simple.

- Put five or six sixteen-ounce cans of whole TOMATOES into a big pot, reserving the liquid. Coarse-grind the tomatoes in a food processor, a short pulse so they come out in chunks and not puree. Now add them to the reserved juice.
- Cut up two or three bunches of GREEN ONION, in very thin slices so that you end up with tiny circles. Now very finely cut up a bunch of CILANTRO.
- Add five cans of diced GREEN CHILES, a teaspoon of GARLIC POWDER, and the onion and cilantro to the tomatoes and their juice. Sprinkle a teaspoon or two of OREGANO. Taste it and adjust seasoning.
- Now start crushing CHILTEPINS (*Capsicum annuum* var. *aviculare*) and add to taste. Add salt. Taste again. Keep crushing chiltepins until it is right for your tongue.

That was the last time I really saw him move, when he was trying to teach me how to make salsa cruda. He knew some things can't be allowed to end.

THE BOTTOM LINE IS ALWAYS SIMPLE, and the way to this line is to get rid of things. I stand at a hot stove and make risotto, a rice dish of the Italian north:

- Melt some butter in oil, then sauté some CHOPPED ONION, toss in the RICE, and coat it with the oil; add the liquid (make the first ladle white wine, then go with broth) a half cup at a time, constantly stirring.
- In twenty minutes, the rice is ready, the center of each kernel a little resistant to the tooth, but ready. Each grain is saturated with the broth and onion and oil flavor.
- Then spread the rice on the plate to cool and eat from the edge inward. Pick a brilliant plate with rich color—I like intense blues and greens, you know—to play off the white. Some mix in A HALF OR FULL CUP OF GRATED PARMESAN to the rice to make it stickier. I just sprinkle some on top and usually favor Romano, because it has more bite. But that is your choice.

The rest is not. After all, we are in Paul's workshop, a thing to be kept clean and simple and direct. The difference between good art and good cooking is you can eat cooking. But the important part, the getting rid of things, it is always there and the kid knew it.

The kid worked. Like most products of the Midwest, I can't abide people who fuck off and don't do things. I can remember my father sitting at a kitchen table in Chicago with his quart of beer, telling me with a snarl that in Chicago we make things, but in New York they just sell things.

I look up at the torn drywall. When Paul didn't answer the phone, his uncle flew from Chicago to New York and took a cab over here to Brooklyn. Clawed his way through the drywall—I look up at the hole he made—and found Paul swinging from the big pipe. He'd left a note and neat accounts on the table, plus his checkbook, so everyone would be paid off proper.

I hum to myself as I look up at that pipe. Hum that song by John Prine about the hole in Daddy's arm where all the money goes.

IT GOT SO HE COULDN'T DO MUCH. One day his ex-wife, Mary, stopped by the ranch to check on him, and he was sprawled in the doorway, half in the house and half out, surrounded by the dogs and cats.

So Mary took him into town. He'd been busy at the ranch despite his weakness as the cancer ate. He'd been building check dams to cure a century of erosion; he planted a garden, put the boots to the cattle, and let the hills come back. He said ranching was over and it was time for the earth to get some other kind of deal. I'd run into him a week or so before at the feed mill and he was chipper. His hair had just about all fallen out because of the radiation, but he said he felt good. He was in town to get a part for the pump.

He was real lean by then, and when I went down to see him at Mary's place, he was stretched out in bed. He wanted to talk Mexico, the people, the plants, the cattle, the way the air felt at night. I brought down some pictures of Mexico and we hung them around the room. He was having some kind of magic tar shipped down from Colorado that was supposed to beat back the cancer, and he was tracking the pennant race also. People would drop by at all hours to see him, since the word was out that he was a goner. He'd smoke a joint with them, talk about this and that, especially Mexico, which he knew was color and sound and smell and taste and a wood fire with a kettle on the coals. Some of the time he lived down there in a shack with a campesino family. When he fell in the doorway at the ranch, half in and half out, he was pretty much set to go back to Mexico. That was on hold at the moment as he tackled dying.

He lasted about a week. I went over one day, and he was propped up in bed so that the tumor blocking his throat didn't pester him too much. He said, Chuck, I got some great news. We just got two inches of rain at the ranch.

Yes. I can smell the sweet grass as the clouds lift.

SHE IS AT WAR WITH HERSELF, the life within her fighting the death without her. And she knows this. And she writes me this. She says, "So after I talked to you, I went out to the cemetery. The sun was out here and it was a beautiful day. Snow in patches hugging the earth in lovely patterns making me realize the earth has temperatures of variation, like a body. I had not realized that before. Then as I drove back, a rage overtook me and I raped and pillaged. I went to where I used to live along the beach and cut branches from bushes I know will bloom (not in obvious places or so they would hurt the bush or tree). Many, many branches that filled up the trunk of the car and the backseat. It took an hour and a half to get them all recut and into water all over my house and closed porch. I've been cutting forsythia and 'forcing' it, but haven't tried these others—redbud, cherry, baby's breath, flowering almond, weigela (probably too late a bloomer), lilac (doubt this one will work) . . ."

As she writes this to me, it is March, a month when boys hang themselves, a month when winter has stayed too long. A month when spring is near and force may be applied.

I DON'T TRUST THE ANSWERS or the people who give me the answers. I believe in dirt and bone and flowers and fresh pasta and salsa cruda and red wine. I do not believe in white wine; I insist on color. I think death is a word and life is a fact, just as food is a fact and cactus is a fact.

There is apparently a conspiracy to try to choke me with words. There are these steps to death—is it seven or twelve or what? fuck, I can't remember—and then you arrive at acceptance. Go toward the light. Our Father who art in heaven. Whosoever shall believe in me shall not perish. Too many words choking me, clutching at my throat until they strangle any bad words I might say. Death isn't the problem. The words are, the lies are. I have sat now with some thing broken inside me for months, and the words—death, grief, fear—don't touch my wounds.

I have crawled back from someplace where it was difficult to taste food and where the flowers flashing their crotches in my face all but lacked scent. My wounds kept me alive; my wounds, I now realize, were life. I have drunk a strong drug and my body is ravaged by all the love and caring and the colors and forms and the body growing still in the new silence of the room as someone I knew and loved ceased breathing.

I remember standing in the room with Art's corpse, so warm, his heart had stopped beating maybe a hundred and twenty seconds earlier, and I stood there wondering, What has changed now, what is it that just took place? And I realized that I had advanced not an inch from where I stood as a boy when I held my dying dog and watched life wash off his furry face with a shudder. I do not regret this inability to grow into wisdom. I listen to Chris saying, Good news, two inches of rain at the ranch. Look up at the stout pipe Paul picked for the rope. Hear Dick slowly trying to explain—in words so soft I must lean forward to hear them—why he cannot pick up a plastic horseshoe in the evening light at the nuthouse. Then these pat words show up that people offer me and these pious words slink away like a cur flinching from this new stillness on the wind.

Almost every great dish in Italian cooking has fewer than eight ingredients. Get rid of things or food will be complex and false. In the garden, there is no subtlety. A flower is in your face and is never named Emily. Be careful of the words; go into the bone garden and then taste desire. So it has taken months and it is still a matter of the tongue and of lust. And if you go toward that light and find it, piss on it for me.

I WOULD BELIEVE IN THE WORDS of solace if they included fresh polenta with a thickened brown sauce with shiitake and porcini mushrooms. The corn must be coarse—ground and simmered and stirred for at least forty minutes, then spread flat on a board about an inch thick and cooled in a rich yellow sheet. The sauce, a brew of vegetable broth, white wine, pepper, salt, some olive oil, and minced garlic, is rich like fine old wood in a beloved and scarred table. When you are ready, grill a slab of the polenta, having first lightly brushed it with olive oil, then ladle on some sauce. And eat. The dish is brutally simple. But it skirts the lie of the words of solace; it does not deny desire.

Never deny desire. Not once. Always go to the garden and the kitchen. Whatever death means, the large white cactus flower still opens in the evening and floods the air with lust and hot wet loins. The mushroom sauce on the corn mush will calm no one, either.

That is why they are better than the words.

AS I SIT HERE, Chris is to the south, Art is to the west, Paul is back east, and Dick is in the backyard by the fierce green flesh of the cactus. These things I know. The answers I don't know, nor am I interested. That is why food is important and plants are important. Because they are not words and the answers people offer me are just things they fashion out of words. A simple veal ragù is scent and texture and color and soft on the tongue. It is important to cut onions by hand. The power of the flower at night is frightening, the lust floods the air and destroys all hope of virtue.

There will be more blooms this spring—the cactus grew at least ten feet last year. They will open around nine in the evening and then close at the first gray light of dawn. I'll sit out there with a glass of red wine and the lights out.

When I tell people about the blooms, about how they open around nine and close before sunrise and do this just for one night, they always ask, Is that all?

Yes. That's all.

Part V

[The world] can only be saved by appetite and appetite of one kind is what is killing it, the appetite to possess things. And the lack of appetite of another kind, the appetite to feel things, is what is killing it.

FROM *INFERNO*

Letter to Barbara Houlberg

The following was taken from a letter written by Bowden to his longtime friend Barbara Houlberg. It was written in the mid-seventies.

START

THE LAND NEVER HELD ENOUGH LAND.
The empty was always full.
The buffalo peddles no surplus space.
The grass invites no guests.
The man suffered blood frontiers with other men.

Killing in the night and killing in the day. The leaf oozed poison. The spine stabbed. The root fought the root. The weak, the old, the young fell hamstrung and gut-ripped to the hungry. And the men, the women, the

children walked north to south leaving a trail of sharp pointed stones and skull-crushing rocks.
Then they came from a there called Europe.
They found a here called the new world.
The land never held enough land.
A lot of feet I guess scrapping over stone age stone heaps scrambling toward home snatches of flesh peace with barking dogs. A million hands zipping along singing a song with bone needles all stitching feet into skins. Back in the wholesome days when folks sat around the cave—seems always snap glimmer of firelight playing across blank faces in the diorama—well, just sat around waiting for History to begin. But the western boot with high heel, scalpel toe? That was designed by the horse. Men who were not Indians wanted to break horses so that they could break land. Legions of them converging from the bump and grind of ports of call, all fastening on the Rocky Mountains and cracking the range's spine like a chicken bone. The marrow of beaver, gold, silver, who cares just take and maybe it can be bought sold weighed measured. This western boot was not made for walking. It breaks things. Now cows are bludgeoned into meat and hide, blistered into leather, fashioned into glove fits; the thing walks off the bench into the street down the dream rut of conquest. The swirls of silver thread? A touch of grace. Of course the boot has slopped over into people without horses who would not break china and the heel stomps Saturday night faces in Detroit as much as Cheyenne. But the Ghost is still in the machine, and the boot knows what the foot has never learned.

The western boot has never left just its footprints. The grass is gone from the desert valleys, the bighorn have retreated into rock, big trees slashed to stump, wells plunged to dry bottom, elk reduced to jerky
Indians reduced to Indians
land reduced to maps
the west reduced to cow country.
Nothing stops this boot.
Now it even kisses barbed wire.

I THINK I'LL MAKE IT through the night thanks to the serenity of the air conditioner roaring in the old motel. The drapes are pulled shut but a sliver of light slips through and plays across her body. I can smell her and hear the curious breathing, a deep inhale followed by a flutter of air, a kind of humming commentary when she exhales. The digital clock glows blood-red at two A.M. and I think I can also hear a hum coming off it, a faint tinny sound that cuts through the chuff chuff of the air conditioner. I do not think about the body on the morgue table.

Once, a local cop told me about crossing the line to view a body in the morgue and found all the stiffs floating in a tub of something with big numbers marked on their backs. The attendant pulled his out with a hook, he said, like a fish for sale in the market. I listened and wondered, Is this too good to be true? And what was the smell like in that room? And was there this chuff chuff sound from an air conditioner? A hum coming off a clock?

That odd flutter in her breathing catches my attention and I put my hand on her thigh and then slide it between her legs where it is wet and warm and the short hairs brush against my fingers. I can tell she is awake though she does not stir. She'll be gone in a few hours. And I'll be back looking for one photograph of one body in that morgue over there, a body that now, thanks to the cop's story, floats in my mind in some tub with a big number on its back. The face will be twisted, the lips apart, and a silent scream will come from the throat. I want that silent scream, but most of the time I doubt its existence. It is more likely that nothing is lodged in the throat, not a scream, nor a sentence, just a brute silence as death descends. But still, I think, it must be odd to be recorded as having drowned and then to discover that one has been tossed into a tub with a number. Assuming such a tub even exists.

THERE MUST BE A WAY to say yes and yet not base this yes off a life of no. There must be a way to say yes where you cross the river, face the corpse and stare into the dead eyes. Just as you accept the broken levee, the flooded and ruined city. The angry skies, the rising human numbers, and seas racing inland. The ice melting, also.

I think without the yes, there is nothing but lies and the ticking of the clock as we wait for the end of our time like a prisoner in a cell.

That is why the snakes matter to me, because of that yes. That is why the bite matters and the pain. And that is why I am here, in this room, looking for the dead.

And that is part of the problem: the room.

Is this where I gather the strength for yes? Or is this the tomb where I wait for no?

THE ELEPHANT TROUBLES ME and I cannot figure out why. There is this small article off the wire about an elephant over there, across that line, a hungry elephant in a circus that cannot afford to feed the beast. So he grazes by the public highway far to the south in this other nation.

I think of the elephant constantly trying to eat, swallowing in a rush, in a desperate move at least to stay even.

I SNIFF THE CLOSE STALE AIR of the room and feel a weight on my chest.

Lately, the best part of my life is this pleasant darkness, the walk down the carpeted hall, key in the slot, then the door opens, the stringent air sagging with soap, bag down on the chair, quick footsteps to close the drapes, the blackness wraps around me, always the clock glowing by the bed, the menu for porn movies atop the television, an ashtray with one pack of matches, the strip of paper across the toilet seat, a stab at one fat button and then the chuff chuff groan of the air conditioner, a tinny blade of sound cutting through the white noise of the machine as it battles with its own internal parts, all this part of a ribbon of highway with every room along every route the same and the blackness the same and the air the same and the clock the same and the cable channels the same. I realize that this is the constant, the blackness, this is the firm and reassuring core, and everything else out there, the towns floating across the windshield, the pumps spewing gas, the bad coffee on the counters with sugar scattered, all that is faint, lacking substance, a thing to be raced through to get back to the room, the next room, the last room, all the rooms.

The job, the phone messages signaled by the small blinking light, the daily specials written on the whiteboards of the restaurants with grease pens, this I no longer believe in. I want to believe in them but somehow they have moved beyond reach. I have no word for my feelings. I am not alienated. I am not lost. I am not angry. There, that is it, a clot of nots, and somehow I cannot muster a single actual word to describe this sensation. I am not depressed, ah, there it is again, another claim of something I am not. Nor do I feel singular even when I sit in the room downstairs in all these motels where they have coffee, some rolls, the television always on to the news and I look at the other faces and see agendas and plans in their eyes, see goals and schemes, even then I do not feel singular. Because I know we all share one thing: we are all living underwater and yet we cannot get wet.

The room is the home, the place where my mind roams and is free. I think I no longer need maps in my nation because all the roads lead to the room and the room is always the same room, down to the air conditioner that sounds, always, as if it is on its last legs.

I am not on the road. There, again that *not*. But I am not on the road. I am moving and yet always in the same place.

I slide my hand down her leg. Her breathing continues its curious pace. I brush my lips against her mouth.

Her eyes open and she says, "Do you want to come on my face? You can, you know."

Excerpt

From *Desierto: Memories of the Future*

Copyright © 1991

THE SLIDES SPLASH COLOR against the white wall as we sit in chairs, drinks in hand, and look at the photographer's shoot. I'm pretty drunk but I'm not the only one. The way to the viewing has been long and pleasant. Smoke curling off the fire, flowers promising spring, the meat searing and crackling out by the ramada. We have had roasted chickens drenched in marinade and cooked over mesquite, fish caught in Glacier Bay and perfectly filleted, rice propped up with garlic and pepper. In the midst of the cooking, a run had to be made to the liquor store. The evening paced itself with pleasures. Out the door, the penstemons are about to bloom, and the furnace breath of summer comes closer.

And then came the moment that night had spiraled toward. The boxes of slides are placed on a small table, the projector ignites its blank eye, the chairs are scattered about the unfinished den of raw wood and new smells.

The photographer is nervous, the weeks of work, the hope of a vision, all this goes on the line now. I am ill at ease at what will come. The desert is a faint word, but the images will assert that they are truly the flesh on all the dry bones rattling against each other within the small word. I worry that I will recoil from the photographs, that I will not recognize my life in the clean frames of the lens. I look up and on the wall is a photograph of Edward Abbey. We all knew him, and we like to drink too. He is sitting on a rock in the desert, a hat on his head, his bearded face serious with thought, and he is scribbling notes about something or other.

I take no photographs; I am the ignorant guest at a professional gathering. The images are perfect, the colors very bright and they scream past my eyes in fiery clots: the cardón big by the sea, the boobies clustered in their nests, sea lions touching noses, an old mission in the sierra lonely with its stone, a face, my God, finally the human face of an old woman who is the caretaker of some church no one prays in much anymore. Then come Roman legions of boojums twisting against the sky, palm-choked lagoons brilliant with color, islands in the sea, a pile of trash left by careless tourists, landscapes as fresh as the day Adam desired a companion to be named Eve. The photographer clicks off one by one. A church blooms on the wall, one ancient with stone and brooding, over that one he lingers. The problem, he explains, is the sign, the huge beer sign right next to the church. He had to climb a hill and very carefully frame the shot to crop out the offending beer sign. The images will all be a book about the desert, there is no doubt of this fact.

All this, I'm sure, helps keep away the loud notes, the garbage cans out in the alley banging away like rats in heat. I'll give you an example of this clatter from the newspaper, Section F, page 7:

> SHOOTING DEATH DETAILED
>
> A naked Apache Junction man, bristling with cactus spines, charged at a Pinal County deputy sheriff and could not be stopped with a nightstick or two superficial gunshot wounds, according to an official report.
>
> Wayne Raux, 31, finally was killed by a gunshot wound to the chest fired by a Pinal County sheriff's deputy near Apache Junction Sept. 19, but not before an early morning, hour-long rampage that included the sexual assault of a woman and injuring another deputy with a large rock, the report says.

I am grateful for the drink in my hand as the last slide dies on the wall and the lights come up again. Then comes the talk. A woman mentions a recent book on the desert, one where a wanderer treks beaches, finds a bottle of scotch that has washed up, throws down his eighty-pound pack, and has himself a drunk. She asks, "Why would they publish an account by an alcoholic who lives off litter?" I think of William Mulholland, one of the real forebears of the fantasy expressed in the movie *Chinatown*. On the day he successfully achieved his theft of water from the Owens River, snaked the treasure across the Mojave Desert into the Los Angeles basin, and unleashed his booty on the city, they made a public occasion of it. As the spillway gushed with the flow, he stood up to give a speech and said to the assembled crowd, "There it is. Take it." Everywhere I go, I can see that they did; every time I see the photographs the crime has been erased.

Finally, I leave and drive down city streets under the overhead lights. I pour a drink in the kitchen and go out and sit on a railroad tie, the night sulking over my head with heavy clouds as I wait for rain, a glass of wine in my hand. There was one shot in the slide show that was not part of the show, just a casual image snapped by a guy who was camped on the coast in Baja. A gray whale was beaching itself, the surf spuming around the massive hulk, that big eye staring out with some understanding the camera could not fathom, the flippers lashing the air. And a small child in a red dress raced into the surf, the one running foot suspended in the air, raced to touch the giant who had suddenly punched into the safe world of the shore. Whales do not belong on beaches, we all know that. But these things happen. There is talk about the picture later, it is thought that it was a female aborting a hard birth, a soul locked in a death dance and come to ground for relief from the sea and the long dying. But then, what does belong in a place, a location, a time? What should be in the picture? *Landscape* seems a word that is swept clean by a new broom before it can be witnessed, an image refined and smoothed, all the edges gone, all the sea lions rubbing their noses, all of our kind exiled from the sacred ground. Based on what we write about the land and the photographs we take of the land, we cannot face ourselves in the mirror.

WORMS ARE STILL FEASTING on Cajeme's flesh when the Yaquis rise again. The structure he put in place survives his death and a new man appears to rally the people, a man called Tetabiate, which in Yaqui means "Rolling Stone." He is the leader who takes the people to the very bottom of their deepest agony. He moves with four hundred Yaquis to the highest peaks of the Bacatetes, places with names like Buatachive, Mazocoba, La Gloria, Aguilas del Chino, Mazatán, and La Pasión. They move into the forts and trenches created under the direction of Cajeme. The Yaquis sweep down and once more set Sonora aflame. Their tracks are sometimes found but almost no one ever sees a Yaqui warrior in the flesh and lives to report the event. During the long war under Cajeme, the Yaquis had dispersed to various mines, ranches, and farms throughout Sonora, seeking shelter from the bloody storm. Since they are working fools, they have no trouble finding jobs. The basic yardstick in Sonora is that a

Yaqui will do the work of two Mexicans for half the wage. Ramón Corral, vice governor of Sonora in 1887 when Cajeme is killed, salutes the Yaqui Diaspora. He is sure the experience will help the Yaquis in "forming a common mass with the rest of the population." Also, he believes, "contact with the white people would extinguish little by little their racial hatred, civilize them and create certain necessities which they could not obtain otherwise except by means of work within the confines of society." Corral is preaching the faith of consumerism, a religion still bleating just outside my door. What he gets is a fifth column. The raiders spreading fire and death from the peaks in the Bacatetes feed off the Yaqui laborers for money, guns, bullets, food, and from time to time manpower. Sonorans wind up giving wages to people who use the wages to kill Sonorans.

Americans show up once again with schemes to develop the Río Yaqui. They write brochures, float stock company scams, and fail totally. It is not safe for strangers on the Río Yaqui. When the Mexican army presses hard, Tetabiate and his people offer to discuss peace terms. And then after a lull the fire flares up again. In 1897 one of these lulls occurs and comes to be called the Peace of Ortiz. All the Sonoran dignitaries are there, including Ramón Corral, who is at the moment serving as governor. It is the fifteenth of May. The Mexican accounts speak of a procession of four hundred warriors carrying white flags of peace. Documents are signed that are supposed to end the conflict forever. Yaqui accounts report events at Ortiz that the Mexican chronicles missed. It seems the Archangel Michael was there and he hovered over the platform as the documents were signed. The Mexican general looked up, saw the heavenly figure, and shit his pants in fright. For two years, there is a kind of armed peace and the government showers the Yaquis with promises and supplies. Outsiders begin to drift into the Río Yaqui. The eight towns send a letter to the Mexican general explaining that they had only signed the Peace of Ortiz because they thought the agreement meant whites and soldiers would leave their land. This has not come to pass, they continue, and therefore "we have no blame for all the misfortunes that there are." Soon Tetabiate is back in the mountains with his warriors and fresh supplies. Attacks against Mexicans resume.

It all comes to a head at a mesa called Mazocoba. It is January 1900 and Mexicans pour all their forces into the Bacatetes. The Yaquis take up position at a fortress they have constructed, a small peak surrounded by cliffs with only few narrow defiles permitting access. Come morning on the eighteenth, one thousand soldiers hit the citadel.

Hand-to-hand combat ensues. Many Yaquis leap from the cliffs rather than surrender. Four hundred dead litter the battlefield, and more than one thousand are taken prisoner. Only 834 of this number survive the march out of the sierra. The government recovers only forty guns. And Tetabiate escapes.

Now the years blur. The government reaches for a solution to this vexing matter of people who will not accept the inevitability of the modern world. The solution is elegant in its simplicity: kill them all. You are walking down the street and you are taken. You are herding cattle on a ranch and you are taken. You come out of a mine shaft after a hard shift underground and you are taken. You are a child sitting in the dust of your yard and you are taken. All over Sonora, Yaqui Indians are disappearing. Sometimes you are shot down like a dog but more often you wind up for a while in the prison in Hermosillo. The governor is said to come by and sit in a chair while you line up for his inspection. Nearby are masked Yaqui traitors and they nod and gesture to signal their opinions to the governor. He lines you up eventually in three formations. One formation goes back to work, another is shot, and the third is sent to the port at Guaymas. Here you are pitched onto some old tubs and begin your voyage. You travel to Yucatán, where the big growers need strong backs for their henequen plantations. The fiber is one of Mexico's key exports and, as in any soundly managed and developing economy, exports are crucial in keeping up the balance of payments that decide who is going to live and who is going to die in the international trade. The aging dictator in the capital is caught in a process that dictates to him: to make the books look right he has to gut Sonora of its key labor force, you and your friends, and send you to Yucatán, where you almost all die within a year. Partly you die because the work is murderously hard. Partly you die because the tropics with their new diseases and conditions overwhelm you. And partly you die of a broken heart. Through the endless wars of the nineteenth century, through the slaughters in the sierra, through the havoc that swept constantly through the eight towns of the Río Yaqui, one thing had persisted and seemed to keep you alive: the family. And now in Yucatán the family breaks up—the man sold here, the child there, the woman somewhere else. Something snaps deep within and then you die. By 1910 a quarter of you, maybe half of you are dead. The rest are scattered in refugee communities from Yucatán to Los Angeles.

You are wayfarers, afraid to admit your real identity, cautious about observing your religious rites, stateless trash floating across the burning ground of this place. You are part of an audition for the century called the twentieth. You are the out-of-town tryout for the new fashion, genocide. You are an early mock-up for a new and growing breed, the DP—the displaced person. You are a pariah and soon the world will provide you with many brothers and sisters as the killing machines fire up. There is only one thing that keeps you from vanishing into oblivion. You never give up. You never stop fighting. You never stop dancing. You never stop believing. How you persist in your faith is a mystery as the year 1910 rolls around and remains a mystery to this day. Scholars of various stripes pick at the carcass of your people and ask questions about your rituals and beliefs. They do this decade after decade and yet they never quite come up with an answer as to why you survive and others do not. You remain baffling, remote, and apparently indestructible. Once in a while you catch on fire and earn salvation with a match and a few moments of agony. You live in the poorest barrios, do the most miserable and difficult work, go hungry often, and live hand to mouth. Yet somehow you breed, keep your language alive, and transmit your culture to generation after generation.

There is an image from those hard years in the first decade of the twentieth century that neatly captures your life then. The governor of Sonora decides that his policies, while sound, are not quite enough to satisfy his appetite for real results. So he mounts an expedition to Tiburón, the largest island in Mexico, floating like a desert dream just off the coast of Sonora. It is the homeland of a few hundred Seri Indians, a native group that in the eyes of Mexicans almost falls off the scale of what they consider human. He tells the Seris that if they are sheltering any Yaquis on their ground, they will suffer greatly. A few days later the Seris come back and give the governor five severed hands of Yaqui men and five braids off the heads of Yaqui women. He is satisfied at this recognition of the authority of the state and returns with his trophies to Hermosillo. The Yaquis take to calling the governor *el segundo dios*, the second God.

In the end, the Yaquis are not saved by the first God or the second God but by something familiar. War. In 1910 the Mexican nation crumbles and falls into a civil war that rages for ten years. And now everyone wants Yaquis for troops. Álvaro Obregón comes and offers them their land forever if they will fight under him. The people form a battalion and become the terror of the campaigns. The killing is something they are seasoned in. They are the guns for hire. They fight against Pancho Villa. They fight for Pancho Villa. Their arms appear under many banners but their conditions are always the same. When they win, they insist on the return of all their lands along the Río Yaqui and to be left alone on these lands until the end of time. The generals always agree to the Yaqui terms.

THEY MAKE US ALL LOOK like cowards and this is not a good feeling. They have survived everything and yet still live at the edges of our towns in the shacks and hovels. The century is winding down and the Yaquis stumble along with their strange dances, their desperate lives, and the occasional flashy suicide. They take jobs, learn some of our customs, fiddle with their own rites, and yet seem never to fundamentally change. They are an affront to every government, social worker, priest, and scholar that bumps into them. So generally they are forgotten and, if remembered at all, seen as a curio on the edge of the real world. At Easter some people come to watch their dances and that is about it.

They are prime evidence of the river of blood, a river without banks, without its name on any map, a river coursing almost secretly across ground claimed by others. Within the Yaquis the living and the dead are both alive and moving, and they are moving toward each other, stumbling across the ground into each other's arms where they are forming a new and unforeseen entity, a people who fail to meet the ordinary definitions of citizenship or territory, a refuse that flourishes and yet is almost unrecognizable. They are an early spring feeding into the river of blood. They have faced the serpent, felt its hot licks on their faces, and obtained power. This power is at first difficult for others to recognize. It is a power that does not hold high office or command armies and navies, nor is it a power that takes over industries or meets in boardrooms. It is the power of the indestructible and the despised. The burned ones. The people who have learned the reality behind the reality, the visitors to the world they have imagined, which is the real world, a world stronger than any currency, more durable than any bond, and more far-reaching than any economic summit. It is the past refusing to go away.

THE RIVER IS RISING. All over the planet the floods come often and the structures we build to contain them prove more ineffectual. It does not matter what kind of dikes we build. We can throw up massive security forces and still the drugs move at will. We can build big steel walls and still the people cross and move and mock the walls. We can create quarantines and still the plagues migrate to new ground and flesh. The world we think we believe in is ending before our eyes and no amount of meetings or discussions will come up with enough sandbags to stop the flow. Our fathers and mothers placed their faith in the new high dams. We sense the rivers cannot really be tamed.

What has been, cannot continue. What is coming, cannot be stopped. The river of blood has been building for a long time and global plans cannot dam its flow and webs of computers cannot in the end protect anyone from its flood stage. We can survive or we cannot survive. Still the river rises.

I SPENT WEEKS TRYING TO find out more about the man who climbed on a mesquite limb, doused himself with gasoline, placed a noose around his neck, drank a can of lye, struck a match and then fired a pistol. He still exists as a shadow in the memory of the town. But no one seems quite able to recall his name, and no one is certain of the year in which he found the purity of the fire. My friend Arturo, the old cop, racks his brain but the name remains just out of reach, floating out there like the smoke coming off the burning mesquite tree. So he exists and yet he does not exist. He is recalled but no one can make his face come into focus or his mouth speak words of explanation. He is a pioneer whose message still is trapped in a code we have not yet broken. I know he is one of us, I can tell by his actions, but I must learn more before his wisdom flows into me like lava. He is one of us because he could see the future and realized there was no place for him in this future. That is why he is not simply a grotesque suicide. And that is why we can neither totally forget him nor consciously remember him. He saw too clearly what we do not want to know.

Rosalio Moisés keeps scribbling in his notebooks. He stays at this work for more than a decade, and when he dies, he still has not finished. But he leaves us a vision. In the late forties he is bewitched and takes to his bed in a delirium. Eventually angels come and he flies with them on his sickbed and wends his way high up in the sierra. There he is introduced to Jesus Christ. Jesus treats him in a kindly manner. He says, "Now I will show you what it is like if you truly follow me." They walk around in a church and suddenly the world falls apart, black clouds boil, lightning sears the sky, a great wind comes up. Rosalio looks up and sees the air full of rocks, sand, big timbers, chunks of metal. And nothing hits and nothing hurts him while he is with Jesus and keeps his faith. Then Christ says, "We will now see the war." And so they walk over to the war. Rosalio sees a great battle, bombs go off, smoke drifts across a bloody field, clouds of gas float full of death, bullets scream. Christ then says, "Now we will go this way." They come to thousands and thousands of candles, each burning and each taper the measure of the length of an individual human life. Next they go to a place of cool streams and many flowers and there are millions of people there, all dressed in white and Christ explains that these are the good people.

Then they enter a desert plain and it is hot and sultry. Mirages ride the waves of heat and everywhere the ground is covered with thorns and cacti. There is no water and the millions of people here look ugly, and their faces are twisted by some inner agony. They can hardly be recognized as humans, some with the heads of birds, some horned like bulls, some hopping around like frogs. Rosalio sniffs and what he smells is like the vapors off a pulque vat.

Christ says, "These are the condemned people. They are here of their own choice. They are here just what they made of themselves on the earth."

After this experience, Rosalio recovers his health and joins a sacred group that participates in the Yaqui Easter celebration. He makes a mask each year and dances for days and does not eat. He has seen the future, smelled the poison gas, dipped his hand into the clear mountain stream, walked the hell of the desert flat. He writes this all in his spiral notebook. He writes it years before I enter the mountains of bone, face the furnace heat of the deserts of flesh.

I have no sacred group to join. Christ has not flown me into the kingdom and shown me my candle or the winds of war or the clean white sheets worn by the saved. And yet I am not without my resources. I do not have to visit the past because the past comes to me.

I do not have to visit the future because it is swirling outside my door. I am moving into the river. The flow carries me along and my will is not at issue.

The man is swinging from the tree and the tree is burning and the tree is mesquite. The river of blood swirls around my feet and is rising. The deep roots are sucking and we are all being pulled up and transmuted and now we will finally face the sun. We are of the wood. Twisted, gnarly, but of the wood.

There is really only one thing left for me if I am to have anything at all.

Dip my hand into this river of blood.

Touch my face.

Feel the burning.

Bone, mountains of bone.

Flesh, deserts of flesh.

CONQUEST

THE NAMES COME FROM OTHER TONGUES. *California* springs from some Spanish dream of gold and pearls; *Colorado* simply means red; *Nevada* stands for snowcapped mountains. Pimas described a place having a little spring with *Arizona*. Navajos meant only land of the Utes: *Utah*. Conquistadors seeking El Dorado wrote *New Mexico* on the map. Shoshones said something with *Idaho*. *Montana* resulted from forcing the Spanish *montaña* to suggest mountains. The Great Plains are littered with Sioux ideas. The *Dakotas* stand for allies; *Kansas* indicates the South Wind people. Omahas expressed flat and shallow with *Nebraska*. Red people is the Choctaw notion buried in *Oklahoma; Texas* a Caddo way of saying, "Hello, friend." Wandering Delawares conveyed "upon a great plain" with *Wyoming*. The arid West is splattered with a babel of languages.

The richness of the words misleads; the color of western history has often overwhelmed the content. The boys who punched cows, the shaggy men who killed the beaver, the Indians who were fodder for cavalry, the miners who searched for a heart of gold, the individuals of exotic reflexes who could dispense small bits of lead at remarkable rates—these humans have had greater impact on modern minds than they had on the land. The grass-shorn rangelands, mine-pitted hillsides, and declining aquifers testify to capital from the eastern United States and from Europe seeking a profitable return. Now such activities are called development; a century ago it was simply destiny. "When Uncle Sam puts his hand to a task," explained one advocate of such policies, "we know it will be done. . . . When he waves his hand toward the desert and says, 'Let there be water!' we know . . ." (Smythe, W. E., 1911).

The chore of concentrating and exploiting resources has gone on beneath the clatter of cowboys and Indians. It is the real stuff of western history, and to look at this process is to gain an understanding of arid lands in general. Because water is scarce, photosynthesis is limited. This means many resources are cycled at slow rates. Humans in the past century in the western United States have used them at fast rates. For decades beeves were shipped east by literally mining the grass and the topsoil. This resulted in devastation of the rangeland, and finally, in the Taylor Grazing Act. Today, management is supposed to keep cattle numbers in balance with the productivity of the vegetation. Clear cutting of the forests led to the same degradation and culminated in yet more federal laws to guarantee a rate of timbering the woods could sustain.

But all resource exploitation does not offer such an easy adjustment to human appetites. Minerals are a gigantic industry in the arid west. Regardless of the rate at which they are ripped from the earth, they are essentially nonrenewable. That is why mining towns end in collapse. The coal beds, oil pools, uranium deposits, and oil shale belts are also one-shot affairs. The energy industry moving into the region can be only a temporary and transitional kind of land use. Water presents a special case. The rivers and other surface supplies are renewed by the rain, and hence, are permanently available. Americans seized this resource first. During the 1930s, 400 million dollars plugged the Colorado with dams and made a wild river a piece of plumbing. In varying degrees, this has been the pattern throughout the west. Since surface supplies were spoken for long ago, Americans have turned to groundwater. Arizona meets 60 percent of its water needs by pumping aquifers. Other states and basins approximate this dependence. The water is commonly pumped at rates faster than natural replenishment. This is called mining.

Groundwater is essentially nonrenewable in the arid west because the economies that exploit it cannot abide a low rate of use. By combusting nonrenewable coal and nonrenewable oil and nonrenewable natural gas, they have managed to lift nonrenewable water at incredible rates. By using water with abandon they can compete with more humid regions, where it is basically a free good. This extractive process, like the looting of ore deposits, soil, forests, and fuels, is the machinery behind the expressions "conquest of nature" and "the miracle of the deserts." Rip away the veneer of western history and this consumption of resources links the centuries.

THE LAST CUT

There seems to be no turning back. As the record of the Covered Wells stick ended in the 1930s, an anthropologist, Ruth Underhill, raced to capture the contents of traditional O-otam society before they vanished. She would ask people about old ways and old ideas. She carefully noted the changes being caused by federal programs, by the entrance of the cash economy among the people, and by the shift from old ways of using resources to new ways. One question flung at her by a Papago made a vivid impression. "Why can't the school teach us to make cake?" demanded the person. "We can buy eggs and milk. We want to make everything the white people make" (Underhill, R. M., n.d.).

The practices and appetites of western industrial societies spread very easily. The twentieth century has witnessed people after people leaving ancient traditions for these new habits with little thought as to the consequences and little control over the process. Scholarship on development has remained largely a futile literature; the movement from a solar-fired economy to a fossil-fueled economy seems to have a life of its own.

Among the Piman people, stick-cutting ceased in the thirties. The water tanks, roads, electric lines, wells, and new jobs produced a swirl of events that gouges and nicks could not order and capture. One stick belonged to a medicine man. He was murdered and his wand vanished. Another was tossed in the trash by a widow. There is a rumor that at least one stick lingers in Papago hands; it is not known if anyone can read it. The records slashed in saguaro are gone because the messages once left in the wood are no longer enough. The mind that could ignore a war and remember a big snow is dead. The desert people, white and O-otam, have joined together in a powerful occupance of the land. They have gathered around pumps.

Excerpt

From
Blood Orchid

THEY APPEARED AT THE time the buffalo went down in the bitter dust with their dark tongues lashing out obscenely for one more taste of the raw, clean breeze in the cold light of morning. Then the black flies soon settled—our hands moving constantly to flick their swollen bodies off our faces, the buzzing crowding our ears—and we went to our knives and had at the hump, the tongue and the sweet organs. We did not think of what was happening then, we were too happy with the raw liver smeared against our lips to worry about the vanishing hoofprints etched in the light powder and pointing to a country where we could not follow. The blood orchids that came at that time were true to their kind, forms that did not seem to live off the land but instead were sustained by outside forces we could not see and have never understood. Their roots ran down the rough bark of our lives and drank our water, their leaves thrust out into the air of our lives and sucked up all the oxygen and soon our lungs collapsed. The flowers . . . I will get to the flowers in a moment.

(*It's afternoon, a storm is whipping off the Rockies onto the high plains. The rains, they have not come, so we are hungry for their fury. The Rocky Flats Arsenal is sizzling a few miles away, the last refuge for native plants on the entire Front Range. I am reconnoitering the Flats, and the place looks as peaceful as a dairy farm. Once they built plutonium triggers here—imagine that six-shooter, partner—and still have eleven tons of the stuff stacked up with nowhere for it to go. The Russkis chickened out, you know, and now refuse delivery. And here we were going to ship it Air Express. There's a nifty little model shop buried in Rocky Flats where they made gifts for visiting physicists—lead-lined jockstraps. Size please, Herr Doktor? God is Lenny Bruce, Yes, She is! I am tired but I will not rest. The orchids never rest, not one second. They are relentless because they feed on us. But they have more will, are stronger, can go the distance. I will try again. I know I must do better. But it is lonely out here. And besides if I am not careful they will put me in the crazy place. Or drug me. To be fair, the drugs have gotten quite good, excellent really. On the street the heroin is so solid that folks have taken to snorting it rather than shooting up. The coke is a powder so white the Aryan brotherhood is said to be in awe of its purity. And the marijuana now has a* THC *factor equal to the lift load of a moon shot. So don't you believe people when they make blanket statements denouncing technology, no siree!! The doctors, bless them, hand out pills like candy to keep strange thoughts from our minds. I am certain these fine chemicals are working. More people in this country are wrestling with dim memories of incest than with blood orchids—a fact. So I must not take cheap shots at the drugs, especially the legal ones that never make anyone happy but do at least dim the lights. Pretty soon, there will just be me and the Prozac eaters.*)

It all happened so very fast, although it took a long time for the roots like snakes to dig into our lives and take our measure and find us wanting. The long cavalcade of buffalo, dark forms swinging into the sun and going over one hill too many, and then the bones white on the ground, skulls formed in a circle like a last prayer, the medicine wheel and yet the patient seemed to keep dying . . . the towns springing up with the smell of raw lumber, the streets annoyingly straight, the whores with colors on their faces and a weariness in their ancient eyes as they peered out the frosted panes at the stillness of a winter night, the snows, big, crippling snows, choking the passes, whipping our faces on the plains and winter-kill elk lying among the aspen with their legs stuck up like saplings toward the steel sky . . . the purr of the electric train at the Black Mesa and the pleasure in firing clip after clip into its robot soul (*pen an essay: call it something about mountains and the correct thinking, all of it in that vogue mode, pensive, the voice aldo contralto*), the lips gleaming as she leans across the hard wooden table, her large breasts sagging and fumes of whiskey pour off her invitation face (*the red-faced warbler at the lip of the spring, poor thing will never make a calendar page: not enough flash, you know. Bye, bye, birdie*). Drunken Indians sleeping like ghosts in the alley—careful where you step! Sundance is raving through the night as his body eats his body (*the white medicine men call this condition cancer: Sundance and I never say this word out loud*) and I go downstairs in the purring elevator and the casino is nothing but whirs and bells and the click of bones on the green felt as we struggle to win what we always lose again anyway. His grandmothers wielded scalping knives at Little Bighorn (*Custer, bless his soul, scribbling that message: "Come on. Big Village. Be Quick. Bring packs. Hurry"*), they saw the arrival of the blood orchids, Sundance gets to be part of the ending. (*Big interesting clouds rising again and again, like giant mushrooms, they say, and everyone looks up out of pride and patriotism and envy*) . . .

Fine sepia-toned photographs hang on the walls as I softly pad down the hallway on Two Gray Hills Navajo rugs and out the corner of my eye photographs of Jackson Hole, the Sierra Nevada, unnamed peaks slide by and look just the way they are said to have looked some fine day a century ago when the earth seemed fresh and the blood orchids were a rumor and a very small one at that . . .

(*Okay, I'll calm down. No need for the jacket and the two dull-witted attendants. I was born two or three weeks before Hiroshima and I believed. Hell; I still believe in one sense: I'm not confident I would have made a better decision than they did. Here, I'll show you with a quote from the official report on the genesis of just one orchid, the atomic bomb: "created not by the devilish inspiration of some warped genius but by the arduous labor of thousands of normal men and women working for the safety of their country." But I know. It has played out. I know. And this has to matter or it really all has been for nothing. I know. You know. We know.*)

The roots getting thicker by the year, at first fine lines like lace on the bark of our lives, the skin of our life, the hopes of our life, and then coarsening as more and more wealth and power and energy surge through and at first the roots begin to look like snakes, then like cables and later like giant aqueducts, the hidden heart pounding to the beat of explosives, this massive web becomes fat and arrogant and when the axe sinks in there is nothing but blood, geysers of blood, thick, sticky, virulent. CAUTION: Do not dab it against your tongue. The lab report is never returned to us, we can only guess. But clearly bad blood.

The bloom is more fearsome. The flower huge and it is artfully constructed so that we see what we wish to see—a woman lush and lying on silk with her legs spread and that beckoning smile on her smooth face, the hair is black, the hair is blond, the hair is long and a tassel caresses a nipple, the hair is short, the skull is shaved and oiled, whatever we wish: or the man is armed, grim-looking, a carbine in his hand, blue clothes, olive drab clothes, mottled clothes of camouflage, he sings "She Wore a Yellow Ribbon," he sings "Over There," he sings "Lili Marlene," he sings "Purple Haze," and smoke curls from his Springfield as he lights up his pipe and the smoke curls from his M-16 as he lights up that joint and beckons, beckons and we go with Ahab and feel the cold skin and sharp barnacles of that big white whale that swims forever in the book none of us can ever seem to finish (*ah, the shame, the shame, we bear over the classics*) and the blood orchids in flower can never be resisted, the allure of the colors, the narcotic effect of the pollen, the giant size of the bloom, the power of the growth with rank green leaves shooting up and blocking the very sun from our eyes and the thing comes from nowhere and seems to bring everything with it, a complete self-contained organism, and when it does not flower, it simply clones itself and replicates like a berserk cell in a petri dish and blood orchids appear everywhere. And then the water goes bad or goes away and the air goes bad and will not move and the earth, the very dirt, mutinies with odd chemicals from some alchemy we cannot comprehend, and the game beats away and forsakes us. And still we get no reports, they are kept a secret from us. For our own good. And the worst thing—we seldom will say this, even to ourselves, no, no, almost never will we say this—is that we become dependent on these blooms, on these huge plants, on the enormity of them and we turn our eyes toward the blood orchids and away from the land and we will say this is necessary, *essential*. We dress for success. Our women fall in love with the blue clothes, the olive clothes, the mottled clothes, and eventually they demand to wear them also. Our children love everything about the orchids, and soon they play with miniature versions and invent games around this new culture in our midst.

Bang! You're dead!

We get regular weather reports—it is hot, it is cold—and then suddenly for five years it is very hot and then for the best part of four decades it is cold, endlessly, bone-chilling cold, and yet the orchids thrive and prosper. They seem immune to what makes us sweat, to what makes us shiver. And suddenly the weather breaks—snap! just like that—and our entire garden seems altered. There is word—whispered at first, then said out loud—that the orchids are ill, that they are dying, or simply that their time is over, a finished thing, and we cannot face these reports and a great fear fills our bodies and we worry about the orchids. We glance back over our shoulders at the land and what we see makes us fear even more and our stomachs tighten and our bowels go loose . . . for the soil is bubbling and burning, the water comes off the mountains like lava, the snows blister our fingers if we touch the searing flakes, the trees yellow and sicken and forget to flower, the buffalo cannot be seen (*they say they are hiding, they say they will never come back to us, they say . . .*), the fish float past our blinking eyes and they are belly-up with a sweet stench rising off them, the skies are empty of birds and dead clots of feathers lie at our feet, and many die of strange diseases, and we grow afraid to touch each other, we fight our instincts, we do not trust the food in the kettle, we fear the woman lying wet by our side, we see the man smiling in the bar as a death threat, and the big blooms keep beckoning, the colors intense, the scent of the flower overwhelming to our frail senses and we do what we have become and we do what little we still know how to do and we mount the flower where she waits and we fuck and we fuck and we fuck . . . fuck . . . fuck . . .

(*Once, I knew a woman with tattoos. The serpents and flowers scrolling across her body were part of her secret self and they could not be seen or even guessed when she was clothed. She dressed very well in expensive sweaters and skirts because her work was professional and demanded such costumes. She had a very nice smile and a wonderful wit and could not speak without an emphasis that implied exclamation points and yet this last fact did not annoy me. Her diet was very careful, she kept a keen eye for all threats to her body be they chemicals or fats or forms of flesh that clogged arteries and stilled the heart. She liked to ride motorcycles and served meals on expensive black china. But she did not do this often since, like so many interesting women of my time, she resented the act of cooking. She wrote notes using purple ink and cut things out and glued them on each page. She did not wish to have children either, and this, like the hostility to cooking, was not unusual. I am used to knowing women who are survivors of some dark time I will never know or imagine.*

Her ex-husband once tried to kill her. He chased her through the house waving a shotgun. He had often beat her but the shotgun was a new tactic and this moment permanently terrified her. She changed states, jobs, for all I know, even her name, in order to distance herself from the night when she faced the possibility of being murdered. She also never trusted her heart again. This also is not unusual. She had grown very adjusted to being maimed in this area.

If I mentioned the orchids, she scorned me, just cut me dead. You see, she wanted to be happy.)

The blood orchids remain to be dealt with, the roots thick, the blood sticky. But lower your voice, do not repeat this. It is dangerous talk. The cold spell is over, this is admitted, however grudgingly. The time of the blood orchids may be passing. But bend your head, we must whisper. . . . We shall overcome, all we are saying is give peace a chance, Johnny came marching home again, make love not war, old soldiers never die, never, never die. Make the world safe for. . . . They are handing out condoms in the garden, they say it will be all right.

The word is out: We Have Won. Time to savor the victory. Walk the metes and bounds of our ground. Careful, don't trip over those huge roots, watch yourself by the flower. They predict a spring this year for the first time in decades. But they warn us it will not be easy. They say the blood orchids cannot be removed. They say we have grown dependent upon them. And if we ask a question they drown us out with bugles.

We have won.

Now enjoy, my child.

(*It is 1527 and Wayna Ahapaq, the head of the Inca empire, takes his rest in Quito. He has just swallowed Ecuador and pauses before chomping on a chunk of Colombia. He is around fifty, fit as a fiddle, and two Spanish captives are being hauled over his empire's 14,000 miles of paved road for his personal examination. He must wonder, just who are these ugly pale guys? He never finds out. Smallpox beats the Spaniards to his door and in a month or two or three about half of his twenty million subjects die. And Wayna Ahapaq is one of the newly minted dead folks. Having lived in that splendid isolation called the Western Hemisphere, he and his fellow citizens have no immunity—and at the moment he falls, about one out of every five human beings on earth is what the newcomers decide to call an Indian. Biological warfare, an early test case. A few years later, Francisco Pizarro hops ashore with a few desperados and some horses and finishes the job we now call the conquest. Toward the end of the sixteenth century, an Indian noble named Pachakuti Yamki tries to make sense out of this rather dark moment. In his account, he has Wayna Ahapaq busy issuing new laws and taxes as he slumbers at Quito with his war machine at idle. Then the news comes to him that a plague has broken out at the capital, Cuzco. At midnight Wayna Ahapaq turns his face toward the sea and looks upon a million people whom he does not know. And he realizes they are the living souls about to die. And then the next day at dinnertime a messenger arrives wearing a black cloak. He kisses the ruler and gives him a small locked box and a key. The boss man tells the messenger to open the box, but the visitor says, nope, he can't do that, the Creator has ordered that only Wayna Ahapaq has that responsibility. When Wayna Ahapaq turns the key and lifts the lid things flutter out like butterflies. Within two days, his chief general is dead, along with many of the best of fighters. The Inca understands. He orders a stone house built, enters it, and dies. I like this story because Wayna Ahapaq has his vision of a million living souls, takes the key, and opens the box. He refuses to be a victim, he assumes responsibility. True, he dies. But he refuses to be a victim, and victims can never fix anything because they cannot fight. And of course, the game is not yet over. Most of the people in Peru still speak Quechua, the language of the Inca, and the ground is not yet safe for those who feel that they conquered it, blood is flowing from a Shining Path. For centuries, many people have faced manifestations of the blood orchids, they have seen strange clouds, felt something seize their bodies they did not fully understand, died painful and surprising deaths. Felt the heel on their necks. And not given in or up. I am not so crazy as I may seem. I have a lineage and I can hear it whispering in my ear. True, I lack a vision of Eden or a belief in such a place. But I have an unending appetite for personal power, for the right to decide my fate. And this sets me at odds with my government, my time, and what all of us have decided is our place—stand over there and wait until your number is called.*)

Ah, but there is so much to mention. There is this huge inventory to go over. We must make sure all the china remains, that no linen has been stolen, that our house is in order. Let us begin: The whale dives, sounding deep, but never surfaces. Then there are the pock-marked hills where God buried bodies we call ore, the toxic rivers, the strangled rivers, the clean, scientifically leveled fields gleaming with white salts and gone sterile as mules, mountains of empty bottles of Mad Dog 20/20, the holes punched for oil, the roar over our heads as the new silver birds fly by, the waters no one will ever drink again from the Rio Puerco (*such a name*), the best movie of all—"Apocalypse Then, Now & Forever." Twenty pounds of barbed wire wrapped around your skull. Who do you love?

It is a very simple plot. We had to kill the thing we love to prove our love.

Lonesome Love, might make a miniseries. I read it in a poem:

> Take any streetful of people buying clothes and groceries,
> cheering a hero or throwing confetti and blowing tin horns . . .
> tell me if the lovers are losers . . . tell me if any get more than
> the lovers . . . in the dust . . . in the cool tombs.
> CARL SANDBURG, "COOL TOMBS," 1918

We had to sacrifice our women to prove our love—so many one-breasted ones now ambling around as testimony to our adoration. Kill the thing we love. That is our central legend, our key holy story, the tale in our sacred books. From the halls of Montezuma . . . it has been a long haul, brothers and sisters. We should rest now down by the river. But please do not drink the water. Let's make it linear, our favorite plotting device: We came, we saw, we were conquered. Julius would understand, he has been waiting for us to get the joke. Or let's skip the A+B+C and go into the swirl of things:

his name is Sundance, he is Lakota, there is a huge stack of *Hustler* magazines by his bed on L.A.'s skid row and he is a very large man, but he keeps muttering about this thing in his bones. The essential story line is in the bones. It is that deep, that basic. Robert Sundance lived our lives before we did. He pioneered our world in special laboratories we called Indian reservations. Long ago, when we still believed in the future, in progress, in hard work, nuclear families, nuclear bombs, and big turkeys at Thanksgiving, he and his friends were drugged, unemployed, and unemployable. They were bored, violent, and almost invisible. They beat their women, abandoned their children, roamed around wreaking havoc. They were us before we even had a clue what we would become. He lived in the West, he served in those wars, he sucked down that air, he drank the water, he is a blood, he is a half-breed, he is dying of cancer, and he can feel the roots of the blood orchids ensnaring him and taking him down. This makes him very angry—but it is too late. Sundance is raving now, it is deep into the night and the pain comes on strong. He is babbling something about scalping knives, the strange curve of the blades. He has killed the thing he loved and now must pay the blood price. His entire story starts and ends with the blood orchids but he is reluctant to admit this fact. We all are. Come here, lie by my side, I will kill you . . . two stretches for manslaughter, yet he survived so that he could live and suffer and pay that blood price.

(*I must be responsible. I am closing in on fifty, I've been around several of those city blocks and have been sternly advised about my conduct by the officers—they were just trying to help, they told me so. I am of the belief that our efforts to protect ourselves and our ground and our rivers and our seas have taken a toll. This volume is suggestive of that blood price. Ah, there, a thesis sentence for the boys and girls in the seminar. Of course, my judgment is seriously impaired. I have lived with war every day of my life. And expect to continue this pace. I could as a child look into the faces of my parents and sense what the world of peace must have been like to feel and touch and know. But this thing they could neither keep for themselves or give to me. Hence, these words as the storm sweeps closer, coming off the Rocky Mountains, several miles from the edge of the Rocky Flats Arsenal where the plutonium will chew the ground for the next couple of hundred thousand years. What the hell, a trade-off.*)

Should we run through some other kind of inventory to make it all safe and clear and untrue? Bases, forts, tests, proving grounds, arsenals, airfields (*how light and fluttery that phrase seems*), war games, wars, gunnery ranges, research centers, underground sites, aboveground sites, MOA's, silos, Star Wars, MAD, Dugway, Los Alamos. And in the name of our Lord and Savior, Trinity. And most importantly, No Trespass, the Prohibited Area, and the very favorite posting of the garden: National Security.

We have achieved our Historical Absolute like good Doktor Hegel promised us so long ago. We have made our entire nation into a reservation with a population unemployed or underemployed, and our merchants eager to supply us with a lot to drink or snort or dose ourselves with. We display a frisky penchant for violence, enjoy an abandonment of everyone by everyone, stare at a future as blank as the president's ass and a past increasingly lost in the fogs that flood our brains. As our bodies become emaciated, our government fattens on our plight and grows larger. They are going to send us to school—apparently forever—so that we can do little jobs around the rez. There seems no end to the work they see for us and they promise that each and every one of us will have six or seven careers in our twinkling lifetimes. There has been some grumbling about the pay, however, and increasingly folks in our cities prefer self-employment—whether with muskets or syringes. There is bold talk that free trade is good for us—free love is no longer permitted, it seems we have diseases—and will make us stronger and quicker and more productive. We are going to get national health care, so don't be scared of the rashes, pustules, tumors, genital sores, and erratic heartbeat. We're going to be one big tribe, the rainbow tribe it's rumored (*they're working out the reading list this very moment*) and at the end of the rainbow, by God there is pot. We have nothing to do and we know it, so we spend our time doing what little is left to do: we wait. Or look backward.

(*There is an artist who is going to place one thousand cast-bronze buffalo on three hundred and seventy acres of Wyoming. All he requires is 450 tons of bronze and $45 million. He will mount the metal herd on swivels and when the wind comes up its force will rush through tubes in the cold, dead beasts and they will moan. The buffalo will stretch over a half mile and form the shape of, what else, a buffalo. The artist desires that his work be visible from the moon. The site the artist has selected is the only known home of the desert yellowhead, a plant no one seemed to notice until 1990. Perhaps, metal yellowheads can be added to the plan. The state endorses this work of art. They say it will be good for tourism. I am not making this up. No one can make up much of anything anymore. The artist says the site is "empty desert." Besides, he explains, "The only way we know the beauty of things is through art."*)

We have one hundred and five million cows, tens of thousands of nuclear warheads, four hundred and thirty-five representatives, one hundred senators, one president for vice, one president for other matters, and liposuction machines.

We outnumber spotted owls, buffalo, elk, deer, antelope, wolves, sea turtles, pup fish, and blue whales. Micro-organisms outnumber us, but we do not like to think of that fact. We have the best orchid garden on the surface of the earth, and the only one that is still intact. And we love to work in our garden. We won't give up this horticulture, we don't know how. We now hold many meetings; we wish, we say, to know the meaning of things. We yearn to drive down the information highway. Everyone is gearing up for this journey. Only no one is willing to go out at night anymore.

Kill the one you love.

Thank God, we won.

Imagine what the defeated now must taste in their dry mouths?

Imagine the problem is not physical. Imagine the problem has never been physical, that it is not biodiversity, it is not the ozone layer, it is not the greenhouse effect, the whales, the old-growth forest, the loss of jobs, the crack in the ghetto, the abortions, the tongue in the mouth, the diseases stalking everywhere as love goes on unconcerned. Imagine the problem is not some syndrome of our society that can be solved by commissions or laws or a redistribution of what we call wealth. Imagine that it goes deeper, right to the core of what we call our civilization and that no one outside of ourselves can affect real change, that our civilization, our governments are sick and that we are mentally ill and spiritually dead and that all our issues and crises are symptoms of this deeper sickness.

Imagine the problem is not physical and no amount of driving, no amount of road will deal with the problem. Imagine that the problem is not that we are powerless or that we are victims but that we have lost the fire and belief and courage to act. We hear whispers of the future but we slap our hands against our ears, we catch glimpses but turn our faces swiftly aside. I am no better. My guts roil with fear. This is how the future comes to me, how I stumble down unmapped lanes and suddenly am in front of that cathouse where she waits unloved, the face of indeterminate colors, the lips smiling and the eyes knowing far too much. I am always walking sometimes in a forest with pink amapas leaning over me and the petals carpeting the ground, sometimes in the desert with every shrub and tree and plant raking my skin with thorns. It is very quiet, soft purr of a breeze, brief bursts of bird song, whirr of insects, and I hear this roar, she comes as a locomotive is flying across the ground, smoke belching, steel wheels screaming, no engineer in the cabin, and behind this engine is an endless strand of boxcars—no tramps looking out because the doors are closed—and there are no tracks, never a single length of track, this express goes its own way. It will all happen too fast for me to react, too fast for me to close my eyes, shut my ears, turn my body and I will briefly face the future. I cannot remember it and be honest because this future is unlike the pasts I like to pretend will be the future. This time the future is alive. And then it will be gone. Sometimes this happens in the night and I see the glow of the lights as it vanishes into the land. This future is palpable, and no charts of economic growth or of population growth can possibly suggest its routes or cargo. There will be no first hundred days for this future, there will be no five year plans. There will be no program. *Imagine the problem is that we cannot imagine a future where we possess less but are more. Imagine the problem is a future that terrifies us because we lose our machines but gain our feet and pounding hearts.*

HER BLUE EYES BLAZE from her eighty-five-year-old face surrounded by tinted auburn hair. The gnarled hands belie her quick tongue. Evie Dubrow came into the movement in 1937, and now she sits in the arena in Los Angeles taking in the tired words from the podium like nectar. I am squatting in the aisle by her chair and listen hungrily for some rumble from the days of sit-down strikes, lockouts, and clubs on the picket line. But they do not come from her. She is the happy warrior, the veteran of early service in the Americans for Democratic Action, the garment workers' union, and as a lobbyist scurrying around Capitol Hill. She likes Al Gore because she liked Al Gore's dad. She liked Barry Goldwater though he'd sometimes stop her in the hall and say, hey, I can't be with you on this vote.

She is the tonic in the hall of a dead movement, a large part of a century sitting primly and gaily amidst the fruits of her labor. When I listen to her, I cannot hear the rock hit the bone, or the sucking sound as the marrow is consumed.

That is the value of the arena full of labor ghosts, to block the eyes and ears. They are the guardians of some kind of fallen system of income distribution, the hagglers over pay envelopes and dues. And they sit in this cavern without a window on the outside world, and if they win, people called workers get a bigger slice of some pie, and if they lose, these same workers get less. No one talks about the bakery where the pies come from, the ovens of the economy. It is sacred now and there is not a single questioning voice left in this arena. They fatten within state capitalism and are content. I crouch by Evie and the huge faces boom from giant screens and the words fall like raindrops. I feel the thing buried beneath the building, the soil, the muck, the bones, the glowing magma crushed and burning in the heart of the globe. Deep beneath my feet there is something permanent and volatile, the forces of life, but here on the surface there is simply a bookkeeping exercise with a division of the spoils and nothing fundamental exists.

I cling to some primitive feeling that gases swirl about on the skin of the earth and feed living tissue and there is only so much of this tissue that can be sustained. That minerals lurk in the hide of the earth, and there are only so many of these peculiar molecules that can be found and gouged from the hide. That fish swim in the sea and only so many can be murdered and devoured before the seas go still and dead. That even a mesquite can reach only so far into the ground before its energy is spent and it can go no farther. That there are limits and that simply discussing a division of the spoils ignores the limits of the treasure house.

I want to grab a pickax and start hacking through the floor of the arena. I am among the cannibals and the black kettle is glowing.

So I am out of sorts.

Love, I don't know what it means, but I roll the word around in my mouth. Love is the answer. Love is eternal. Love is lust—no, can't say that anymore. Lust is not even lust. Hack through the floor, shoot a bazooka through the walls, break on through to the other side, find the union maid, feel the roots coursing through the earth, walk into the farmyard and have the old lady strip me and boil my clothes. Cut the rope swinging off the pipe.

I leave Evie to her labor pleasures and I go out onto a patio where a fat cook from the snack bar sits all in white and gobbles his cigarette as union heavyweights in very good suits consult their cell phones and make plans for good dinners.

I sink into a chair and soak up the sun and accept the wonder of it all. A weary woman sits across from me. Her dad was union, she is union. Her kids are a blank. She is UAW out of Detroit, she is black, she is an organizer and she is worn down by the success of it all.

She tells me not to sit in the sun. I ignore her.

She tells me that she visited Tijuana once, just a hop, skip, and a jump south of where we sit, and it damn near broke her heart. She left the tour of the American-owned factories in the Mexican border city and went into a home and found a family living in one room.

She tells me, "It brought back memories, lots of memories, of my childhood in the early forties." And then she falters at the memories of being a black person in a city where no one wanted black people around and the filth and hunger of the lean times.

She tells me now, "These kids walking around with hip-hop clothes, chains drooping from their pants, cell phones clipped on their pockets—union wages paid for those things."

She stops talking at this point and looks wistful.

I understand. That is why I want to hack through the floor of the arena and find the earth and then in the earth find the root and then follow the root until I hear a sucking sound and feel the flow yet again. Two things I believe: the past is not over. The future is not over.

The present is the real question. It may be over.

PACIFIC AIR SWEEPS ACROSS the sands near the saltworks of Guerrero Negro in Baja California. The small plane lands on a dirt strip by the sea, the runway a glaze of clay surrounded by small dunes of sand. An old man stumbles out of a shed as she climbs from the pilot's seat. I walk over and ask for aviation fuel and he scurries away like a crab dragging the heavy black hose, and pushing before him a small metal platform for reaching the tanks in the wings. She ambles away in her tight Levis and black leather bomber jacket, her long black hair blowing in the wind. The old man looks up at me, his face a wasteland of gray stubble, the teeth rotten and dark.

He asks, "Is she good to fuck?" Right away it is out in the open, the reason a person comes to Mexico, or the thing that quickly drives a person away. I remember a moment a couple of months back, down at Cabo on the tip of the peninsula. We'd landed the plane and I walked into the air terminal and this guy says to me, "You want some coke?" and I think, I'm getting out of here. So we fly north to a farm town on the Pacific side named Todos Santos, All Saints, and land on a little road in the garbage dump. The plane gets stuck, and a bunch of guys show up out of the garbage and push us out. We hitch a ride into town, have a couple of beers, she's high as a kite from the landing in the garbage, and then we find this lodging called Hotel California right across from the local pool hall. The whole town is based on sugar cane, *panocha,* and they make nice flat cakes of the syrup. I couldn't be happier, *panocha* is Mexican slang for pussy. We walk along the dirt streets and come to this restaurant that is like a giant ramada, thatched top resting on columns and a low concrete wall circling. The whole thing nestles in a depression with vines and trees staging a tropical riot. The table is metal and naked light bulbs hang down and we order platters of shrimp and some more beers, and then I notice her staring over my shoulder, her eyes locked on this table where this Mexican couple, the guy in his forties, the woman past thirty, are locked in a moment. The man is talking endlessly, his head bent down toward the tabletop, talking that steam of sadness and worldliness that Mexican men like to dish out to their women. She sits there, her abundant body about to burst out of her clothes, her flesh reeking with desires, and nods her head carefully. Her blouse is unbuttoned and huge breasts promise to topple forward and go splat on the cool metal tabletop. The man keeps his low rumble of words going. This goes on for an hour and he never stops and she never skips a beat in doling out her attention, or ceases to exude this musk.

When the woman leaves, I look hard and long at her hips. Outside I can hear the faint sound of the Pacific swells crashing into the curve of clean sand beach. Then we walk back to our hotel, buying a six-pack of Tecate on the way, and strip and lie on the bed with the window open. It is hot and there is no cooling system and for hours we fight and grow sullen and I sit on the side of the bed and look through the window and see the night wash across the trees and vines and hear people's voices laughing and smell that musk, and the beers are warm now and taste bitter in my mouth. Sometimes, I love this country.

The town of Guerrero Negro, the Black Warrior, is ugly, a company town for the largest saltworks on earth, one now owned by the Japanese. Huge pans have been carved out of the sand, the sea floods in, is trapped, evaporates, and the white blaze of salt stares up. Then it is loaded on barges, hauled out miles across the ocean to Isla Cedros, loaded on big freighters, and disappears into the maw of Japanese life. The wind never stops blowing here, the sand is always in the air, the streets moving walls of dust, the shops and houses forlorn out on the barren sands. The desert is just a happenstance, a platform where looting takes place, a thing ignored in the frenzy of capturing the salt. The desert ends here, surrenders to the big waters.

I have come to see the whales, the Pacific grays that plunge down the coast from Alaska to calve in Scammon's Lagoon, the site of the saltworks. Whales and barges somehow negotiate around each other. Longer than we know, the cows have come here to drop their young in the lagoon while the bulls patrolled outside its mouth like warships. It is like the salt, like everything in the desert, something that could go on forever, until we discovered it. They arrive around January and some linger into March. No one knew they came here until a captain stumbled upon them in the mid-nineteenth century. He found the entrance to the hidden lagoon and the rest was blood in the water and strange cries.

Now, people come to watch, pay to go out in small boats and touch. For the time being we are busy murdering the oil beds and the whales get a break until their turn comes up again. From the plane window, they are shadows in the green water, the huge cow, the small young, two pods nestled against each other in a gigantic nursery. Scientists and tour guides run the lagoon, and while the saltworks still grinds away day and night, those seeking nature and nature's ways flee their jobs and come here to look into eyes the size of pizzas. I am no different.

I'm in this cafe tackling a fish dinner when I notice a guy sitting at another table mainlining *cervezas* in the heat of the afternoon. He drinks three Coronas fast but picks at his *pulpo coctele*. The beard is trimmed, the shirt white with blue stripes, the slacks tan. He looks across the cafe and asks, "How do you say 'times time'?" He translates for the Japanese who own that hefty chunk of the salt. He is the Mexican intellectual, the Marxist, the man who has written articles, done time in the intense conversations of Mexico City. His grandfather was a captain with Pancho Villa—and died before a firing squad. This is a common background of horror that every Mexican can produce when the occasion warrants it. Now he is back in the desert, back to his native town, this hellish outpost of salt. He says, "I love Baja."

He tells me I must stay to see the sunset.

Why? I ask. The town stares out to sea at an almost permanent fog bank brewing just off the coast, a dull morass of swirls.

"For the grays," he explains, "all the grays."

He continues on about his pueblo. Ah, of course, he must touch on the drugs. Have you heard of Caro Quintero? he asks. Well, he has several ranchos near here out in the desert, places well guarded with buried oil tanks by secret airfields. The life. He does not seem disturbed by this fact and I know what he will say if I ask about it. He will tell me that if Americans wish to kill themselves with this vile poison it is not his affair or that of his country. That they are very poor, and have deep problems, that they are two nations, European and Indian, trying to heal ancient wounds, a festering memory of a rape. Besides, the desert is good, Baja is home, and these other matters, whether *narcotraficantes* or capitalists lusting for salt, these other matters cannot touch the deeper life, the one that holds him in its thrall. I agree. Not because I believe this argument, this act of faith actually, but because I am living it. I am watching ruin, and yet savoring life. I am complete. At one time, I thought such a state would require solutions, or at least absolution. But now I realize all it requires is hunger, the hunger to belong to something that is worth giving my bones to.

Two or three years ago, the man in the cafe tells me, his brother was the town doctor. A man was found dead in the desert and there was nothing left of this man except for some bones and a few bottles of American medicine. A man, I suspect, like myself, someone who had gone into the desert for reasons he could not really explain or deny. All this, the bones, the pill bottles, was brought to his brother in a plastic garbage bag. The remains told nothing and the American consulate discovered nothing. No one missed the man in the garbage bag. Finally, he and his brother took the bag of bones down to the sea where the desert tasted the salt water and they cast the remains upon the waves.

"We gave him," he says almost wistfully, "a faraway."

I KNEW NATURE BEFORE I ever knew the word. Blue sky, green tall grass, air heavy with moisture and smell, my mother in a thin cotton dress hanging clothes in an Illinois spring. The limestone blocks of the house cool and pale, the barn huge and thrashing with odors. Chickens clucking and grubbing bugs, the cattle lowing, apple trees in leaf, and down at the milk house spring water softly flowing around the full cans. The creek green and slow, carp jumping, and cattails snaring the shore here and there. My nose sucks everything in, my eyes blur with the smear of green. I see a snake gliding through the grass and follow. I hear the scream and then my mother's rough hands on me boosting me from healing ground. I am alarmed by this interruption. The sweet shit of the barn smacks my face, the sun on my skin, blue sky above and the smells of spring, soil breathing and releasing rot into the heavens. I am two years old, I've checked, and this is certain.

I begin to have adventures with a snake I ride about the countryside. My parents are entranced by these tales and I do not understand their laughter. My first crayon drawing is of a worm thinking of a man. When I die I will see that blue, smell that green raw grass, and feel that sun pouring on an Illinois hillside by the old limestone house. Years later, in my twenties, I drove past and the house and everything was gone, leveled and hauled away. I remember little but that instant, the thin dress clinging to my mother, the rush in my nostrils that would make cocaine such a disappointment. The slick body of the snake in the green.

I LOOKED IT UP and this is what He said: "And the LORD God said unto the serpent, Because thou hast done this, thou art cursed above all cattle, and above every beast of the field; upon thy belly shalt thou go, and dust shall thou eat all the days of thy life."

Imagine no knife, no fork. The tongue split and no hands to help you grab the roast.

I want to eat the dirt and lick the rock. I am loyal if nothing else.

SEEING IS NOT LOOKING. One of the five senses, a finger ripping out the eyeball and opening up the world to view. The road sees its way clear and the road writhes on yellow sand under gray sky. Dunes rolling west, huge sand breasts rubbing against the wind, and these breasts incised with the track of sidewinders searching the sweep of the land. The mountain is sinking right before my eyes, the jagged range slipping under the march of the dunes. The Strange Range on the tongues of my kind. The road, really thousands of roads, and all of these highways the marks of snakes under the endless sky. Look and sand eats at the eyes, bites the face, rubs raw the yearning stone of the range dying before my eyes as the dunes come and take and go on and on. The rock looks gray, the sand yellow, the scrub huddling, trying to grab onto the shifting piles of sand, and everything moving, always moving, and when the moon walks across this ground at night, still it keeps moving, and when the stars scream in the night, the moving never stops, not for a second, not even for the scream of the stars. The planets are ignored also.

This is the place of the looking. But the seeing, that is another matter. The camera clicks, the image becomes fixed, the sheet of paper fresh from the laboratory, the print ready for framing and yet a lie of tame colors, a thing I pitch into the wind here and watch it flutter away to the death it portrays.

I am huddled against a rock looking west into the sand and the shaking and hustling of the dunes, my body frail against the rock, my body dead against the twitchy energy of the sand. My eyes peering out from slits as the sand eats at me. Seeing, something besides looking, seeing is going down and in and like the Strange

Range itself the seeing begs that I be buried alive under the waves crashing against the stone walls of the range.

Colors shift, the gray and the yellow go by the boards, the looking leaves me, and now comes the seeing, the rainbow things smearing across the ground, not coloring the surface but being the thing, this rage of color boiling out of the particles, erupting from the stone, coming into my eyes like an ice pick and opening up my brain to waves of the color. Purple snakes on red dunes under a green sky as the black stars scream and are ignored, so too the pink planets. Seeing, a thing too important for the eye, a thing denied the cameras, a thing never to be caught on film. I sit on the rock as it explodes and gushes colors. The sand moves and will take the Strange Range and take me. My eyes lie on the moving dunes. My empty sockets take in the scene.

THREE DAYS AGO, weather whipped me like a dog. But then, in that burst of fury a few days back, came these living moments, a few minutes that were actual. I can regain those moments at will. They went like this: The dust storm initially moves out of the Growler, over Papago Wells, through gaps of the hills and spills into the Tule Desert, moving relentlessly but without haste, marching toward me and I watch as mountains, then hills, then distant mesquites, then nearby creosote bushes and then myself disappear into the stinging winds of sand and dirt. All this three days ago, I think, my calendar keeping has seriously declined and I wear no watch in this place.

When the storm takes me, I can see maybe ten feet, breathing becomes a labor, my face stings and I wheel with my back into the wind and wait for the fury to pass. The storm pulls off, and a feel of rain hangs over my head, the air a gauze wrapped around my face. Sand clings to my legs, the dunes roll, a flesh of particles, and black rocks from the lava pock the curves molded from sand. Doves sweep past toward a roost at dusk, the storm pulls back and to the east black walls of rain hang over brown and white walls of dirt kicked up by the wind of an hour ago.

A stillness descends, the air is dead, spent by its works, and weighs like lead on me. My groundsheet shines blue on the sand, my thin sleeping bag is at ready for the cool hours just before dawn, and the stars are not yet out. I hear the rumble of trucks from the highway in Mexico a scant mile away. I see the scar of an outlaw road cut through the desert for smuggling. I see the café across the line where I have sat for hours at a time with tired truckers and wide-awake drug dealers. Brown skin, fried chiles in the air, hot coffee and cold pop, plates of beans. Just south of the café waits a small airfield where loads come and go feeling their way through the caution of American radar. For fifty miles in any direction my feet know the paths.

The first time I was here, years ago, the feel was not this way. It was winter that time, the moon a frozen rock beaming white light onto the dunes, the highway somehow more silent then because there were fewer of us and we moved less frequently. That lost world seemed uninhabited and I slept on the dunes in fear of snakes and strange sounds and the demon power of the moon. I did not belong then, but that was why I had come, out of a sense of longing. And I knew less then, I had not walked the ground or stood on the secret airfields or seen the bodies, blood still seeping from the fresh gunshot holes in the chests and heads. There were at least a billion fewer of my kind on earth then and my eyes were not as hungry and my heart was not as large and my skin was not as scarred and my needs then were slight, something contained within the words nature and the natural. I had not come to hate those words then, had not taken a knife yet to their lying sounds. I was still learning the names of plants and birds and types of rock then, still bewitched by place names tossed off carelessly by earlier people as they trudged over the hills and through the valleys. That first night, I remember the light winds, the cold, the lack of mercy in the face of the moon, but mainly I remember fear, a fear of being in this place and out of place. Now that has long gone. Now the sandstorms, the thirst, the snakes feel correct. But the place has gotten too small, the sound of trucks rumbling too loud, the sign of my own kind too common.

You must bear with me, here, I'm trying to sort this out. I have lost my fear, lost my sense of boundaries and borders, stabbed those words again and again, and come back to settle some accounts. I need something that is here but this thing I need is not contained in the categories I have been taught. This thing I need is not order or harmony or balance or peace.

FLOATING

Golden light pours on the scrubbed wood floor in the kitchen by the wood stove as they bend over the chair driving brass tacks to hold down the green fabric on the seat in the August of a summer and out the window, wood sash and glass framed in small squares, out there the sky is blue and oaks brush the horizon, a green fur of the leaves, soon dusk will come and the fireflies but now the tap tap tap of the small upholstering hammer, a wood handle and brass head, my father with a hand-rolled cigarette in his mouth, my mother fussing to keep the fabric smooth, and near at hand a brass ashtray cut from the fired end of a cannon shell from faraway, out there on the oceans of the world during the last war, the one before the next war, and I can hear men in the house, all young men in blue starched uniforms and with bibs and white sailor hats and they drink from quart bottles and smoke short strong cigarettes and smile at me as I toddle around, and they don't know what to do with themselves because they are still alive and when they drain those quart bottles day after day and week after week the others come back and stare, and this comforts them and frightens them and so they drink and drink and my mother can barely stand this, cooking for a mob, the men drunk in the morning and the night, and my father hears her out but does nothing because he knows even though he will not say this knowing; knows that this must continue until it ends, that there is a blood price to be paid and so his huge stone farmhouse, fourteen rooms plus outbuildings, teems with the living who drink with the dead.

Maybe it never begins but if it does begin, I think it begins at that moment, the world of green and blue pouring through the century-old glass, the tap of the hammer, the pies cooling on the counter, the low smoky comfort of the wood stove that never grows cool, the men broken but held together by bottles, the ocean whispering from the sawed-off cannon shells, the fabric of life unraveling before me and yet caressing my face.

That is the floor of my optimism, all from a room and afternoon and time that was vanishing as fast as I swallowed it, a war fading, the sun sinking, the pies cooling, the wood stove soon to be replaced by gas, the pump in the yard to become a pipe to a faucet, the privy to be abandoned, the farm to be fled, the roar of the city to fill my ears, the sky above to fill day by day with airplanes screaming and the fields and the creek and the rank growth and rich earth to move away from me and yet always stay near, as close as fireflies floating in the last moments of a summer dusk.

There is blood also, constant killing of beasts for the table. Constant small words about the dead and the fear and the dread of dying any instant.
And song.

I want to wear that crown of glory,
When I get home to that good land;
Well I want to shout salvation's story,
In concert with ohh the blood-washed band,

That is how it begins for me and I have never envied other beginnings.

Because everything was in place in my beginning, there was no other, no rupture, no evil, no innocence.

Fireflies, floating, like the glow off the cigarettes as the men sit in the growing dark of the farmyard with their bottles and loves and tears.

LOOKING EAST FROM MY BUNK with a tiny cup of espresso in my paw, I catch him looking west. He is over there in the black rocks on the other side of this national park being born in my cyber dispatches. He would not approve of the cyber stuff, that lonely satellite over France, I'm sure of this. I'm not sure he'd approve of France. He used an old beat-up typewriter and listened to classical music. And hated machines. We used to argue about this and that, but one thing we always argued about was the public's appetite for the natural world. He'd cite some goddamn poll that showed eighty percent of the folk just loved all this stuff about plants and animals. See, he'd say, things are coming around. I'd stare back and say these results don't mean much because they are not connected to actions. Or appetites. He'd quietly grunt back. I'd tossed a monkey wrench into his little pool of calm and he had damn few such pools and no need to hear my quibbles. That was years ago, before the hurried journey, the fresh-dug grave, the pile of rocks, the burial without benefit of a cemetery or the lawyers. Back before he became a vulture wheeling over my head when I least expected it. Now I'm further down the line, increasingly share his need for some thin reed of hope, but alas, I am still resistant to this balm brought by opinion polls. Still troubled by the lack of appetite behind the numbers.

I suppose I should make it abundantly clear that he is dead and that this fact has no meaning for me. I look east across this empty desert, he stares from his grave looking west and we are both here. I lack a spiritual side but I know what I have just written is true.

The ground keeps shrinking. The use of the ground keeps growing. The faces grow more and more numerous. The animals that I'itoi drove away when the locomotive roared into this country over a century ago, well, the animals keep moving deeper into some secret country but the space for this secret country shrinks by the hour. Besides these woeful facts, the notion of reserves keeps getting undercut. Nothing set aside seems big enough, at least according to the studies. No park, or island or refuge has enough size to be self-sustaining, to be safe from deterioration. The park now living inside my head and in those unseemly dispatches to cyberspace would run five thousand square miles and yet I know in my bones this is not enough. The other side of the border, those few miles to the south where those damn trucks are raising a ruckus on the downgrade, another seven thousand square miles of land and sea has been plopped under the umbrella of some kind of protection by the Mexicans and even when this is added to my five thousand—and the two would-be reserves essentially touch—I know it will not be enough to guarantee survival for the various beasts and plants festering around me as I sprawl here in the darkness.

Did I mention the trucks? Yes, those trucks rumbling in the night, rolling down the pike, highballing, deadheading, air brakes kicking up a racket, those trucks, brown hands on the wheel, big wheels keep on turning. They are coming at me, at us, they are the thing to spook not just this night, but all the nights. The trucks are hungry and need some place to roam. Pedal to the metal, brown face behind the wheel, yea gods, so many of them, cranking out the miles, make that kilometers, heading my way. I see the truckers now in my own mirror when I shave. I am resigned to all the pollution numbers, the surging human numbers, the various webs and fabrics and matrixes being slashed by killers in the night, the bad news by the bushel, but I continue to have a hard time with the fact that the truck raising such a racket in the night as I sprawl here in my official wilderness sipping espresso from my exquisite cup, that I am driving that damn truck. Yes, I am.

I'm standing in the dirt by a house in a bleak neighborhood in Juárez on the line, got a fresh can of Tecate in my hand, and the notebook is sprawled on the hood of a car and I'm scribbling while the trucker jabbers at my side. It's Saturday night and that seems to be a global condition. At my side is a forty-six-year-old long-haul trucker, the real McCoy, and he is wearing old soiled britches, a moustache, and sandals. His gut is spilling out over his pants, his eyes are swimming in beer, and he is on a roll telling me about the road in Mexico and what it takes to get down that road. He's had his share of accidents, there was that bad curve and the bus where he left eleven dead and fled on into the night and kept to his schedule. He shrugs off the gore and screams.

Look, you gotta understand the work, he explains, waving his beer in my face and laughing. He makes this run, over a thousand miles, from Juárez on the line with El Paso, Texas, to la capital, Mexico City, the heap of twenty million odd people. For the trip, he prepares: a twelve-pack of beer and some excellent cocaine, the beer of course to level out the marching powder. The road is open, he revs up his engine and storms south. There are no stops except for gas and he's got a thousand miles or more to cover. At the truck stops, he pumps beer while the gas goes in. Sometimes he gives women a ride for the standard fee, a blow job. He never rests, not even a catnap. And when he finally threads his way into Mexico City and drops the load, his eyes the size of tortillas by then, he gets four to six hours while they set up his new cargo. Then turnaround, and boom, back to Juárez, more coke, and of course, beer and good Samaritan moments when he gives rides to women who cannot afford bus fare.

We are standing by his house, a cement creature that looks forlorn but inside a light bulb dangles from the ceiling and there are beds everywhere for the kids and his woman is cooking something, the aroma floats into the yard. He's doing okay, he's got this house and the kids and the woman and the work, man, it's getting harder with the years, and sometimes now he uses grass instead of beer to level out that cocaine because, you know, too much beer isn't good for you but despite the pressure, he is making it. He dreams of driving in the United States where the roads are safe and you don't hit near so many buses.

His brother, from the Los Angeles area, is standing by the trucker as he explains his life. The brother left seventeen years ago, got a job in LA, and is doing okay. He comes back, of course, to eat the dirt here and be home. He's bought a house lot and is going to build one of these days. This trip, and he just arrived a few hours ago, he piled his fourteen-year-old boy into his old Chevy and lit out on the interstate after dark. He took that big road that runs near the line, the American artery that frames the northern border of my wilderness, my desert of yearning, and Jesus, after a couple of hours he couldn't handle it, too tired after a week of work, so he puts the kid behind the wheel, and falls asleep. He awakens as they cross the swatch of dunes, those loving sand piles of my desert, and he glances over and sees his son is cruising down the Interstate at ninety-five miles an hour, his fourteen-year-old head barely clearing the steering wheel, and man, he felt good, going home, the night air sweet, and his boy feeling the roar of speed.

He throws back some Tecate, his trucker brother laughs at the tale, and I realize I'm looking in a mirror, that I am among my own people. And I don't mean anything clever by this, I mean something simple. That we share the same appetites, that we are clawing through the ground toward something, that we are coming and God help my wilderness with the likes of us on the loose. That I'm skeptical of that beer/cocaine diet since it seems to me that marijuana and cocaine provide a more balanced nutrition but these are quibbles compared to our love of speed, our understanding of the edginess of things, and of our war against balance and harmony and our disbelief that lambs lie down with lions and live.

We are an appetite, billions of tongues, hey, honey, sure I'll give you a ride, and all the names and cultures and passports don't mean a damn thing if you are a snake or a Gila monster or a mountain or a desert because we are coming, hear that air brake shredding the night on the downgrade? Smell the cab full of stale beer and smoke? We are coming and whatever our hopes for ourselves about nature and nature's ways, we are a force to be reckoned with. There is no way to square our plans with our numbers and no way to corral our appetites within the tidy borders of our ideals. It is not something that can be handled with words like overpopulation and underdevelopment and urban planning and global economies, it is something that has always been out of whack with these rational notions and now, as we spawn and grow huge, this inherent distance between speed limits and our foot on the pedal grows more obvious as our big cocaine eyes take in the night. Systems expand to maximum power, the whole ecosystem is heading toward climax and that biological end of history, and here, sit on this bench and take in the vista, read that thoughtful park sign explaining the rich texture of the botanical assemblage, and my God, watch out, a truck is coming through and oh, Lord, I'm behind the wheel.

AND EVEN IF IT WERE BIG ENOUGH, and it is not, they will come and they are we. Our numbers are said to be six billion and we yearn to be ten billion. They tell me there is no avoiding these numbers and these throats devouring all manner of things. Then there are these matters of ecology, conservation, recreation, carrying capacity, pollution, inputs, outputs, biodiversity, Jesus, an endless list of this and that to attend to lest the thing be unsound. I fall asleep listening to the reports from these various fronts and I refuse to go to the meetings or join the clubs. I watch no nature programming on television, which oddly enough seems to focus exclusively on one organism dining on another, do not read the magazines, turn my ideas away from the pornography of the nature photography, burn the books of nature essays to test Lord Kelvin's laws, and leave more than my footprints. I also worry that people with a deep interest in the natural world seem to lack a deep interest in burlesque, make-up, high heels, and the kama sutra. There are simply not enough push-up bras on the trail, or wine corks for that matter. I'd even like to find a few martini shakers here and there. And I worry about the herbal teas driving out the jolting cups of coffee.

Can the natural world be saved if we are not animals?

Or better yet, can the natural world be saved once we utter that damning phrase of segregation: the natural world?

Rembrandts can be saved. Rare Chinese vases can be saved. Fucking buildings can be saved. All these things can be saved by diffidence and demonstrations of good taste. But not this mess out here, this belching, thorny, shitting, fucking mess. It can only be saved by appetite and appetite of one kind is what is killing it, the appetite to possess things. And the lack of appetite of another kind, the appetite to feel things, is what is killing it. I used to think it could be saved from our numbers if there were a way to convey it all as a wet panty. Now I fear no one wants a whiff. The very phrase, bird watching, has had me worried for years. We simply watch too much and touch not enough.

But my dead friend was adamant about those opinion polls, about this rising tide of sentiment. I see the allure. According to a poll where I live, 84 percent of my fellow citizens want the very park I want. The newspapers endorse the park. It is, like sunny weather, a very popular thing.

But almost no one has ever been to this place, the ground I want to make a park, where I now fiddle with my espresso needs. It is too hot, it is too hard, it is too something. Off the beaten track, God forsaken, full of venomous beasts, inconvenient, yes, inconvenient. Not that I really want a horde to come here but still I can't help but notice that almost no one has ever been willing to venture into the place. And those that drive by its huge empty edges have almost no memory of the experience. When asked, when probed about their recall of looking out the car window into this big empty, they draw a blank.

I am sitting in a fine restaurant on top of a tower, the restaurant revolves thanks to some Herculean mechanism, I am eating Ahi tuna, rare, and the fellow facing me is an expert birder, he's just seen his first ruddy dove, by God, and he's born and bred in these parts, spent a lifetime in this desert, and I tumble things around to this reserve, to this park in my head, and his face goes blank and maps are fetched, and, ah, yes, he puts his finger on this huge hot pan of dirt and it is a blank to him, a place unknown, or barely known except for car rides where he has glanced out the window and even then, I can see him struggle to dredge up some kind of image from those car rides and idle glances. The restaurant keeps spinning as I look out over a huge desert city and the desert itself no longer exists except as a report of distant things.

Looking east while he is looking west, I can't shake this belief, tiny cup in my hand, bitter taste in my mouth, the night still hanging overhead, the dawn a theory with no facts yet to back it up. Somewhere behind me in the rockpile, that three-legged sheep with knowing eyes. Her white white skin. Bones singing. And he is looking west while I look east and between us is this immensity of five thousand square miles without a single resident that can vote in an election. The polls look good, to be sure. But something chemical is missing and that missing thing is the only real prayer of saving anything. To have that chemical, there must be appetite and of course, all the appetites are devouring the earth itself. It is not a pretty picture but the pretty pictures are devoid of appetites, are passive, shallow, and lacking in scent. And are not true, not true to the ground or the forms of life scratching on the ground.

Afterword: Excerpt

From *Some of the Dead Are Still Breathing*

LULLABY

I KNOW MY DADDY'S RICH and my mom is good-looking and she's half buried by the tangle in the garden, there by that row of pole beans, the leaves dark green, the pods hanging, but the dirt, a humus that is rising from the clay of this ground, that slick clay that puddles up the water and sucks the tires down after the heavy rain, is buried now under a splotch of black from the manure off the Holsteins, the tons shoveled out of the henhouse, all this turned under, dark ground now, the garden's an acre, the sun hot and the humidity without mercy and the spring seeps in, the summer comes, and then the fall and everything grows and yearns and the rot adds up and the clay disappears from view and the soil goes black, ground my daddy says is richer than two feet up a bull's ass and then he gets a quiet smile and bends over and fingers the soil, and my momma's good-looking as she fills that pail with fresh snap beans, the dirt rushes up, arrowheads come out every spring with the turnover of the ground, tips sharp and nicely napped, and you hear the bows long silent, hear them in that instant as you bend like my momma over there by the pole beans, and the next row is tomatoes, the leaves rank, run the fingers and the aroma clogs the nose, the fruit green and there, see the red one, pluck, take that up also to the limestone house on the hill.

Fish are jumping, slap, hear that, jumping in the creek down the hill, bursting out of the green water, gills sucking in the sweet air under the big willows leaning over the clean slate of wet, and then smack and they dive out of sight, jumping, going to do that until the end of time, and you don't know why and stare and learn the world's marvels before you know words or can form them in your mouth and sizzle, grease in the pan, black pan, seasoned iron, the meat hits and browns, supper is coming, the stove old iron also, wood fed, and Grandma is bending over, but she ain't blood, just so old she's called Grandma, one of those ragged people come in from the cold and hunger and she bunks in the wooden addition tacked on to the stone house, keeps a shelf there with gallon jars full of salamanders and other strange creatures all floating forever in alcohol and on the same shelf the diaries where she scratches out the sunrise and moonset and how many eggs the hens laid and other details that manage to make a life into order.

The water comes from a pump by the sink and there is that other pump in the yard.

The outhouse has three holes.

The clay sticks and coats the skin after the rain and the air rank with fragrance, scent, aroma, stench, suck it down and lap with the tongue, take it in and touch me. Touch me. My daddy's rich and my momma's good-looking and the stone on the house is rough-cut blocks, the stove is hot, men stand outside in navy uniforms for that photograph, a small print with scalloped edges and my God, these things cost a lot of money and there they are in a line all navy blue, Buck and Jim and Slasher and Bud and some are kin and some not but all are blood and the drinking is heavy and my daddy is rich and he's gone all the time and my momma's good-looking and she's cooking like a slave and men are drinking because they are all scared, that North Atlantic passage, an uncle on a drunk missed his ship out of New Orleans and it vanished without a trace out there.

The waters had long settled and calmed over the ship he missed as he spoke to me, and I could see his broad shoulders still shiver at the memory. When I was six or seven, he turned to me in a union hall and told me he'd kill me if I ever crossed a picket line. And my God, my momma's good-looking and she's bent over in the garden and the peppers are coming on strong, the carrots fat, the turnips a row of knobs in the black ground and the breeze is wheezing through the woodland to the south and no one at this moment can smell the stench off the refineries or the coking mills, the air is wet feathers as she plucks two hundred chickens a year for the table, the neck on the stump, swing of the hatchet, the hot water and wads of old newspapers, blood on the green grass and then one day she sees a weasel inching into the henhouse and stands on the back steps with a .22 and drops the beast with one shot and when she brings down the rifle the look in her eyes is of dread and disgust and the woodstove always seems warm, skins of animals on the floor as rugs and out the back door, across the garden, past the henhouse and the big barns, walking along the line of the woods and then the bluff and below is the plain with the river and down there, forgotten by everyone, is the line where the past still lurks in a dolomite prairie that came to feel the sun when the great ice retreated twelve or thirteen thousand years ago and the waters called Lake Chicago drained suddenly south and gouged and raced down new channels and began building with dirt the delta and bayous that became the bench for the creation of the dead city taken by the big wind one roaring day in the heat of August, there, in that nest of plants, a sole survivor almost for the region, a place left alone because those dolomite soils are no damn good for farming even though someone downhill and out there on the land created a functional steel plow in 1835 and the murder of the vast prairies began, but not here, the soil is too feeble and up on the bluff, the clay can be farmed but no one is ever happy with the results and so my daddy's rich and my momma's good-looking and I first feel the sun on my face in a place where the mammoth felt the temperatures begin to rise and its doom come on the warming breeze, and all this some thousands of years ago, and downriver the dirt piles up and up and New Orleans becomes a possibility as the ground under my feet erodes south in a fury of the melting ice and I'm a child and the world is solid, the house stone, cows lowing in the meadow by the creek, supper's on time, the wood stove never cools, the barns are huge and sweet hay smell in the air, the men on a Saturday afternoon sitting under the apple trees in the orchard on old wooden chairs and drinking quarts of cheap beer, rolling cigarettes and hashing the last war and the next one and dancing around the fear and staying silent on the empty chairs for the friends who did not come back and there's an elephant table in the house, a flat top and then a full-blown carved pachyderm below, solid mahogany, come back from Africa and I can't remember which uncle or cousin was ducking bullets there, ashtrays, solid brass and big from those cannon shells that the men cut down at sea as souvenirs and everything is old, real old, no one has had a dime for a long time because of times they all call hard and then, of course, came that war, and the rugs are not rugs but the skins off Holsteins that stopped being good milkers and went to meat and the floor, rugs of Holsteins with the hair on, all black and white splotches and when you crawl across them you smell the fields and life, and the men drink under the apple trees and my God, one day the fruit is getting ripe and the crows rip into it and one of my uncles steps off the porch and ropes a black bird dead, hangs that corpse from a limb in the orchard and they stay away because, my uncle says with quiet respect, "They understand," and everything seems so solid, ain't never gonna end or change, and all the while beneath us are the layers of silt from that old Lake Chicago and the limestone from the silt of a forgotten sea and the mammoths whispering in the graves and saying, Be sure to get a helpin' of flowers and the Indians filing west to dust and dreams and leaving ground where they'd buried tens of generations and then the canals came and the factories and the stone house, carp jumping all the while, and the men stir slightly in their chairs and then settle back and don't care what comes next just so long as it is nothing like what has gone by and one uncle comes back and my God, he's been years in a tank rolling through North Africa, then Sicily, and then up that boot of Italy and it's real strange because during the hard times he walked off from his woman and his children in the Dakotas, couldn't feed himself much less them because the rains did not come, the clouds of dust rose like God over the plains, rose so high and mighty that on the coast they call east, the light got dim at noon, so he took off, joined that army, the war came without his permission and it was years in a tank, that tin can with guns, but still he'd gone up that land firing where the Italians live, tasted the food and probably other things I was not to know, tasted and come back alive with this new squash, zucchini, and it goes into the ground there by the limestone house and the meadow with cattle lowing and the world gets new and bigger and my daddy's rich, my mom is good-looking and she leans out the window of the house and says, "Dinner's on the table."

The old valley floor shelters purple meadow rue, old witch grass, big bluestem, raspberries, and feral plums, and over the rank green floats Hine's emerald dragonfly, and there is leafy prairie clover, there are egrets, kingfishers, and the stench of those refineries. I was born in a place so worthless the old world survived because the new world could find no way to work the land. I was born on the edge, the line where the ice stopped and then melted and the seas rose and the mastodon died out after twenty million years and the mammoth, after a million and a half, gave up the ghost and went where we all go in time. This is the line, here the ice stopped, before that, in the long gone, the seas washed ashore here and the big house, where the woodstove glows and the pies are on the windowsill cooling, is made of rough limestone blocks carved from the dead of the long-gone sea, and the ice melts, the valley is gouged, the rivers come out of the ground, come out like the dead on resurrection morning and the soil of my birthplace heads south and forms the place where all that jazz comes from and the refineries come because of a big hole in the ground at Spindletop in Texas, a gusher of oil that needs to be cleansed and then burned. I can as a child at night see the flares in the refinery as they burn off byproduct and the mills roar and the stacks shoot black into my sky and that is how it starts, everything that is my life, here on this line where the ocean left its dead and the ice came and then the ice went and the mammoths were no more, arrowheads coming out of the ground each spring plowing, old tomahawk heads also, the smells never leave me, and I spend my life living on this edge, the place where an energy explosion comes into the world, one that changes the face of life itself, first the rivers, then the canals, then the railroads, then the oil and just across the valley that big nuclear laboratory and everything is here, like surf crashing onto the coast, here all the messages of the big waters can be touched in the limestone in a house made of bones from a dead sea, and all I see is green and blue and the earth floats as scent everywhere and the garden is one acre, the fish jump, my daddy's rich, spends each weekend patching holes in the inner tubes of the worn tires, fencing with sweat running down his face, and then the train into the city and the money and in all those scents I find a path as inevitable as the mammoth becoming bones and then powders that heal the wounds of our wars and the only song my rich daddy ever sang to me was "Hard Hearted Barbara Allen" and my God, the thing is blue and green, at first, yes, it is blue and green, because

It was in the merry month of May
When green buds they were swelling
Sweet William came from the west country
And he courted Barbara Allen

and then it goes well and then it goes bad and Sweet William sends his servant to fetch Barbara Allen and she sees him in his sickbed and says, "Young man, I think you're dying," and he turns his head to the wall and sees death and then to the graveyard he goes and

Then lightly tripped she down the stairs
She heard those church bells tolling
And each bell seemed to say as it tolled
Hard-hearted Barbara Allen

and so he sings it and the sweat runs down his face and the sky is blue, the world green and hush, little baby, don't you cry.

For some of us, everything begins with a lullaby.

Rock-a-bye-baby
On the treetop
When the wind blows
The cradle will rock

and began rocking in the seventeenth century when someone walked off the *Mayflower* and met the Wampanoag Indians, then there was that Thanksgiving, the murder of turkeys, the magic of corn, and the tribe carried their babies in cradle boards and would hang them from trees when the women worked and so

When the bough breaks
The cradle will fall
And down will come baby
Cradle and all

and these songs never get out of your head and these feelings never go away and the cotton is always high and the living is easy and you believe no matter what mean street you are walking at the moment, once the melody starts, the voice purrs in your ear, you believe and at that moment, for a brief instant, you cease to be the fool that the world accepts.

The photographs tumble out, a pile of images with blood staring up at me, the old house, limestone in the sun, the creek, the barns, that first dog, the trailer in the woods where my uncle drinks and I run through the woods with his German shepherd, the boys back from the wars, the first big one, then that second big one, then some over in Asia, spiffy in their uniforms and whiskey eyes and cigarettes burning in their hands as they stare unsmiling at the camera and think of not ever thinking again, and the air is fresh, spring air, smoke curling up from their hands and down the hill the gas flares, the mills thunder, and by the ruins these shreds of original prairie survive because they are beneath notice, Jews hiding in some Berlin cellar waiting out a war, and there has never been a line that mattered, not between nature and whatever is not nature, between war and peace, between the lullaby and the steer slaughtered this morning, now the quarters hang on hooks in the barn, the flesh wrapped in cheesecloth, the meat cooling while flies buzz, the rough boards smeared with blood, and up in the house, the women frying the liver to go with the eggs and potatoes.

There has never been distance, just lullabies.

I float down a stream, bottle of wine in my hand, otters on their backs pacing the slender bow of the canoe, a storm slowly filling the sky overhead and I hit the marsh and glide among the wild rice and quack of ducks and one photograph is of my aunt on her eightieth birthday, she's got a cigarette in her hand and ignores the big cake and I know she wants it over so the poker game can begin and the whisky come out and the next shot is of her farm, the bleak buildings making bold on the endless sweep of the plains and one of these mornings, yes, one of these mornings the song comes again and

Oh, do you remember Sweet Betsey from Pike
Who crossed the wide prairie with her lover Ike?
With two yoke of oxen, a big yellow dog,
A tall Shanghai rooster, and one spotted hog.
Hoodle dang, fol-de-dye do,
Hoodle dang, fol-de day.

crossing out there, right behind the red barn on the lip of the endless plains, leaving for something better, believing, saying yes, and oh, Betsey is all yes, yes, yes

Out on the prairie one bright starry night,
They broke out the whisky and Betsey got tight
She sang and she shouted and danced o'er the plain,
And made a great show for the whole wagon train

and I can see my aunt's hand move in the still photograph, reach for that whisky, start cutting the cards and the wind can howl, no matter, the game will go on till all hours and the future will be made plain as the cards are dealt and everyone knows the song, knows it in their bones and it has many names and places but still the song says

Oh Shenandoah! I long to hear you,
Way-aye, you rolling river
Across that wide and rolling river.
Away—we're bound away
'Cross the wide Missouri!

Yes, we are, and the cotton is high and the fish are jumping, hear them? And the songs keep coming and I flip through the photographs, a century or more of blood slaps against my face and my daddy is rich, my momma good-looking.

You have no right to a better deal than a whale or a mammoth or that Hine's dragonfly, all but extinct, skittering over the tall grass in the shred of prairie down the hill from the big limestone house. Aquagirl is out there somewhere, the big ships with nets are killing, the snake is waiting by the path and listens for the footfall of a mouse, and the room awaits and can suck the life out of life, and the room is necessary but then, rise and leave and take Sweet Betsey and cross the wide Missouri, because one of these mornings you're going to rise up singing. Yes, you will.

In an ancient photograph my mother is eight, maybe nine, wears the rag of a dress, hair cropped short, and she is outside holding the reins to a team of horses hooked to a plow and her face has no smile as she rips the prairie apart and my momma's good-looking and there are long nights and they touch our lives and that is how we see the light.

And after ten hours of labor, the doctors said nature was not working out this time and then came the sterile void of the surgical theater, the whir of the saw, and suddenly my child in my arms and those tiny fingers. I counted them, a kind of inventory males do, and then he is swaddled in his mother's arms. I remember placing my little finger in his palm and feeling his hand curl around it.

We are always reaching out to touch a world we neither fully trust nor flee. We see things but they do not seem to really exist until our fingers brush against the fur or the stone and confirm they are real. A friend taught drawing by having students feel a walnut in a brown paper bag and then making a sketch informed only by the sensations of their fingers. I spend a week down by the river blundering across sheets of limestone and shale, the bones of ancient times that form most of the ground there, and I keep rubbing my hands against the rock as much as looking at it. A desert flat never really exists for me until I walk through the brush and feel the thorns rake my legs.

One afternoon I walked into a slot canyon called the Devil's Garden and saw a sprig emerging from a crack in a boulder. I gently touched the tiny leaves and then rubbed my fingers against the brown rock. I was my son as a babe in arms curling his fingers around my finger.

Years ago, the morning my son was born, the body of a contract killer was found on the outskirts of my town. I spent months looking into the life of the man who wound up a corpse under a mesquite tree. He was twenty-seven, had killed fifty or sixty people. He began his murders at age thirteen in a Mexican border town. Locals told me he'd been abused as a child and they recalled seeing him fly through the air as he was tossed down the hill from his parent's hut. He wound up afraid of guns and did all his murders with a screwdriver or scissors. As my son struggled toward birth, the killer was being kidnapped in the parking lot of a shopping center and moved to his desert future just west of my town. That same evening, I stood out under the stars and gave a talk to nature lovers about a nearby mountain. I motioned with my hand and said that up there, in that darkness, a lion was padding by and watching us and knowing our scent and we live ignorant of this other nation. Later, a biologist told me I'd had too much to drink.

The morning my son was born, I stopped by the grocery where my mother worked and told her she was a grandmother. She left her job and went to the hospital with my christening robe.

I returned to that same hospital about three years ago for the dying. My mother was nearing ninety and had a cardiac about dawn. They'd put her into the intensive care unit. Now the moment came to switch off the life support. My sister and I stood on each side of the bed as our mother slipped from coma to the place we call death. The lines etched in pink or green on the various machines slowly went flat.

We each held one of our mother's hands as she died. I kept slowly massaging her palm and gently squeezing her fingers. With my other hand I would from time to time caress her face.

I'll make it simple.

It is never safe.

It is always sensual.

We can see it with our eyes.

After we have tasted it with our mouths.

And after my son curled his tiny hand around my finger, I leaned down and sucked in his scent.

And after my mother's hand went limp in mine, I leaned down and kissed her face.

Gonna spread your wings, take to that sky, yes, feel the wind and rise up toward the stars, Melville's at his desk looking out the window at the mountain and his dreams are dying as he puts his dream on the page, the white whale is still in the ocean deep and so is Ahab, plowing the endless blue waters and staring with eyes of wonder at the dead oceans that they both now sound, and once for a commencement address I simply read from the long goodbye as Molly Bloom lies in her bed and wonders at the emptiness of life and the feel of life and why life is not simply her breast yearning and she says yes, yes, yes, and after I finished there was silence and then voices objecting to what the woman said and how she spoke of her body and I thought lullaby, remember those lullabies and you won't be afraid in the darkness of your lust and love and clean sheets, and I'm told it is hopeless,

I'm told someone must suggest a fix, a solution, a way to avoid the way and yet the path is plain, been going down it hundreds of thousand of years, maybe more, no one has kept good notes, going down it, going over Jordan, going downriver, the silt riding and building that delta and then the city and all that music and gumbo of love and violence, the wind rises, the waters rush in, and I enter houses with mud and mold and no one comes here anymore and the feel is of a life gone wrong, of love betrayed and the mammoths come out of the ice with bellies full of flowers, and still, as my coffee cools, the cardinals build the nest under the blazing sky and I open a notebook and the words are in my father's hand, some slender leather-bound pad he carried in his vest, and his hand scratches out quotations he wants to keep and the first is by Martin Luther and says, "Who loves not women wine and song will live a fool his whole life long," and my daddy's rich and his hand writes down, "Far better to kiss the clay than curse the May," and he is gone with the mammoths and the little leather notebook says it was patented in 1904, a time when the valley below was still lush, a time before the refineries came and flared flames in the night, and the seas teemed and I had not met Aquagirl and left port to die or find a reason to live, and I have no idea what people mean when they say hopeless.

My daddy's rich but he don't look good and I'm near the sky in the Shoshone mountains, the snow comes in the night following a cold rain and I freeze in my bag while far away across the wide Missouri and other rivers, the man in that White House resigns and flees to the other coast where he sits and stares out at a dying ocean, and I come down from that night and call home and find the report is not good and begin to drive and drive and hit the Thunder Basin, a spill of grass and wind that rubs the horizon, antelope everywhere, and history has not happened, and the antelope run sixty miles an hour and are chased by cheetahs that vanished from this ground ten thousand years ago when the mammoths left us after a feed of flowers, and finally I hit the desert floor and park, walk into the house, and my daddy's rich and sitting there at table with a cold bottle of beer and we say nothing and then a week or so later they cut out the cancer and the long dying begins and now I read the notes he made as a young buck coming up, go through his old letters and my momma's good-looking and the beasts shuffle past into some mist and I cannot follow, no, I cannot follow but I mark the trail because I will be back and take it up and when he was dying my aunt came from the city now dead and they sat and her new man drank Jack Black, the old man rolled his cigarettes and she was working the river on a boat, gave me my first bite of okra on earth and none of this makes sense, leave the room and follow that trail into the mist, the one that crosses water and goes far out to sea where ships gather with huge nets and yet on the land, the cardinals pulse north and their young rise up singing and they spread their wings and take to the sky, follow that trail into the mist and find Sweet Betsy dancing drunk in the moonlight of the plains while wolves howl,

and,

Too-ra-loo-ra-loo-ral,
Too-ra-loo-ra-li,
Too-ra-loo-ra-loo-ral,
Hush, now don't you cry!
Too-ra-loo-ra-loo-ral,
Too-ra-loo-ra-li,
Too-ra-loo-ra-loo-ral,
That's an Irish lullaby.

because we cannot get it out of our minds, it scores us like a diamond on glass, and nothing can harm us, daddy and momma are standing by, and yes, that word, always yes, yes, yes, and I keep going back to the room and the negative floats in front of my eyes, the print dripping from chemicals and I stare and try to make out what happened and I know in my mind and heart the negative does not exist, just as I know the boy was tortured, strangled, and dumped in the river and I will always know this and cannot deny this and so I will be in that room for a while and then leave, snuff out that cigarette, kick the bottle across the floor and hear it skitter and go, yes, go and find that negative that does not exist because the boy died and the mother is in tears and the facts must be honored even as they are erased, the mammoth shuffles off to doom with a belly full of flowers and we miss the point, just as we miss the yes in her eyes.

Can I ask you a question?

Just what is it you don't understand?

Just what is it you need to know?

Just what is it you want?

I think the sea is endless. That's why I ran away to sea. After the storm—the vomit running down the deck, the bodies flying against the bulkhead—I lay in my bunk, the sweat pouring off me from the leaden tropics. I have a bottle, it is not my watch. I study the moisture beads on the metal walls, my body stripped and sweating. She enters and stands before me. The clothes begin to drop from her body. Her breasts stare at me, the hair between her legs, the long hank off her head. She smells very sweet, I do not know why. But she does. And she has no taste of salt.

"What would you like me to do?" she asks.

I'm on the desert flat and the buck antelope stands ten feet before me, his harem a short way off and I am blocking him, his eyes dark and bulbous and burning into my face and as I move aside he goes off with his harem, ever watchful for the cheetah that has been missing for ten thousand years and I keep going through these boxes, an old letter falls out from 1918, my grandmother is in her twenty-eighth year, the honey crop failed because the clover failed, all the turkeys died out of spite, the letter says so, but the geese are fat and a success, and then it is 1919 and the Spanish influenza is killing everyone still and she dies, dies not even knowing what is stalking the land, this plague that did not come from Spain but erupted out of Kansas and she will be dead for over eighty years before the scientists determine it was really a bird flu, and my mother becomes a motherless child and is marked forever, but she hitches up the team, works the fields, and I hardly ever hear a breath of this, hardly a word but find it all in a box after my mother has rolled over Jordan, find another letter from her uncle who is over the ocean helping to smash the Germans for good and he writes my grandfather that it is God's will, and he writes that our death is set at our birth, and he writes that we can do nothing to change the date set for our dying but must submit to it because it is the way of the Lord, and I am close by the line, they are sleeping on the street or under the trees down by the river, and they tell me of their journey north, tell of the men who tried to kill them or rape them or rob them and they are rolling over Jordan as soon as night comes down but they are so very hungry and I start handing over money, ten dollars, twenty dollars, forty dollars and they stream toward stands selling tacos in the street, and there are many words for them and their fate, studies of migrations, failed economies, declining resources, words that clatter on the floor of the bar like small change, and I turn to leave and get into my car and they claw at the windows like animals and follow me as I plow down the rutted street and flee from what is everywhere but now is hot breath on my neck.

I'M OVER JORDAN, I'm just going over home and the fish are jumping and the cotton is high. I was baptized in holy water in my mother's faith. I open an envelope and out tumbles a business card and on the back in my father's hand are explicit instructions that he is to be cremated and there is to be no service of any kind and none of any religious nature.

I did not obey him because death is for the living and my mother lived and so he had to endure the death she desired and my momma's good-looking.

I stare through the glass into the room as three doctors apply the paddles and then the surge of energy slams into her body and she is naked and right before my eyes she flops like fish hauled onto the deck of a ship and they do it again and again and bring her back and my momma's good-looking and I say yes, put her on the machines and so hush little baby and I keep her alive for hours and hours so that others can gather round and then—did I tell you my momma's good-looking? The cotton's high, also—the machines go off and she fades away and finally it is summertime and the fish are jumping and I enjoy the warm nights and try not to forget and try not to remember that moment with the paddles in the antiseptic room.

I once was stunned by heat and sprawled in the desert and hallucinated a wall of ice studded with mammoths and dire wolves and saber-toothed tigers rolling past me in the midday sun, clawing at the land and reclaiming it and making it the way it was when they stormed across the grass and shattered the calm of the forest.

In the long ago, I decided to write this thing and it took much longer than I planned and became something I did not know at the beginning.

That morning she stood leaning against the doorjam, bare-breasted, the hair black, the skin brown, nipples dark, and a smile riding easy on her face. Her teeth were very white and even. I turned away, I am always making this mistake, I turn away from the glow of that flesh. I turn away from myself, yes, that is it, from myself. I know it is fear, I am not a fool. How many women have there been? This is always asked. The trouble with this question is that it has an answer. And good questions do not have answers, they can barely break themselves into words. I noticed the faint moustache of dark hairs on her upper lip and wanted to lick them. There seems no end to it, and I have work to do. The aroma from the green coffee cup caressed my face and then I felt her hands on my shoulders, the fingers small but strong, her bare skin against me, and she said, "I'm crazy too." I could feel her smile grow huge then, and smell her, smell her good clean skin. She had just washed, her hair hung in clumps. Her clothes rode loose on her generous hips and it seemed as if they would fall at the faintest flick of a finger. I rolled a swig of coffee around on my tongue.

Going over Jordan and there is never a promised land because we are already in the land, the only land. Going over Jordan and then maybe we can face where we are and learn to be here and not flee at the first burn of dawn. Enter the mouth of the gigantic snake and in a day or maybe in weeks emerge, come out still walking east toward the light and have the new tools and songs and that food for the spirit, all this because we fear the snake and yet overcome this fear and enter the mouth. But, we are warned, not until we are ready. And yet I think we cannot wait much longer, no, it is time or time may run out for us.

There can't be a summing up, a set of commandments, a safe and sacred way. That is the path to ruin. There is appetite, there is the shift of things, the change in weather, the melting of the ice, the new rivers gouged, and the songs we make up to help us keep going.

And it is all words words words and she said that last night of her life, she was leaning back in the hospital bed, the voice frail, the face worn and tired of everything, she said, "I dreamed of your father last night," and then she let this hang in the clean air like a cigarette ring that is and then drifts away and never happened. And my father had been dead for over thirty years and there had been little mention of him for decades. Once, she told me out of the blue, "I never was afraid when your father was alive." And now she dreams as she enters the last night of her life and is on the edge of ninety, she dreams of my daddy who is rich and my mom is good-looking and I sit in the chair by the bed and know she is going over Jordan and why not since she actually believes in the river and believes in the other side and a part of her is happy because I think she always worried I'd get killed and then hell, she'd have two gone and be left alone in the fear and I'm going to see my father, so the old gospel song says, and going over Jordan and the whale's out there but so is the drift net and she dreams of my father and I know the dream is yes, I know the dream is past fear, I know she's got a bellyful of flowers and my momma's good-looking and the politics and the churches can't touch it, try to cover it up, they are things used to block the sun as it rises and shines down on this green ball of dirt and you'll spread your wings and nothing the priests say or the holy men do can change this or explain the feel of flight and the sunless realms are in the rooms not in the life and so go go go, and I sit by the bed and finally she falls asleep.

And then come dawn, I get the frantic call and rush to the hospital and they are smacking down hard with those electric paddles and the machines come out so folk can gather and you'll take to the sky.

My father used to tell me this story when I was a boy about an old man who had wandered much in life and would come to the saloon in the small town where my daddy was raised and get drunk and then he'd dance all by himself and twirl and finally this dance would end with him kicking the red-hot potbelly stove. Each time, he'd ruin his foot and limp for days or weeks. And if you asked him why he did this dance and kicked that iron stove, he'd say, "You have to. It's *The Sea Wolf*."

Yes.

The smell comes off the woodstove, a pie is in the oven, apple with lots of cinnamon but tart, and a guinea hen out in the yard is inches from my sister and looks to be about to peck her eye out and my mother races to the porch and drops the bird with one round, and then that sadness floods her eyes. The breeze comes up, the sky blue, grass green, fish jumping in the creek and the garden is big and the snakes are here and the apple orchard fronts the farm and no one fears the offer.

The morning will come and then nothing can harm you, your daddy, he's rich, your mom is good-looking.

Hush, little baby, don't you cry.

One of these mornings
You're going to rise up singing
Then you'll spread your wings
And you'll take to the sky

But till that morning
There's a'nothing can harm you
With daddy and momma standing by
GEORGE GERSHWIN, "SUMMERTIME"